THE SECRET LANGUAGE OF SUCCESS

THE
SECRET
LANGUAGE OF
SUCCESS

Using Body Language to Get What You Want

DAVID LEWIS

Galahad Books · New York

First Galahad Books edition published in 1995.

Galahad Books
A division of Budget Book Service, Inc.
386 Park Avenue South
New York, NY 10016

Galahad Books is a registered trademark of Budget Book Service, Inc.

Published by arrangement with Carroll & Graf Publishers, Inc.

Library of Congress Catalog Card Number: 89-30238

ISBN: 0-88365-894-1

Printed in the United States of America.

*We respond to gestures with an extreme alertness and,
one might almost say, in accordance with an elaborate
and secret code that is written nowhere,
known by none and understood by all.*
Edward Sapir

Contents

Introduction   1

Twelve Things This Book Will Help You Do Better   3

ONE   The Secrets of Silent Success   5

TWO   The Art of Impression Management   16

THREE   Silent Speech in Action   20

FOUR   The Four Minute Barrier   32

FIVE   The Importance of Self-esteem   37

SIX   Falling in Love – With Yourself   46

SEVEN   Creating a Memorable Image   54

EIGHT   Anatomy of an Encounter   71

NINE   Close Encounters   93

TEN   The Hidden Power of Your Handshake   115

ELEVEN   Successful Self-selling   131

TWELVE   Love-signs   153

THIRTEEN   Power-plays   177

FOURTEEN   Reading Others Right   205

FIFTEEN   Dress Success   231

SIXTEEN   The Thirty-one Rules of Silent Success   237

Bibliography   243

Acknowledgements   245

Introduction

There are scores of books, and thousands of learned papers, on body language – or non-verbal communication as specialists prefer to call it. Some are highly technical, a few very readable, many intriguing and informative. Together they can tell you almost everything you want to know about silent speech – except the most important thing of all: *how to use it*!

Putting the vast amount of information they contain into practice is like attempting to master a foreign language from a dictionary. All the words you need are available at the flick of a page. The difficulty lies in knowing how to use them properly. Are some words more persuasive than others? How can fluent sentences be constructed? Should certain words be avoided?

This book will provide answers to these and other key questions about the effective use of body language at work and play. It is a practical guide to using this powerful medium for achieving greater social and professional success.

To make it as immediately useful as possible, I have extracted thirty-one basic rules for successful silent speech. These are explained in the relevant chapters and also collected in the final chapter. If you are mainly interested in enhancing your silent speech skills as rapidly as possible, without concerning yourself with *how* and *why* each rule was formulated, then I suggest you turn straight to chapter sixteen.

As with any skill you cannot become proficient in body talk merely by reading a book about it. Practice is essential to make your silent speech eloquent. Just like learning to speak an unfamiliar spoken language, you'll probably be slightly hesitant and awkward at first. But after a short while this new way of using your body will become smooth and effortless.

Silent speech is important to you. It significantly affects your chances of succeeding or failing in any social encounter, whether personal or professional. Research suggests that only some 7 per cent of the meaning in any conversation is contained in the words spoken.

1

The majority of information is communicated by means of a complicated mixture of appearance, posture, gesture, gaze and expression. Furthermore a large part of the effects these produce operate below the level of awareness. They influence mood, attitudes, expectations and motivation without our ever being conscious of the fact. This offers a potent instrument of persuasion to those able to use it effectively.

In an increasingly fast-paced and competitive world silent speech skills can prove the key to social and professional attainment. You can control the messages being sent while accurately interpreting the signals being received. This ability to read another's body talk accurately is especially important in situations where you suspect attempts to conceal stress, mask anxiety, disguise deception, camouflage indecision or hide hostility.

When it comes to success and or failure *what* you say often matters far less than *how* it is said.

Twelve things this book can help you do better

1. Make a positive impression on others.
2. Sell yourself successfully during job or promotion interviews.
3. Feel more confident in social situations.
4. Get what you want – when you want it.
5. Persuade others to adopt your viewpoint.
6. Communicate your ideas more powerfully.
7. Develop warmer relationships.
8. Negotiate deals confidently and effectively.
9. Avoid being dominated.
10. Take control – without being overbearing.
11. Instantly put others at their ease.
12. Know what others are really thinking.

CHAPTER ONE

The Secrets of Silent Success

Success is all a matter of luck . . . ask any failure.

Anon.

Before I met Alex, a top salesman for one of America's Fortune 500 insurance companies, his colleagues had assured me he was probably the most persuasive man I would ever meet. As one put it, 'Alex could have convinced *Titanic* passengers they'd only stopped to take on ice.'

So it was something of a let-down when I heard a taped presentation Alex had made at his company's annual sales conference. While there was nothing wrong with either its content or its delivery, his speech seemed unexceptional. I felt slightly disappointed. Was this man really the crown prince of persuasion?

It was only after watching Alex in action that I realized how he had gained his reputation – and how well justified it was. Within moments of meeting him at a party he had made a deep and favourable impression both on myself and the group of guests I was with. Effortlessly and charmingly he took command of the conversation, spent ten minutes chatting pleasantly and then moved away. After he had gone my fellow guests were loud in his praise. 'What a delightful man,' one woman commented, while another remarked it was easy to see how he had become so successful.

As a psychologist with a special interest in non-verbal communication – I had recently completed a three-year study of infant body language* – I was both impressed and intrigued by Alex's performance. How had he achieved such a swift and powerful impact? His conversation had been witty, but no more so than that of many other guests. Nor could his charismatic presence be explained by excep-

---

The Secret Language of Your Child, St Martin's Press, Souvenir Press.

5

tional looks. Alex was neither strikingly handsome nor physically memorable in any other way.

The secret of his success clearly lay in his mastery of silent speech. What the tall, fair-haired thirty-year-old *said* was far less significant than *how* he said it. While Alex's spoken language was ordinary, his use of body talk was extraordinary.

My opportunity to discover more about Alex's impressive social skills came three months later when I was asked to carry out a study into techniques of silent selling. The idea was to record a series of sales presentations and make a detailed analysis of the non-verbal signals which either aided or detracted from success. Alex was one of those who volunteered to take part in the study. 'I have a special interest in the subject,' he told me, 'because I deliberately worked on my own body language in order to become a more efficient salesman.'

Alex explained how, some years earlier, he realized that his ability to sell face-to-face was less impressive than his skill in telephone sales. 'It wasn't that I was terrible, only less successful than I knew I could and should be,' he commented. The clue to his lack of success came while watching a video of his son's wedding. A lengthy sequence showed him talking to the bride's father. 'It struck me that my posture was poor, my use of gesture excessive and my facial expressions distracting and inappropriate. I suddenly realized that this could be holding me back when making a presentation.'

To check his theory, Alex bought a video camera and studied recordings of himself in various situations: during casual conversations, while making a sales pitch to one or two other people and during group presentations. After identifying what he considered his major non-verbal faults, he set about correcting them. 'I viewed hours of recordings of speakers of all kinds, taken from newscasts, training videos and my own tapes of presentations by those I admire,' he explained. 'I studied the way professional actors sold themselves to an audience, and even attended mime and dance classes to increase my body awareness. Gradually I developed a greater non-verbal fluency and with it more confidence. Before long my success in face-to-face selling had outpaced my achievements when selling by voice alone.'

Alex's achievements were impressive. But they had taken far more time, trouble, energy and effort than most people would be willing to invest in perfecting their body language. What I sought to discover through the study was whether the same excellent results could be attained faster and far more easily.

Studying silent speech

Although we started exploring formal presentations in front of groups, ranging from half a dozen colleagues in the intimate atmosphere of a company office to an audience of several hundred strangers in a conference hall, the research soon moved from boardroom to living-room, and from lecture theatre to bars, restaurants and clubs. Anywhere, in fact, where people gather to make friends and influence others.

What the research clearly showed was that, as with the spoken word, body talk is a smoothly flowing language with its own special pace, rhythm, vocabulary and grammar. Just as in a verbal language there are 'letters' which, when correctly joined, form unspoken 'words'. And such 'words' are then linked to create the 'phrases' and 'sentences' by which messages are exchanged. Putting the result to practical use, by running training workshops, proved to me that silent speech can spell the difference between success or failure in most social encounters. But fluency in silent speech is not something you are either born with or must for ever be without. All its many signals can be learned, practised, and perfected.

The silent speech of success and failure

We've seen how improving his body language helped Alex to far greater success in his profession. Now let me describe two individuals whose lack of silent speech fluency caused them to be much less successful than their skill, knowledge and experience merited.

Why Arnold and Tricia failed
Before he learned to use silent speech effectively, Arnold could walk into a room without being noticed and leave without being missed. An amiable, intelligent, well-meaning and eager-to-please individual in his mid-twenties, he made no more impression on others than a shadow in a coal cellar. He wryly told me there was an office joke about an empty car arriving and Arnold getting out.

But for Arnold, an accountant with a major computer company, this inability to make his presence felt has proved anything but funny. He believes it lost him a promised promotion, denied him jobs for which he was ideally qualified and left him lonely and friendless. 'I try very hard to make people notice and like me,' he explained sadly during an early training workshop. 'But somehow I just get ignored.'

One thing Tricia could never complain about is being ignored. She has similar social and professional problems to Arnold but for entirely different reasons. A dynamic woman in her late thirties, she's been nicknamed Typhoon Tricia by colleagues at work. Her presence is so overwhelming a few minutes in her company are exhausting. A friend once told her, 'I have to feel terribly well to enjoy your company.'

Despite excellent qualifications, a fine work record and ample experience, Tricia fails to make a favourable impression at promotion interviews. Despite being a friendly woman, she is unable to sustain close relationships. Men tend to find her intimidating and women overpowering. So what is going wrong? How is it that Arnold, Tricia and millions of other hardworking, experienced and basically friendly men and women find it so hard to make a positive impression on others?

Let's examine Arnold and Tricia's body language in detail to see where they make mistakes, and what general lessons the rest of us can learn from them. Here's the report I prepared on Arnold after his first attendance at a training workshop:

Report on Arnold

Arnold is a slightly-built young man with pale blue eyes, a pink rather baby face and sparse fair hair swept back from a high forehead.

He enters the room quietly, almost apologetically. His movements are very slight, rather irritatingly fidgety. Now and then he will clutch at and massage his throat with an abrupt, nervous gesture. While speaking to you his eyes appear to be staring over your shoulder into the middle distance or else he is looking at his feet.

When speaking his face shows little animation or expression, all his facial movements being very restrained. On the few occasions he smiles, his lips do little more than twitch and the smile is never reflected in any other part of his face. His shoulders sag and he has very poor posture. His hands remain hanging at his side for the most part and he occasionally plucks nervously at jacket or trousers. He walks slowly and stares at the ground while doing so. There is no colour or animation in his voice.

Tricia, needless to say, made a totally different first impression:

Report on Tricia

She burst into the room as if making a stage entrance. Her gestures are equally dramatic and rather disconcerting. When speaking her face is animated and expressive. Yet those expressions often appear unrelated to what she is saying.

When telling an amusing story about a colleague, for instance, her features suddenly assumed an expression of deep gloom even though she continued to recount the anecdote. A few seconds later, however, she started telling us a very sad story. It was as if her face was a stage on which over-enthusiastic scene-shifters had changed one set before the actors had finished the scene. Especially irritating is her refusal to yield her turn in a conversation. If you try and comment, reply or change the topic your words are simply drowned. While speaking she gesticulates with hands and arms waving wildly. This is especially oppressive since she insists on standing far closer to you than feels comfortable. But if you attempt to back off even slightly she immediately takes a step forward herself.

Bad body language is commonplace

Arnold and Tricia are far from unusual. And even those who are far more non-verbally skilled still fail, for the most part, to use silent speech to best advantage. In fact, my studies suggest that only 1 in 100 adults has any great degree of fluency. What's more, verbal skill is no guarantee of silent speech eloquence. Often, indeed, the professional speakers are among the least non-verbally effective. You can check this for yourself by simply turning down the TV sound while watching politicians or others with reputations as powerful orators. Once the impact of their words has been removed what remains is frequently far from impressive.

Most people are not only inefficient at sending and receiving non-verbal messages but are hardly aware that such a subtle and elaborate system of communication even exists.

Why silent speech is a secret language

There are three reasons why so much about silent speech remains hidden and why I feel justified in describing it as a secret language:

1. The messages act sub-consciously
Many body talk messages communicate below our normal level of awareness. They act on the subconscious mind, exerting a powerful influence on how we think, feel and behave without our ever being aware of exactly what is producing those reactions.

The photographs below illustrate one of these subliminal effects.
If you are a male, glance at the first two pictures and say which one
you prefer; if you are a female use the second pair. Make this choice
before reading further.

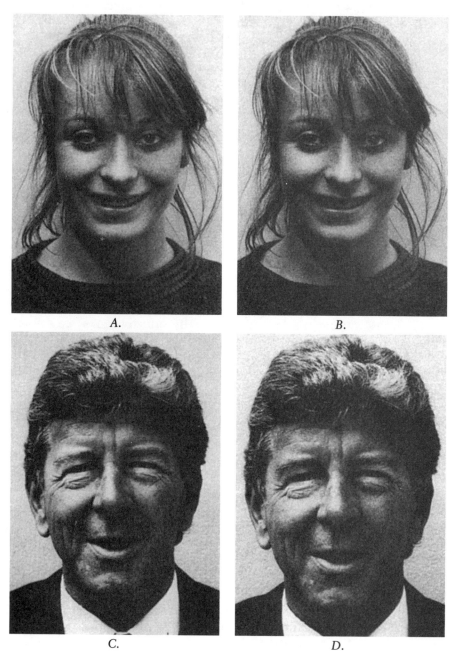

A.

B.

C.

D.

Most heterosexual males and females prefer (B) to (A), most women (C) to (D), although they are usually unable to explain why. The explanation is simple. Both these images have been retouched to make the pupils slightly larger. In (A) and (D) the retouching has been used to make the pupils appear smaller. What difference does this subtle adjustment to the image make? As we shall see in more detail later in the book, the size of the pupils varies according to our degree of interest and physical arousal. When we meet somebody attractive, our pupils get larger. If you chose one of the images with the larger pupil size, it was because you subconsciously associated that dilation with an expression of 'interest'. Because the man or woman in the photograph appeared to 'like you' better in those photographs, you responded more warmly.

Incidentally, many heterosexual males find they dislike the man in photograph (C) more than (D). This is because they interpret the artificially dilated pupils as an indication of sexual interest on the part of the model and, feeling threatened, become anxious or hostile. Women, on the other hand, find no such threat in picture (B) and tend to prefer it because of the extra degree of liking implied by the wider pupils.

Much of body talk is like that. Instead of comprising the large, easily observed signals such as expression or posture, it involves brief, subtle messages that exert their powerful effects below the normal level of awareness.

The case of Clever Hans

The potency of these tiny non-verbal signals was interestingly demonstrated at the turn of the century by the case of Hans the counting horse.

Hans was owned by Herr von Osten, a Berliner, who had trained him to do simple arithmetic by tapping his front hoof. Such was the animal's prodigious ability that its fame quickly spread throughout Europe. Contemporary reports suggest it was an intriguing and baffling act. Not only could Clever Hans perform addition, subtraction, multiplication and division, he was even able to solve problems containing fractions and factors. Without von Osten uttering a word, Hans could count out the size of his audience or tap the number wearing hats or glasses, or respond to any other counting question asked.

Later, Hans was taught the alphabet and, again by tapping out hoof beats for each letter, was able to answer anything he was asked. Hans quickly attracted the attention of scientists and a commission was set up to establish whether this was a case of clever trickery or equine genius. Hans performed before professors of psychology and physiology, a circus owner, vets and cavalry officers. Von Osten was banished from the room, but Hans was still able to provide the right answers with apparent ease. The commission announced itself satisfied that the horse really could understand arithmetic and languages. But a second, rather more perceptive, board of enquiry put an end to that belief. They asked the horse questions to which no single member of the audience knew the answer. For instance, von Osten was asked to whisper a number into the animal's right ear while another member of the audience whispered a second number into his left ear. Under these conditions Hans remained dumb. The explanation was simple. Hans wasn't especially bright, but he was very observant and highly skilled at reading human body language. When Hans started to answer a question, the audience became tense. It was only a slight increase in arousal, too slight for the human eye to detect, but perfectly noticeable to the horse. Then, when the correct number of hoof beats had been tapped out, they would relax again. Hans noted the change in non-verbal behaviour and stopped tapping.

'Hans's cleverness', comments Dr Mark Knapp, 'was not in his ability to verbalize or understand verbal commands, but in his ability to respond to almost imperceptible and unconscious movements on the part of those surrounding him.'

2. Too many messages

The second barrier to recognizing the importance of silent speech lies in the astonishing quantity of non-verbal information produced during even a brief exchange. Ray Birdwhistell, professor of communication at the University of Pennsylvania, offers the following thought experiment to illustrate just how much data is generated:

Imagine, he says, two humans in a complicated box which enabled us to record all the information flowing into the container which could be received by the occupants. This, he estimates, might amount to as many as 10,000 units of information per second. 'Probably the lifetime efforts of roughly half the adult population of the United States,' he comments, 'would be required to sort the units deposited on one tape record in the course of an hour's interaction between two subjects!'

With so much potentially available information we can only afford to pay attention to a tiny fragment of the total. How we direct that attention depends, to a great extent, on our expectations and previous experience of such encounters. A policeman, for example, will be trained to focus on different non-verbal clues to those observed by a doctor, therapist or casual observer.

This filtering means that only a tiny proportion of the available information is ever consciously perceived, even though it can be observed and may well exert a subconscious influence.

3. We overlook its importance

Up to the age of around three, children rely mainly on non-verbal messages to communicate with one another. As a result they are skilled in its use and interpretation. Then spoken language takes over and silent speech is largely lost beneath the weight of words. Yet although we are unaware of its impact we remain very open to its influence. Albert Meharbian, professor of psychology at the University of California in Los Angeles, has calculated that only some 7 per cent of understanding derives from what is actually said, 38 per cent coming from the tone of voice in which it is said and 55 per cent from the silent speech signals.

The importance of non-verbal communication has also been stressed by Ray Birdwhistell, who estimates that the average individual actually uses words for only ten to eleven minutes daily, with the standard spoken sentence lasting around two and a half seconds. He considers that when two people are conversing, less than a third of their communication is verbal, with more than 65 per cent of the social meaning being conveyed by silent speech signals. This means that during a typical exchange, whether it be a casual conversation, an intimate encounter, a vital job interview or delicate and crucial negotiations, more than half the messages received and sent will be visual rather than verbal.

The eyes have it

One reason for the importance of visual information in any exchange, and the reason why success of all kinds so often depends more on silent speech than verbal eloquence, comes from the relative importance of the visual and auditory systems. Faced with the hypothetical alternative of going either deaf or blind, more than 95 per cent of people opt for deafness.

Although it is impossible to measure differences in the quantity of information gathered by eyes and ears, some idea of their relative importance can be gained by comparing the size of the optic and cochlear nerves which connect them to the brain. The eye's optic nerves contain eighteen times as many neurons as the cochlear nerves of the ear, suggesting that around eighteen times more information flows along them. Furthermore the retina, the light-sensitive layer at the back of the eye, is actually an outpost of the brain itself.

The distance over which the two systems operate offers a further clue. The ear is highly efficient up to twenty feet, while one-way communication is possible up to a hundred feet so long as the speaking speed is slowed down. When two people attempt a normal conversation at this distance, however, the limitations of hearing over seeing quickly become apparent.

By comparison the eye can detect a tremendous quantity of detailed information at a hundred feet, and remains effective for human communication at distances of a mile.

The relative speeds with which sound and light travel are 1,100 feet per second at sea level for sound waves compared to 186,000 miles per second for light waves. And while the range of sound frequencies over which the ear is sensitive is fairly limited – between 50 and 15,000 cycles per second – the eye can detect light at 10,000,000,000,000,000 cycles per second. As a result the information provided by our eyes tends to be far more precise and much less ambiguous than that available through the ears. All of which has caused many researchers to suggest that, as information gatherers, our eyes are a thousand times more effective than our ears. Which implies, of course, that silent speech should enjoy a similarly dominant position over the spoken word. The fact that it does not seems largely the result of mankind's social evolution.

Silent speech and left-brain dominance

As is fairly well known, in the majority of people the left side of the brain is specialized for speech. Damage to two crucial centres – Broca's and Wernicke's – results in an inability to speak (expressive aphasia) or to understand the spoken word (receptive aphasia) despite intact vocal and hearing mechanisms. The left brain is also best at tasks demanding logical, deductive reasoning and the sort of technical wizardry which is so highly valued in the modern world. The resulting left-brain dominance may be responsible, at least in part, for the emphasis on verbal rather than visual signals in human communications.

But this over-reliance can lead to confusions and misunderstandings, many of which might be avoided were we to become more aware of accompanying silent speech messages. 'Words not only fail, or cheat, or prove unnecessary,' comments non-verbal specialist Warren Lamb, 'they sometimes convey so little that it is better to look than to listen, and a great deal more interesting.'

Using silent speech

As I have explained, the effective use of body talk is as crucial to social success as being able to speak your native language fluently. By mastering its various messages you can take control of almost any exchange, whether formal or informal, intimate or public. The method by which this may be achieved is termed *Impression Management*. What this is and how it can mean the difference between succeeding and failing I shall be explaining in the rest of this book.

CHAPTER TWO

The Art of Impression Management

It is probably no mere historical accident that the word
person, in its first meaning, is a mask. It is rather a
recognition of the fact that everyone is always and
everywhere, more or less consciously, playing a role . . . It is
in these roles that we know each other; it is in these roles
that we know ourselves.

Robert Park, *Race and Culture*

The mere mention of Impression Management makes some people
throw up their hands in horror. They consider it sinister or manipulative, protest that it will destroy spontaneity, encourage deceit,
promote deception, destroy true feelings and turn warm human beings
into insincere puppets. The majority of such criticisms come under five
main headings, and since these concerns may – at least to some extent
– be in your own mind, it seems sensible to consider them before
proceeding further.

Criticism 1: It's only acting

The argument here is that, because Impression Management involves
changing or improving silent speech, those concerned will stop
behaving naturally and start play-acting.

Strangely the same criticism is seldom directed against language,
elocution or public-speaking classes designed to enhance ability with
the spoken word. If, for instance, a teacher taught students the right
ways of holding a conversation in French or German, there would be
no suggestion that he or she was simply coaching them to speak their
lines. Exactly the same can be said about learning and using silent
speech efficiently.

To communicate successfully through a greater understanding of body language is no more play-acting than setting out to inform, persuade, dominate, entertain or amuse others via verbal fluency.

Criticism 2: It's not spontaneous

No it's not spontaneous — when first used. But neither is any foreign language spoken by a student who has only been practising it for a short time. Initially your attempts at silent speech will tend to be slightly uncertain and hesitant. But with only a little practice the new signals will be used as smoothly, effortlessly and instinctively — although usually to far better effect — as those employed from infancy.

Criticism 3: It's manipulative

Yes, it is! But so is the spoken word. Like it or not we are all involved in attempts to manipulate one another. Whenever people meet, except on the most fleeting and casual basis, they seek to impress each other. One reason why it's often hard to remember somebody's name after hearing it for the first time is that we are so busy making an impression during the first few moments of a meeting that insufficient attention is paid to what's said.

We converse to obtain something we desire in exchange for something which is desired of us; companionship, sexual favours, a job, a contract, a reassurance, agreement, acceptance, understanding, information or insight. But in every case, if you dig below the surface meaning of the words some element of manipulation will almost always come to light.

We can draw a further comparison between silent and spoken speech. Imagine you meet an attractive person at a party and want to be seen in a favourable light. You give your best performance by striving to be as charming, complimentary and entertaining as you know how. You crack your best jokes and utter your wittiest anecdotes. You recount stories whose purpose is, generally, to portray yourself in the most favourable light; as courageous or caring, clever or cunning. In doing all this you are deliberately setting out to manage the impression made. You are presenting what sociologist Erving Goffman has called 'front': that part of our personality we present to the world at large. 'Regardless of the particular objective which the individual has in mind and of his motive for having this objective,' comments Professor Goffman, 'it will be in his interests to control the conduct of others, especially their responsive treatment of him — when an individual appears in the presence of others, there will usually be some reason for him to mobilize his activity so that it will convey an impression to others which it is in his interests to convey.'

Yet at no time do we feel ourselves to be play-acting or consider our approach either lacking in spontaneity or unacceptably manipulative. We are simply expressing, as efficiently as we know how, a natural desire to communicate successfully. The same holds true when using silent speech for Impression Management. The difference is that the body language comprises expressions, gestures, eye-contact, stance and posture rather than words, phrases and sentences.

The only question, therefore, is whether one tries to manipulate the other person efficiently and successfully – in other words persuasively – or incompetently and ineffectively.

Criticism 4: It's insincere

There's an old George Burns joke about the secret of successful acting being sincerity: if you can fake that you've got it made! But, if truth be told, there's more than a little sincere insincerity in every conversation. 'You look ravishing,' the polite guest assures her jaded hostess. 'You're in great shape,' one old friend tells another at their school reunion, ignoring the couch potato's bulging stomach and sagging hips.

Neither our personal relationships, nor society as a whole, could survive more than a few hours of truth telling. To this extent, there will always be an element of insincerity in any exchange, whether it involves the spoken word or silent speech.

In fact, as we shall see in chapter fourteen, it's far harder to deceive anyone who is trained to interpret silent speech. Almost a century ago Freud made the point that even when people lie effortlessly with words they betray their innermost feelings in a host of silent ways which are apparent to the trained observer. If it is your intention to delude or deceive others then a knowledge of silent speech will certainly help you do so more successfully. But, equally, the same insights can make you far more conscious of such attempts, allowing appropriate counter-measures to be taken.

Criticism 5: It's obvious

If that were true then there would be no excuse for not being highly proficient in silent speech. Unfortunately, as we have seen, this is simply not the case. Understanding and using body language efficiently is not just a matter of common sense, but of knowledge, skill and practice.

When people raise this objection, I am reminded of the story of a computer scientist who decided to write a program that could make him a fortune on the stock market. For years he laboriously keyed in every known fact about dealing in shares, until his machine's memory banks contained the distilled knowledge of a thousand leading brokers. He then asked the million dollar question: What must I do to make a fortune out of stocks and shares? Lights flashed, magnetic tapes spun, electrons raced through their microchip pathways, and up flashed the answer: 'BUY LOW – SELL HIGH!'

The theory is obvious, making it work in the real world is somewhat harder.

Before seeing how to use body talk in everyday encounters let's take a closer look at the sort of signals people exchange and the meanings these messages convey.

CHAPTER THREE

Silent Speech In Action

In a sense, and in so far as this mask represents the
conception we have formed of ourselves – the role we are
trying to live up to – this mask is our truer self, the self we
would like to be . . .we come into the world as individuals,
achieve character, and become persons.

Robert Park, *Race and Culture*

Let's explore the ABC of silent speech to see how the various messages
it conveys can be used in effective Impression Management. Non-
verbal signals can be divided into four main categories:

1. Emblems

These are signals which may be directly translated into a word or
words within a particular culture. Examples include the thumbs-up
sign; two-finger victory signs; the thumb and first finger formed into a
circle to convey OK – scuba-divers use the same Emblem to signal
everything is fine; miming eating or drinking to convey hunger or

Three widely-used Emblems

(i) Thumbs-up – everything is fine. *(ii) Victory sign.* *(iii) OK – used by skin-divers.*

Technical Emblems used in television studios.

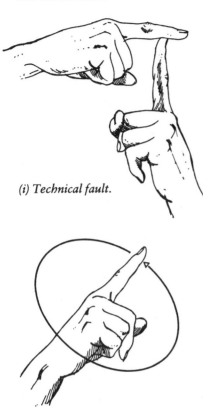

(i) Technical fault.

(ii) Transmission in progress.

(iii) Material must be cut.

thirst; and placing the two hands together against the side of the face to show tiredness.

Many Emblems are specific to one culture and cannot be accurately interpreted outside it. To communicate the idea of suicide, for instance, the South Fore of Papua, New Guinea will clasp their throat with one hand; Americans point one or two fingers at the side of their head to symbolize a pistol; while the Japanese make a vigorous arm movement with fist clenched.

The number of Emblems in a particular culture varies considerably. In the USA there are around 100 in regular use, while Israeli students, with more than 250, are said to use the most.

Formal Emblems are often incorporated into specialized silent speech systems, such as those used by television studio floor managers to communicate with their On Air presenters. A technical fault, for instance, is signalled by placing a horizontal first finger of the right hand onto an upright first finger of the left, forming the letter T.

A finger inscribing a ring in the air symbolizes the red studio light and warns that the programme is being transmitted, while the same finger making a spiral in the air means time is running out. A cut-throat sign orders, 'Cut the speaker off: that material can't be used'.

Not all Emblems are signalled using fingers, hands and arms. A wrinkled nose may be used to indicate disgust, shrugged shoulders uncertainty, a shaking head refusal. Emblems can be used singly, or strung together to create short sentences. Imagine, for

21

instance, that you walk into an office where a receptionist is talking on the phone. By means of Emblems she silently apologises for being engaged, invites you to sit down, expresses her irritation at the length of the call and indicates that the managing director will be with you in five minutes.

Most easily decoded are those Emblems which:
1. Involve directions: 'Go over there,' 'Come here,' 'Sit there.'
2. Issue commands: 'Be quiet,' 'Stay calm,' 'Follow me.'
3. Convey a physical state: 'I am hot/cold,' 'He's stupid/crazy.'
4. Contain an insult: 'Screw you,' 'Go to hell.' This is often done by displaying a single, raised, finger.
5. Indicate a response: 'Yes,' 'No,' 'I promise,' 'I like it.'
6. Describe emotion: 'I am angry,' 'I feel sad.'
7. Offer a description: 'Busty woman,' 'Slim figure.'
8. Ask a favour: 'Give me a lift,' 'Money please,' 'Feed me.'

So far as Impression Management is concerned, Emblems have limited value. But knowledge of them can still prove helpful in three ways.

Using Emblems successfully
First, using an appropriate Emblem can help you gain acceptance to a particular group or culture. Here the Emblem serves as a type of identity badge indicating that you share their beliefs or attitudes. It acts in much the same way as the use of thumb pressure in a Masonic handshake. When travelling abroad or seeking to integrate yourself with a closed group, judicious use of its Emblems can prove invaluable. However, you should beware of using an Emblem which implies a status, position or knowledge you do not actually possess. If, for instance, you attempted to pass yourself off as a Mason through a knowledge of their secret handgrip – which is now a fairly poorly-kept secret – other checks and tests would quickly reveal you to be an imposter. At which point, of course, your deception would cause far deeper and more lasting damage than any benefits you might have hoped to gain. The same applies for any sort of quasi-secret Emblem whose use is properly restricted to fully initiated members. However it is still an excellent idea to be observant about any unusual Emblems and, where this can be done without deception, to employ them as appropriate.

Second, a knowledge of Emblems can help you avoid inadvertently sending the wrong message. In Arab countries, for example, shaking the head from side to side means 'yes', while moving the head upwards and clicking the tongue indicates refusal, not assent. A friend of mine who was offered a sheep's eyeball at a banquet in the Middle East and shook his head vigorously to indicate – as he supposed – a polite but firm rejection of the morsel, found to his horror that several were then supplied by his generous host and he was obliged to swallow them all.

One finger screwed against the side of the forehead to indicate madness is little more than a fairly mild insult in many countries. In Germany, however, the same Emblem is considered so offensive that people using it can be arrested for causing a breech of the peace. In Italy making the sign of the cuckold, by pointing the little finger and thumb at another male, would be considered so offensive that the injured party was justified in using violence.

A knowledge of national Emblems can also defuse anxiety and remove confusions when travelling abroad. In Saudi Arabia, for example, a man kisses another on the top of his head to signify apology. In Jordan and some other Arab countries flicking the right thumbnail across the teeth is a sign that the person has limited funds. Libyan males will twist the tip of their forefingers into their cheeks if chatting to a beautiful woman.

Finally, knowing your Emblems and being alert to their use can help you discover intentional deception. The English wife of a teacher stayed in the Middle East while her husband went to work in Europe. While he was away she had an affair with one of his Arab students. On returning home the husband asked whether she had met the student: his wife guiltily denied that any meeting had taken place – by jerking her head upwards and clicking her tongue!

Peter Ekman, who has made a special study of Emblems, compares such blunders to verbal slips of the tongue; slips which, Freud believed, often reveal a person's true feelings. He describes a woman becoming stressed during a tough interview with her employer. Although unable to express her dislike for him openly, the woman subconsciously betrayed these negative emotions by displaying 'the finger' along the arm of her chair for several minutes. I shall talk further about detecting and making use of such clues when I explain how to read others right in chapter fourteen.

2. Illustrators

Illustrators are linked to speech and can be used to emphasize a word or phrase, indicate relationships, draw a picture in the air, pace an event and impose a rhythm on the spoken word. Although they are often made with the hands and arms, any sort of body movement which plays a role in verbal communication can be described as an Illustrator.

People vary enormously in the number and types of Illustrators they use, some nationalities depending on them to a far greater extent than others. People living around the Mediterranean consider such gestures

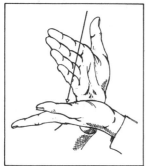  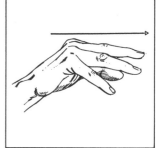

*Illustrators emphasize, indicate, pace and
impose a rhythm on spoken words.*

24

essential to any conversation: 'To tie an Arab's hands while he is speaking', comments anthropologist Robert A. Barakat, 'is tantamount to tying his tongue.'

William Condon, whose slow-motion analysis of human interactions forms one of the foundation stones of non-verbal research, believes that all normal humans show synchrony between speech and body movements. Indeed such synchronous actions between voice and muscles are essential to successful communication. One of the disturbing features of both Arnold's and Tricia's body talk was an absence of such synchrony. In Arnold's case the use of Illustrators was too limited, while Tricia's were not only excessive – they distracted from what she was saying verbally – but also out of step with the rhythm of her speech. As a result, although few people actually realized what was happening, holding a conversation with her was as tiring and irritating as watching a badly dubbed foreign film in which the actors' lip movements and the words uttered fail to match.

Sometimes the Illustrators used by one person, together with other aspects of their silent speech, will mirror those used by his or her companion. Fluent silent speakers like Alex do this to an extraordinarily high degree without apparently realizing what is happening. Mirroring is, however, one of the most potent and valuable silent speech skills you can master. With a little practice it will come naturally and spontaneously, transforming your ability to capture others' attention and arouse their favourable interest.

In her book *Inside Intuition* Flora Davis describes what she saw while watching one of William Condon's slow-motion films. A male employer and female job applicant sat facing one another and chatting. When projected at normal speed very little of interest seemed to be happening. But when slowed down the extent of their synchrony became clear: 'The two began to lean toward each other,' she says. 'They stopped at the same split second, both raised their heads, and then they swept backwards together into their chairs . . . it was very much like the elaborate courtship dances of some birds.' Condon's favourite way of describing such synchrony is that the participants were like puppets pulled by the same strings.

As we shall see in chapter eleven increased synchrony between a couple is a sign of developing affection and intimacy.

When Illustrators are out of sync one or both parties will find the exchange stressful and unpleasant, although they will be unable to explain quite what is going wrong. You can use this, if you wish, deliberately to stress another person during an exchange. Equally, by achieving synchrony you can enhance the atmosphere and take command of the situation.

An intriguing example of the need for synchrony presented itself to me while I was researching body language in children. The mother of a baby with cerebral palsy was finding it extremely hard to grow attached to the infant. There seemed to be no bond between them. Then a therapist taught her to mimic the baby's jerky, palsied movements. This reintroduced a measure of synchrony into their exchanges and a far warmer relationship was able to develop.

3. Regulators

Regulators are turn-taking signals which also have an important role to play in starting or ending an exchange. Handshakes, for example, serve as Regulators. But they also convey an important message about power and status. In chapter ten, for example, I shall be explaining how to use the handshake to indicate either dominance or subservience at a first meeting.

Regulators can also be used to speed a speaker up or slow him down, indicate he should continue or request him to yield up his turn to another.

The most frequently used Regulators are head nods and the use of gaze. Rapid nods convey the message to hurry up and finish speaking, while slower, more deliberate nods request the speaker to continue and indicate that the listener finds what is being said interesting and to her liking. The correct use of Regulators during conversations is essential to making a good impression. You may recall that one of the silent speech handicaps from which 'Typhoon Tricia' suffered was her seeming blindness to turn-taking signals during conversations. Instead of responding to silent speech requests to stop and yield the floor to another speaker, she simply talked on and on. 'Effective turn-taking may elicit the perception that you and your partner really hit it off well,' comments Mark Knapp, 'or that your partner is a very competent communicator; ineffective turn-taking may prompt the evaluation of "rude" (too many interruptions) or "dominating" (not enough turn-yielding), or "frustrating" (unable to make an important point).'

When yielding a turn, the speaker not only drops his voice, slows the tempo of his speech and possibly even drawls the final syllable but usually also glances down, lowering either the eyes or head, or both. At the same time the use of Illustrators is likely to cease. Then, at the moment after the last word is spoken, the listener is given eye-contact in an invitation to take over the conversation. If this fails to produce a response, the speaker may raise an eyebrow or touch the other person. People who want to speak will also use Regulators as a means of requesting their turn. A commonly employed silent speech signal is an upraised finger, which conveys the impression of an impatient listener attempting to deflate the speaker's flow of words.

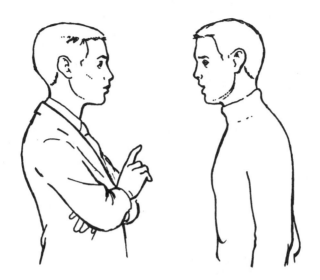

*An upraised finger regulator signals a desire
to break into the conversation . . .*

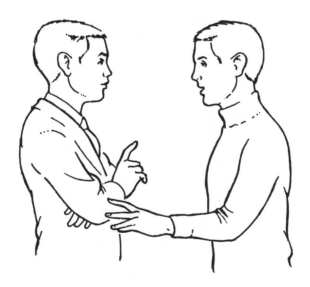

*. . . a light touch to the arm indicates the
speaker intends to keep talking.*

This gesture with the finger, which is often accompanied by a sharp intake of breath, is probably modified from the raised hand in class. It is a throwback to childhood days when that was the only way you could get permission to speak.

When two people are well synchronized one will take over smoothly and effortlessly from the other. There is a clear rhythm to their dialogue. However where synchrony is poor the transfer can be fumbled, like clumsy relay runners dropping the baton at the changeover. Then the speaker may stutter into the conversation – 'I . . . I . . . I . . . will . . .' – instead of slipping smoothly into the exchange.

To maintain your turn in the face of requests to yield the floor a different set of Regulators is used. Eye-contact will be avoided, making it far harder for the other person to interrupt. A light touch may be applied to the other's arm or hand, an instruction to 'hold back a moment, I haven't finished'. The touch may sometimes include a gentle patting movement as though soothing the other's feelings. But however politely done, such a touch is the equivalent of clamping a hand over the other person's mouth. By using such Regulators you can maintain the floor during negotiations or discussions in which it is in your interest to maintain the upper hand.

Finally there are turn-denying Regulators, used to refuse an invitation to speak. These include remaining relaxed and avoiding eye-contact.

To watch Regulators being used with superb skill to control the response of a large audience, or an antagonistic TV interviewer, watch a truly polished professional politician in action. Such people have developed Impression Management to a fine art and, in the right circumstances, can manipulate the mood and responses of their listeners with the skill of a supreme puppet-master. In *Our Masters' Voices* Max Atkinson reveals the public speaking strategies of political leaders to demonstrate how they signal their desire for applause from the party faithful. Analyzing a segment of videotape of Margaret Thatcher addressing a Conservative Party rally, he describes how, after looking down, she closes her mouth and clears her throat: 'These things . . . appear to be retrospective signals, or confirmations, that the time has indeed come for the audience to show their approval. By closing her mouth so noticeably she indicates that she has finished for the time being, and by clearing her throat she shows that she is putting the few seconds break to good use . . . anyone in the audience who has still failed to notice that it is time to applaud is therefore provided with two final reminders as to what should now be done.'

The effective use of Regulators will enable you to take charge of any exchange, whether it is an intimate dinner for two across a candle-lit table or a rousing speech to an audience many thousands strong.

4. Adaptors

Adaptors are movements, gestures and other actions used to manage our feelings or control our responses. They usually occur in stressful situations and reflect earlier, often more childish, coping methods. Normally we are unaware of them, even when habitual. If feeling upset, for instance, you may pull at an ear lobe, massage your hands or tug at clothing. Arnold, who often felt anxious in company, had the unconscious habit of massaging his throat — which became tense and dry whenever he felt stressed. This accounted for the abrupt and disconcerting hand movement which I described above.

A commonly used Adaptor, which has its origins in the nursery, is a head-grooming movement which many adults use at times of uncertainty. The back of the head is massaged with a downward brushing action, usually involving the dominant hand, i.e. the right hand in a right-handed person. This originates during conflicts between very young children, similar to those shown below. Here one child competes with another for possession of the playschool tricycle. An adult appears and forces the previously victorious youngster off the trike.

As he surrenders his position to the younger, smaller child the boy backs off then raises his left hand (he is left-handed) in a gesture which is part defiant and part defensive (see over).

29

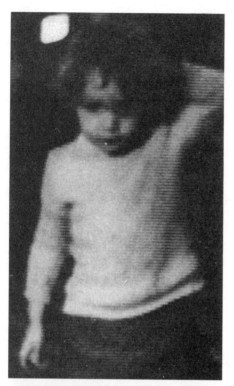

After losing his claim for a playgroup tricycle, Stephen retreats, raising his arm in a gesture which is partly aggressive and partly defensive. In adults it becomes . . .

. . . a head-grooming gesture used when unsure what to do next.

This is often seen in what psychologists term an approach-avoidance conflict, where the desire to advance is countered by an equally powerful urge to retreat. Under these conditions a child may raise one hand halfway between a striking (far from the head) and protective (close to the face) position.

With adults similar approach-avoidance conflict is revealed through head-grooming. If you notice this Adaptor, or catch yourself using it, the message being sent is one of doubt and conflict. The person is unsure whether the best course is to launch an attack or beat a retreat.

You might see it, for instance, when a motorist is being given a parking ticket, when an employee is receiving a dressing-down from his boss, or when a woman is being criticized by her partner.

CHAPTER FOUR

The Four Minute Barrier

The present moment is a powerful goddess.

Goethe, *Tasso*, 1790

How long does it take to make a first impression? An hour, a day, a month or a lifetime? Unhappily for anybody who believes he or she can build an impression over weeks or even years, the evidence suggests that the upper limit is around *four minutes*. While this may sound an absurdly brief amount of time in which to reach a lasting judgement about another person, some experts argue it is actually *too optimistic*. They believe that an enduring evaluation is often made within the first 120 seconds of an encounter. And this applies whether you are trying to impress an attractive new companion, close a first deal with a client or land a much-wanted job.

Four minutes to interview success

'First impressions are crucial in everyday life, and interviews are no exception,' comments Dr Bernard Kingston, director of the careers service at Sheffield University. Just how crucial has been demonstrated by Dr Neil Anderson of Aston University's Management Centre. He asked professional and lay interviewers to watch a videotape of a simulated interview. After four minutes the tape was stopped and the candidate's personality assessed. The remainder of the interview was then played and, at its conclusion, another personality assessment completed. When the two sets of ratings were compared there was little to choose between them. Within four minutes those watching the video had arrived at lasting judgements about the candidate.

This argues strongly for the potency of silent speech since, as Dr Anderson points out: 'In the first few minutes of the interview it is the interviewer who is speaking for the most part as introductions are made and the scene set ... the interviewee is consequently non-verbally active, responding through cues such as eye contact, facial expressions, head nods and gestures.' After further experimental research he concluded that in arriving at a judgement about the candidate the greatest attention was focused on the face and eyes. These areas, it seems, provide most of the information used to assess another's personality.

Nor can one take comfort from the belief that any biases during the interview will be balanced by such objective evidence as formal qualifications, references and an impressive work record. Studies have shown that these count for far less than making a favourable impression and being judged a 'good person' to employ. Research by Drs Ray Forbes of UWIST and Paul Jackson of Sheffield University, for instance, has shown that the candidates most likely to succeed are those most skilled at Impression Management.

The importance of candidates being able to sell themselves is demonstrated by a recent UK study which revealed that the majority of companies depend on interviews as their *sole* method for choosing and hiring staff. 'It is astonishing that although research on the selection interview since 1915 has almost unanimously pointed to the interviewers' susceptibility to all manner of biases, companies remain so inefficient and unsophisticated in their interview practices,' remarks the research director, Dr Richard Ford.

Four minutes to friendship

A similar finding, this time for the informal encounters which occur at parties, clubs or during casual meetings, has been reported by New York psychiatrist Dr Leonard Zunin. Based on years of careful observations he concludes that, 'The first four minutes is the key to establishing lasting social relationships, family harmony, business success and sexual pleasure.' During this brief period there is insufficient time to impress with the spoken word. Virtually all the information exchanged is by means of silent speech.

Research has also shown that once we have come to a judgement about whether or not we like the other person this conclusion is resistant to change. Rather than alter our opinion we distort incoming information in a way that makes it support our initial assumptions. In one study, college students were presented with a brief description of a guest lecturer prior to his appearance. These differed by just one phrase. In some he was described as 'rather cold', in others as a 'very warm' individual. The students, who received one or other of these, did not know that two descriptions had been circulated. After the lecture those who received the 'warm' version rated the lecturer as more sociable, popular, humorous, humane and considerate of others than those receiving the 'cold' description. It was also found that the 'warm-cold' variable directly affected the students' behaviour. More than half those who believed him to be 'warm' took part in a discussion which followed the lecture, while only a third of those given the 'cold' version did so.

Remember all these students attended the same lecture. The only difference lay in their evaluation of the speaker's personality.

Beliefs not only affect judgements and behaviour, but can even distort what we see. Some years ago a paper in Minneapolis published a photograph of a pair of breasts under the caption, 'Can you identify this famous star?' For days after they published letters of outrage from readers protesting that such a pornographic illustration should appear in a family newspaper. On day four they reprinted the photograph, this time showing the whole head and shoulders of actor Johnny Weismuller, star of the Tarzan movies and a champion-class swimmer, the cause of his well-developed pectorals!

The power of first impressions

When somebody responds favourably to you at a first meeting then the enduring nature of initial impressions clearly works in your favour. But suppose that encounter was disastrous. What happens if, for various reasons, you messed up the meeting? The depressing answer is that removing a dismal first impression could prove a long, hard and perhaps futile struggle.

The case of George
George is a tall, burly individual with carrot-coloured hair, a curly red beard and an abrupt manner. His gaze is keen and his eyes piercing. Unless they get to know him well, most people evaluate thirty-three-year-old George as aggressive and intimidating. Casual acquaintances described him to me as rude and domineering. Surprisingly his family and few friends assured me he was a gentle giant, warm, caring and very shy. After getting to know George I collected a list of all the positive aspects of his personality as seen by those closest to him, and showed them to people who knew him only slightly. Would these testimonials change their minds? In most cases the new facts made not the slightest difference. 'Even rude and aggressive people must have good days,' was a typical response. 'I would still hate to get on the wrong side of him because he's bound to have a terrible temper.'

Part of George's problem stemmed from his burly physique and bright red hair. These triggered a stereotyped response from people at first meeting. Because he was so obviously physically strong, people assumed he must also be dominant, while his carrot-coloured hair caused them to believe he had a fiery temper.

We all make such snap judgements, of course. It's part of the continuing message everybody sends out to the world. Plump people are automatically considered affable, tolerant, calm and sociable. A lean physique conveys the impression of caution and nervous tension. people with glasses are viewed as having above average intelligence, long hair is associated with a liberal outlook, fair women are stereotyped as 'dumb blondes', while tall men are considered powerful and virile. What fortune-teller ever told a woman she was going to meet a *short* dark stranger!

But there was one other thing which caused George to be regarded as aggressive. I mentioned that his eyes were piercing and that he gazed long and hard at people while talking to them. As we shall see this is often used as a means of conveying hostility. But George intended no aggression. He was merely long-sighted and too vain to wear his glasses. He stared in order to make out what the people talking to him looked like!

To transform George's image it was only necessary to improve his silent speech signals and tactfully suggest he correct his vision with contact lenses. As a result George was able to manage the impression he made for the first time in years. After only a few weeks of practice his private life had been transformed. Now, instead of turning people off by unwittingly making them feel intimidated and hostile, he charmed them with his combination of strength and gentleness. 'You must have lobotomized George to calm him down so much,' one of his colleagues challenged me when we met six months later.

It is hardly tactful to point out that in George's case, as with so many of my other clients, anger – like beauty – lies mainly in the eye of the beholder. The sad part of the story was the George still had a hard time persuading those who had originally summed him up as aggressive of their misjudgement.

'Non-verbal communication is rather like a code,' says Dr Zunin, 'which we must learn, analyze, refine, modify and enhance to achieve more satisfying relationships.'

RULE ONE FOR SILENT SPEECH SUCCESS

Manage every second of a first meeting. Do not delude yourself that a bad impression can be easily corrected tomorrow. Putting things right is a lot harder than getting them right first time.

To create the most favourable image keep in mind the points discussed in the last chapter. Do not be concerned overly much about what is said during formal encounters. Being a good listener is actually a more effective way of making a good impression than being a gifted speaker.

Be aware of any negative feelings your appearance – however unfairly and unjustly – triggers, then work to overcome them. But also be conscious of positive judgements which your appearance may create and build on these strengths. I'll be describing practical ways of achieving both goals in chapters six and fifteen.

CHAPTER FIVE

The Importance of Self-esteem

What we are, that only we can see.

Ralph Waldo Emerson

You only get one chance to make a first impression. And, as we have seen, the time available for impressing your personality on others is shorter than most people realize. Before you can create any sort of impression it is, of course, essential to be noticed. As Arnold discovered to his cost, there's a great deal of truth in the songwriter's query, 'How can you win the world if nobody knows you're there?'

I am reminded of the man who bought a high-spirited colt. Being tender-hearted he wanted it trained only by kindness and sought a trainer with a reputation for being gentle to his animals. Having been recommended to one, he was horrified when the man's first act was to smack his startled colt across the nose with a whip.

'I was told you used only kindness in training horses,' protested the outraged owner.

'Oh, I do,' the man assured him. 'But first you gotta catch their attention!'

Some people adopt a similar approach when trying to make an impact on others. Like Typhoon Tricia they seek to attract attention by using sledge-hammer tactics.

Projecting a successful self-image demands perception, confidence and the ability to control any strong emotions, such as anxiety or irritation. It means presenting yourself in a way that matches the desires and expectations of your audience. It requires the development of what stage people call 'presence', that special sparkle which transforms a person into a personality.

While everybody has the ability to create a favourable and lasting impact on others, few bother to do so. There are various reasons for this neglect. Sometimes their reluctance to stand out from the crowd is due to shyness, modesty or concern that becoming the centre of attention will result in unacceptable demands being made on them. In other cases I have found that a certain arrogance underlies their refusal. 'People must take me or leave me as I am . . .' they insist. While this is a perfectly legitimate viewpoint, it means that in many situations they'll choose to leave you. Which could mean lost chances, missed opportunities and frustrated goals.

Suppose a candidate turned up for an interview with a conservative company dressed in torn jeans, a grubby sweat-shirt and sporting a bright-red punk hairstyle. Would one applaud his individuality or wonder at his sanity? It's the same managing impressions through using effective silent speech signals. In any situation you must ask yourself – what do I hope to achieve from this encounter? If your ambition is solely to stand out as a unique personality, there is no reason why your body language or your appearance should not be as bizarre as you like. But if your objective is to be seen as an individual and to attain goals of winning the other person's favour, co-operation, understanding, assistance or whatever else you desire, it is *essential* that your silent speech signals satisfy the demands of that situation.

In short, the secret of successful Impression Management is to match the *impact* your image creates to your goals. This requires a sensitivity both to your surroundings and to the self-esteem of the other person. Body language acceptable at a lively party would clearly be inappropriate at a boardroom meeting. Similarly, if you wish to win the co-operation of somebody with poor self-esteem it is tactless to present yourself as overly confident or dominant. If your intention is to dominate and control that person, however, you should project a high degree of self-assurance and mastery of the situation.

The three key factors determining which type of image is best suited to a particular situation are:

1. The goal

Ask yourself – What is it I desire from this encounter? Try and formulate your goal in one or two short sentences. Is it friendship, intimacy, collaboration, co-operation, loyalty, support, acceptance or what?

Often, of course, you will have multiple goals. Be careful that these are not in conflict with one another, or your silent speech signals are certain to be so as well. For example, seeking warm friendship and unquestioning loyalty is clearly to strive after incompatible responses.

2. *The situation*

Ask yourself – What behaviour is expected in this situation? How are others behaving? How do others expect me to behave? While there are occasions when you can deliberately violate group expectations and demands, for instance when demonstrating superior status during a power-play (see chapter thirteen), a general rule is never to be excessively different from those around you.

While this may sound like a recipe for tedious conformity, and will be dismissed as such by many, the reality is that except for the few people to whom society extends a special licence – such as artists or pop-stars – for eccentric conduct, odd and unusual behaviour generates tension and antipathy rather than affection and admiration. And even the licence extended to eccentrics has strict limits placed on it. In a sense their eccentricity is made acceptable by being seen as part of their conformity to the role they have chosen to play.

3. *The other's self-esteem*

As I shall explain in a moment, the best rule to follow when seeking co-operation is to match your level of esteem to that of the other person.

While this may sound little more than common sense, many people fail to appreciate the need to vary the kind of impact they make according to those three key factors. As a result they are more likely to lose control of the encounter and, instead of managing the impression being made, find themselves becoming anxious at the prospect of failure, humiliation and rejection.

These negative thoughts trigger what is termed the 'Red Light' reflex, a primitive mechanism which evolved at a time when mankind faced daily threats to physical survival. Once the Red Light reflex comes into play, your emotions quickly overwhelm your ability to deal with the situation in a calm, rational and logical manner.

The Red Light reflex

You are walking down the street when a car backfires. It startles you and triggers the Red Light reflex. The table overleaf shows what happens to your body, together with an approximate timescale – in thousandths of a second.

Time since noise	Response
12 milliseconds	Jaw muscles tighten.
16 milliseconds	Eyes and brows contract.
20 milliseconds	Shoulder and neck muscles contract. This raises the shoulders and brings the head forward.
50 milliseconds	Elbows bend, hands start to turn palm downward.
60 milliseconds	Abdominal muscles contract. Rib cage is drawn down, stopping breathing.
70 milliseconds	Knees bend and turn inward. Ankles roll feet inward.
80 milliseconds	Muscles of crotch tighten. Toes lift upward.
90 milliseconds	Heartrate increases.
100 milliseconds	Mouth dries, digestion slows.
150 milliseconds	Breathing becomes irregular.
200 milliseconds	Palms start to sweat.
250 milliseconds	Face grows pale.

In less than one second the body is transformed from a state of relaxation to one of high arousal. It becomes crouched and flexed by a cascade of nerve messages which flow down from the face via the neck and shoulders to the trunk, arms, legs and toes. This response is initiated by a collection of neural cells in the brain stem – to be exact the reticulospinal tract, which originates from the ventral pontine and medullar reticular formation. 'It happens before we can consciously perceive it or inhibit it,' comments Dr Thomas Hanna, director of the Novato Institute for Somatic Research and Training. 'It is our primitive protector, whose motto is, "Withdraw now, and think about it later." Survival demands an immediate response. We do not have the luxury to reflect at length on how dangerous the sudden threat really is.'

After this initial, high-speed reaction to being startled the body can remain tense for minutes or even hours. Some chronically stressed individuals remain in an almost perpetual state of physical arousal.

But it doesn't take an unexpected sound or objective danger to trigger the Red Light response. Anything which is perceived as putting us at risk – and this includes psychological threats – can lead to increases in arousal. The way in which these changes are interpreted, however, varies according to the way in which that situation is interpreted. Given a similar event, one person may become anxious and another angry, as these case histories reveal:

Anxious Anne

Anne was born and raised in a small provincial town. She moved to the city in her late teens and held a variety of menial office jobs before getting temporary employment as a secretary in an advertising agency. Being bright and enthusiastic, she soon caught the attention of the creative director and was taken on as a full-time employee. After three years Anne was promoted his personal assistant, then made office manager. Shortly afterwards two senior partners left to form their own agency and invited her to join them. A year later they made her a partner. The agency specialized in promotional work using big-name celebrities. Which is where Anne, now aged twenty-seven, unmarried, quiet and somewhat introverted, first began encountering silent speech problems.

Although she was completely relaxed and at ease in the office or when dealing with clients on a one-to-one basis, Anne hated the exclusive social gatherings the job obliged her to attend. Still a provincial girl at heart, happier in trousers and a sloppy jumper than high fashion, she became acutely self-conscious in such surroundings. High society made her feel under threat and so triggered her Red Light reflex. Interpreting the increased bodily arousal as anxiety she became tense, clumsy and tongue-tied. She fumbled for words, never knew what to do with her hands, and moved awkwardly.

'I feel completely out of place,' Anne told me at our first meeting, 'I feel sure all those famous and influential people look down on me. They think I'm just a jumped-up little secretary who got lucky. Frankly I feel a complete fraud.'

Videos of Anne's body language at different gatherings showed how significantly different her silent speech signals became under the influence of the Red Light reflex. At informal gatherings, in the office or when socializing with friends, she was relaxed, expressive and well co-ordinated. When mingling with the great and famous, her posture became stiff and tense. Smoothly flowing movements were transformed into abrupt and poorly co-ordinated gestures. Her naturally expressive features took on the appearance of a death mask.

All these changes were, of course, the outward and visible signs of Anne's inward and invisible anxieties. In later chapters I shall explain how to achieve control over these inner states in order to prevent them interfering with the image you desire to project. In chapter thirteen I will explain how, by deliberately putting people under stress, you can attain ascendancy over them during a power-play. Finally, in chapter fourteen, I shall be telling you how to identify and interpret such messages in order to gain a psychological advantage over others.

The result of Anne's anxiety was that others became uneasy and uncomfortable in her presence, although, as is usually the case, their ignorance of silent speech meant that they were unable to explain the precise cause of their discomfort. This is a common response, since – unless you are skilled in reading silent spech – the effect of another's inappropriate body language operates below the normal level of awareness.

As another's anxieties make you increasingly uncomfortable, your own silent speech signals reflect this tension. These signals, in turn, affect the other person, thus rapidly raising levels of discomfiture over the encounter. C.H. Cooley captured this constant interplay of signals when he wrote, 'Each to each a looking glass, reflects the other that doth pass.'

Because strong, negative emotions are distressing, the impression you make is bound to be unfavourable. After such an encounter people are more likely to say, 'There's something about her which makes *me* feel anxious,' rather than, 'She was obviously nervous.'

Angry Arthur

Arthur is a thirty-two-year-old self-made millionaire. In an almost classic rags to riches story, he started life as the youngest out of six children born to an impoverished factory worker. He had little education and left school at the age of fifteen to take unskilled jobs on building sites. But Arthur was ambitious and smart. He worked hard and became an expert bricklayer. By scrimping and saving he accumulated sufficient capital to invest in rundown, urban properties. When prices boomed he suddenly found himself extremely wealthy. Shrewd investments put him into the millionaire class by the time he was thirty. But wealth was unable to buy him social poise.

Like Anne, Arthur felt unhappy and ill-at-ease in the circles in which his money and position now required him to move. Unlike Anne *his* response was not one of self-doubt and anxiety but frustration and anger. What aggravated him most was the fact that this inability to make a favourable impression lost him the chances of lucrative deals. 'I felt certain they despised me because of my background. It made me furious. Perhaps it shouldn't have done, but it did.'

Arthur's response to the threat of rejection, his own trigger for the Red Light reflex, created silent speech signals which others interpreted as hostility. As a result they responded either with anxiety – he was a tall, strongly-built individual – or anger. Even when he was doing his best to be charming, friendly and co-operative his body language communicated dislike or disapproval.

Anne and Arthur's self-images were influenced by a powerful belief: in Anne's case that important people despised her for being a 'jumped-up little secretary', and in Arthur's that his humble origins made others reject him. While on some occasions these beliefs may well have had a basis in truth, what mattered was that both Anne and Arthur behaved as though these assumptions were valid, whether or not they had any genuine grounds for doing so. They therefore allowed certain situations and encounters to trigger their Red Light reflex and so drastically affect their silent speech signals. The result was a self-fulfilling prophecy as each projected an image based on their preconceptions of other people's reactions to them: Anne acted in a way which really did cause people to wonder how on earth somebody so apparently unsophisticated could ever have become a partner in such a high-powered agency; Arthur constantly found himself involved in furious rows and gained a reputation as an impossibly aggressive person to do business with.

As well as adversely influencing their body language, these beliefs filtered the information arriving at their brains and led them to pay more attention to any silent speech signals which seemed to support their beliefs while ignoring those which contradicted them.

Because Arthur was, justifiably, proud of his background and saw no reason to pretend to be something he was not, his initial response to the suggestion of Impression Management training was defensive and dismissive. 'I am not going to play-act,' he protested angrily. I was able to assure him that nothing of the kind was either necessary or even advisable. All that was needed was to prevent the Red Light reflex from dictating the kind of image he presented by controlling his silent speech signals. He also needed to become more sensitive to the body language of others so as to interpret their messages correctly.

With practice and training Anne and Arthur were able to transform the negative impression their inappropriate silent speech signals had previously made into a positive presence.

Matching your image to the encounter

In some circumstances projecting the most effective image means being quiet, unobtrusive and apparently passive. I say *apparently* because what you will actually be doing is engaging in *active* passivity rather than being submissive. That is, your behaviour will be a matter of deliberate choice rather than unavoidable necessity. There is a world of difference between a troop commander who orders a feigned retreat in order to ambush an unsuspecting foe and one whose men flee in a panic-stricken rout.

In other situations you may need to project a far more powerful image in order to achieve the desired result. This could involve deliberately setting out to dominate the others by means of a carefully-orchestrated power-play conveyed through silent speech signals. How this may be done will be described in chapter thirteen.

In every encounter your objective must be to remain firmly in control of events, to manage successfully the impression being created and the impact being made.

Matching self-to-self

The surest way of making a favourable impact is to make certain that the level of self-esteem present is matched to the individual whose impression you wish to manage. When dealing with a group, match your level of esteem to that of the most influential person present. If your intention is to dominate that person, of course, then you should present yourself as more confident and self-assured than they are. How this can be done will be explained in chapter thirteen.

The importance of matching self-to-self when developing empathy and liking was demonstrated in a study by psychologists Jay Hewitt and Richard Abloff. They assessed self-esteem by means of a questionnaire and then showed their volunteers answers from men and women who had supposedly obtained higher, lower or the same scores as themselves, and asked them to choose one as a companion. If given a free choice, the majority favoured those with scores equal to their own. When compelled to choose between low or high self-esteem partners, they generally selected the latter. However high self-esteem women were more likely to be shunned than equally assured males.

In later chapters I shall be explaining how, through the correct use of a wide range of silent speech signals, you can create an impression which perfectly conveys the most appropriate level of self-esteem.

Let me summarize the three key points made in this chapter, since these form the foundation on which to build body talk success.
1. Creating an Impact Image means making your presence felt in the most favourable way.
2. For effective Impression Management the image projected must be appropriate to both the situation and your desired goal from that encounter.
3. Always seek to match the level of self-esteem your silent speech signals are conveying with those of the other person, or the most influential individual, present.

The surest way to make others form a bad judgement about you during the first four minutes is to feel badly about yourself. The starting point to ensuring a fast, favourable, first impression is to fall in love — with yourself. In the next chapter I shall explain how to kindle the flames of a lifelong romance.

CHAPTER SIX

Falling in Love – With Yourself

To love oneself is the beginning of a lifelong romance.

Oscar Wilde

It's natural to desire love, admiration and respect from others. Only a fool deliberately sets out to alienate those around him. But where does one begin? How can you create the charisma necessary for making a positive impact in just four minutes? The answer is to start with what you know best and can work on most easily – yourself. With your beliefs, attitudes, assumptions and – above all – the opinion you have of yourself.

If you feel good about yourself then you will tend to assume others will also like you. And if you believe you are likeable, people are going to share that belief. As psychiatrist Harry Stack Sullivan put it, 'It is not as ye judge that ye shall be judged, but as you judge yourself so shall you judge others.'

This simple truth was demonstrated by Dr Rebecca Curtis and Kim Miller at Adelphi University in an experiment where people's beliefs about whether or not another person liked them were deliberately manipulated. Sixty students were divided into pairs and spent five minutes getting to know each other. They were then separated and some of them were informed, untruthfully, that their companion had either liked or disliked them. Later they were reunited for a ten-minute discussion and their silent speech signals observed. It was found that the type of signals sent depended on whether a student believed he or she was liked or disliked by the other person. When students believed their partners *disliked* them they gave less eye-contact, moved further away, leaned back rather than forward in their chair and appeared less relaxed. This behaviour was mirrored by their companion. When receiving warm, empathic signals, they responded in kind. If the body language sent messages of dislike, that was what their own silent speech signals reflected. But the researchers also discovered that people who felt positive about themselves were much less vulnerable to such misinformation. They continued to send out warm, friendly silent speech messages even after being told the other person didn't much like them.

How you look matters far less than how you feel

Let's be clear. Having a positive self-image should never depend on attaining some cultural stereotype of what it takes to be handsome or beautiful. 'I'd have no difficulty feeling good about myself if I looked like Robert Redford,' a slender and depressed twenty-four-year-old called Tom told me ruefully. 'But who could feel good looking thin and weedy like I look?'

As a matter of fact I could tell him exactly who would feel good looking as he did: an overweight fellow-student on the training workshop called Simon, who had confided to me the previous evening that all it would take to make him fall in love with himself was a slim body '. . . like Tom's'.

Not long ago I was on a lecture tour of the United States. It was an exhausting schedule with workshops starting at 8.30 each morning and flights to a new location every evening. In five days I spoke to audiences in Denver, Colorado; Claremont, California; Columbus, Ohio; and Atlanta, Georgia. Accompanying me on much of this trip was a good-looking tennis pro and athlete called Roger Crawford. In 1984 he was one of the runners who carried the Olympic torch in San Francisco. Roger is young, dynamic and bursting with talent. He is also multiply physically handicapped. When he was born, surgeons told his parents he could never be expected to walk. One of his legs was so badly deformed it had to be amputated. His arms are stumps, and he has just three fingers and three toes. Part of the Archilles' tendon from his amputated left leg was grafted into his left hand to produce a claw. He plays tennis by wedging the stump of his right arm into the racket and using the left stump to hold it firmly in place against his right forearm.

In public he rightly makes no attempt to conceal any of these disabilities, and heads turn. Walking with him through airport departure lounges was to run the gauntlet of shocked stares and, occasionally, disapproving looks. Yet Roger's multiple handicaps have never prevented him striving for and achieving athletic and career goals. At Loyola-Marymount University in Los Angeles he was awarded a Bachelor of Arts degree in communications. Now, as a professional speaker, he travels thousands of miles a year. 'I would rather have one leg and a positive attitude than two legs and a negative attitude,' he explains. His message is, 'You can see my handicap, but I can't see yours. We ALL have them.'

For many people their worst handicap is to believe that the only way they will ever be capable of liking, let alone loving, themselves, is via a total body transplant! But until you can love and respect yourself, it's impossible to feel confident and assured. Charisma, presence, an impact personality – call it what you will – arises from what's inside you far more than anything on the outside. So let's make a start by running a check on how good or bad you currently feel about yourself.

The self-love test

Rate the following statements on a scale of 1–5, where 1 = not true at all and 5 = very true.
1. I adore having my photograph taken.
2. I always tell the truth about my age.
3. I would/do try to conceal grey hairs.
4. I enjoy being the centre of attention.
5. I would not mind making an informal speech.
6. I take care over my grooming, even when alone.
7. I watch my weight.
8. I exercise regularly.
9. I would not be embarrassed to strip on a nudist beach.
10. I do not mind undressing in a public changing-room.
11. There are no parts of my body about which I feel ashamed.
12. There is nothing about my appearance I wish to change.

Now total your score:

12–25: You do not seem especially happy about your body and would probably like to make changes.

26–35: You seem fairly happy with your body and the way you present yourself in public, but probably have some features you wish could be changed.

36–60: You have confidence in your body and feel good about your appearance on most occasions.

The Mirror Test

If you scored less than thirty-five on the test, explore your feelings about the way you look in greater detail by examining each part of your body independently. Here's what you do: undress and stand in front of a full-length mirror. Now rate each area shown on the illustration opposite on a scale of 1–10, where 1 = very dissatisfied and 10 = very satisfied.

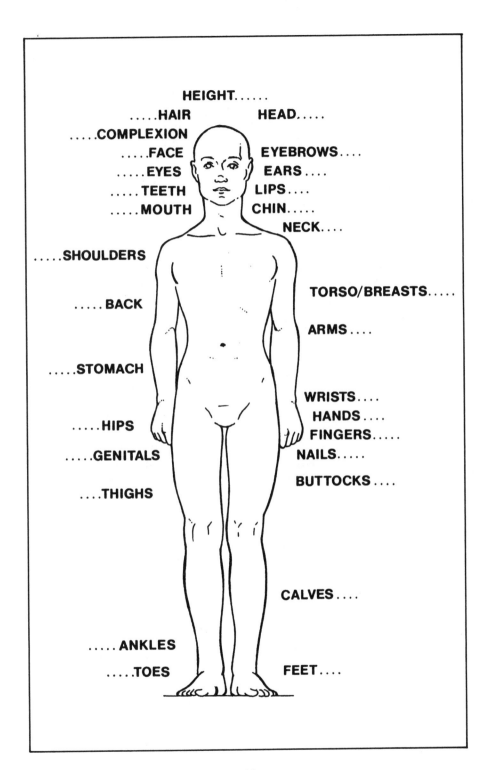

HEIGHT......

.....HAIR   HEAD.....

.....COMPLEXION

.....FACE   EYEBROWS....

.....EYES   EARS....

.....TEETH   LIPS....

.....MOUTH   CHIN.....

NECK....

.....SHOULDERS

TORSO/BREASTS.....

.....BACK

ARMS....

.....STOMACH

WRISTS....

HANDS....

.....HIPS   FINGERS.....

.....GENITALS   NAILS.....

BUTTOCKS....

....THIGHS

CALVES....

.....ANKLES

.....TOES   FEET....

What your total score reveals

30–60: Very negative. Most parts of your body are viewed with dissatisfaction and this unhappiness over the way you look will, inevitably, have an adverse effect on your confidence and self-esteem.

61–120: You feel *negative* about your appearance. Some parts of your body clearly arouse great dislike. The extent to which this will undermine your self-esteem depends on the importance you attach to those imperfections.

121–150: You feel *ambivalent* about your looks. Some aspects of your appearance please you more than others. Build on these good feelings to enhance self-esteem while taking what practical steps are possible (see below) to remedy anything you regard as a flaw.

151–200: You feel *positive* about your looks. This is a healthy body image to possess and should make it easier for you to sustain a strong level of confidence and self-esteem.

201–300: You feel *extremely positive* about your looks. Make certain you are not overlooking aspects of your appearance which, although satisfactory to you, are either less attractive to others or pose a long-term health risk. For example, some people are very satisfied with their looks despite being several stone overweight.

While it is healthy to feel good about yourself, turning a blind eye to obesity may not prove so helpful. Apart from the risk to your physical well-being, in terms of heart problems and the increased chances of developing diabetes, excess weight triggers stereotyped judgements in others.

Why not ask your partner to rate you on the same test, without letting her, or him, see your own scores? It may well be that parts of your body with which you feel perfectly satisfied are viewed rather less positively by others.

If your score was below 150, the following comments will apply. The lower your overall rating on the Mirror Test the more relevant they become. Anything less than a positive score means there are parts of your body causing intense dissatisfaction which you yearn to change. In some instances significant improvements may be achieved by means of diet, exercise, good grooming or in extreme cases plastic surgery.

Other aspects of your appearance can be altered either very little or not at all. In such cases the first thing to do is to come to a more realistic appraisal of your appearance. What seems like a devastating defect to you may appear appealing to others. A useful check is, once again, to ask your intimate partner to rate your body on the same scale, but without letting him or her see your own scores. Now compare results. You may well find that areas of the body with which you were very dissatisfied look attractive when seen through another's eyes. This should give you a confidence boost and allow you to become more objective about your supposed imperfections.

Many hate their looks

Dissatisfaction with the way we look, and a desire to make changes in our appearance, is very widespread. Studies have shown that a majority of people would like to change their appearance in some way.

In a survey of 2,000 *Psychology Today* readers conducted by Professor Thomas Cash and his colleagues at the Old Dominion University in Norfolk, Virginia, 72 per cent of men and 93 per cent of women admitted to being unhappy with their looks. Weight was the cause of greatest concern, with 41 per cent of males and 55 per cent of females expressing dissatisfaction over how they looked. The area of the body least liked was the mid-torso region. More than half of those completing the survey felt unhappy with their stomach or hips.

Such dissatisfaction also tended to be an enduring feature of people's lives. Nearly half those who were unhappy with their looks while teenagers remained discontented as adults. On the other hand 87 per cent of men and 78 per cent of women who regarded themselves as attractive during their teens continued to do so.

How silent speech betrays poor self-image

If your total score was less than 150 pay particular attention to any features rated at 6 or less, since these represent somatic hot-spots. These are areas of your body, aspects of your appearance, about which you have either negative or ambivalent feelings. At times of stress, inner unease often focuses on this part of the body, especially when it includes the head, neck or hands. A man unhappy about hair loss, for instance, will often employ grooming *adaptors* when anxious or uncertain. He may nervously stroke his hair, usually with a sweeping movement from the forehead backwards, pat it, run his fingers through it or smooth the hairs to cover a balding patch. Similarly a young adult who feels embarrassed by a spot on the chin will unconsciously pick at the blemish when in a state of uncertainty or discomfort. Other grooming adaptors include stroking a beard, smoothing the eyebrows with the first two fingers of either hand, licking one's lips, massaging the throat, rubbing the back of the neck, manipulating the ear lobe or tugging at the fingers. All these movements are termed *auto-contacts* – the term used when other people do the touching is *allo-contact* – and they serve to get rid of internal tensions while also providing a certain amount of reassurance by covering, or concealing, that part of the body we dislike the most.

When reading others right (chapter fourteen), be on the lookout for *auto-contact* adaptors, especially at moments of crisis. They often identify aspects of that person's appearance which cause the greatest unease, either because that part of the body is looked on as ugly or because it is subconsciously regarded as posing some sort of threat.

The mouth is the most frequent target for auto-contact, probably from concern that some damaging admission or embarrassing gaffe may emerge. This is yet another of the many echoes from early childhood found in adult body language. When a small child makes some comment which he instantly regrets, the normal reaction is to clasp a hand over his mouth as if to hold back further blunders. Precisely the same response is seen in adults when they have said something unfortunate. If the hand hovers around the mouth during a conversation, it's usually a sign that the person is uneasy about the situation and guarding his or her words with care. This may be through a sense of delicacy if discussing a mutually painful subject or because he or she is attempting to deceive.

But auto-contacts have another purpose: that of bringing direct comfort in a distressing situation by means of massaging a sensitive area of the body. Small boys, when stressed, will often clasp and manipulate their genitals, either directly or, more often, through clothing. For adults the mouth, another organ rich in nerve fibres and capable of providing immense tactile gratification, provides an acceptable substitute. They will suck, pluck, pick or chew at their lips, rub them with finger or thumb, or suck their fingers or some other object such as a pencil.

Hair-rubbing and massage are frequently gestures whose purpose can be either the attempted concealment of a disliked feature or a comforting massage. While stroking or supporting his forehead the harassed business executive is attempting to recreate the comforting caress of his mother as she soothed his brow when a baby.

Studies have shown that city-dwellers use more self-massage than people living in the country, while women employ hair-grooming adaptors three times as often as men. Males, on the other hand, are more likely to rub or support their temples. The reasons for these differences are not known but could be due to the extra stress of living in a busy urban area and the generally greater concern which women show over their looks.

Reflect on, or observe, your own behaviour at times of conflict, uncertainty or upset. You will almost certainly find that you seek out a particular part of the body for attention. Notice what score you allocated that on the Mirror Test.

What self-touching reveals

If you observe others engaging in auto-contact it is reasonable to make these assumptions:

1. The person feels emotionally aroused. You can often decide whether that arousal takes the form of anxiety, anger or uncertainty from the context.
2. It is possible that the feature selected for auto-contact is disliked. In this case the type of contact is likely to be either concealing – perhaps by covering the feature with the open hand – or aggressive. A teenager with a spot on the nose may either try to hide it with his or her fingers or attack it by picking and scratching.

CHAPTER SEVEN

Creating a Memorable Image

Self-love rightly defined is far from being a fault. A man who loveth himself right will do everything else right.

Marquis of Halifax, *Miscellaneous Thoughts and Reflections, late seventeenth century*

Unfortunately most people not only fail to love themselves, but often hardly seem to be on speaking terms! Julian, who attended one of my early workshops, was an excellent example of such self-loathing. And because he didn't much like himself, he was a very difficult person to like. On the body image scale above he achieved one of the lowest scores I have ever recorded, just thirty-six points. Which meant that on almost every feature measured he was scoring the minimum possible score, indicating extreme dissatisfaction. The only feature with which he was remotely satisfied were his eyes (score seven). 'I think', he said modestly, 'I have quite nice eyes.' It was hard to tell, however, since most of the time he kept them hidden behind dark glasses. Julian made an impact on the group all right, but it was an entirely negative one. Interestingly the next lowest score recorded on the body image assessment was Arnold's, whose story I told in chapter one. He managed sixty-seven.

To make a positive impact on others it's important to have a love affair with yourself. That doesn't mean being so completely wrapped up in your feelings, or so captivated by your appearance, that you have no time for anybody else. Greek mythology warns of the dangers of self-worship in the story of Narcissus, the handsome youth so entranced by his own good looks that he drowned while trying to reach his reflection in a pool. By falling in love with yourself I mean possessing the same sort of respect, acceptance and tolerance that you feel towards anyone of whom you are deeply fond. Often people who can express such tender emotions towards their partners are unable to extend the same warmth to themselves. They seem to have little respect for their looks, abilities or attributes, they are unable to accept many aspects of their personality and they are intolerant of their mistakes, setbacks and blunders.

Only by learning to love yourself will you ever be able to radiate the confidence, energy and enthusiasm needed to make a lasting and positive impression on others. 'Learning to accept and approve of ourselves, faults and all, will inevitably attract approval from those around us,' says Patricia Cleghorn, a specialist in developing self-esteem. 'Cast your mind back to the last time you went out feeling good about yourself, and ten to one it was an evening you enjoyed because the people you were with responded positively to you. People tend to think of us as we think of ourselves.'

A healthy self-image, with its associated feelings of competence, confidence and worth, is essential in order to make a positive impression on others. And that image is intimately tied to the most tangible and visible aspect of our being – the body.

If we feel good about the way we look it is very likely we shall also have high self-esteem. If we feel bad about our shape, height, physique, colour or facial features then it will be much harder to remain confident and assured in social situations. As psychologist Don Hamachek points out, 'To a very large extent our self-concept develops out of the reflected appraisals others have of us. People respond not only to what we say and do, but also to our appearance – clothes, grooming, physical attributes. We form opinions of our emotional states, personal abilities and attractiveness largely from the feedback we get from others. In a very important way our bodies come to occupy a central role in our perceptions.'

A score below 150 on the Mirror Test in chapter six suggests that to enhance self-esteem you should bring about improvements in the way you feel about your body. In chapter fifteen I shall be discussing grooming and dressing for success, since both are key elements in achieving positive self-esteem. Here I want to explain how to create an Impact Image by enhancing five key aspects of your appearance over which it is possible to exert considerable control. These are *posture, body shape, fitness, muscle tension* and *facial expression*. By enhancing each of them, using easily mastered exercises, you will dramatically increase the power of your presence.

The importance of posture

Watch the average man or woman walking down the street and you won't be surprised to learn that back pain has reached epidemic proportions in the Western world. Some 80 to 90 per cent of adults seek help for this condition, which is the single most common reason why people visit their doctors. It is also the main cause of worker absenteeism in the United States, Sweden, UK and Canada. The reason for this and many other health problems can usually be traced to the effect of poor posture on the spinal cord.

The spine consists of thirty-three bones, of which the top twenty-four are able to move freely while the lower nine are fused. These are stacked one on top of the other to produce a highly flexible column which, when posture is correct, is perfectly aligned and held in place by ligaments, tendons and muscles. When posture is poor this delicate balance is destroyed. Slumped and rounded shoulders cause the stomach and pelvis to be pushed too far forward, tightening back muscles and producing chronic strain, fatigue and discomfort.

To demonstrate the importance of correct posture on spinal health simply hold a match upright on a hard surface and attempt to break it. You'll find it surprisingly strong. But angle the match even slightly and you'll find it snaps easily. The same thing happens with the vertebral bones. When your whole weight is directed downward, as nature designed, the spine is extremely strong. But when curved even a little out of true it is significantly weakened. While the bones are unlikely to break, they can slip out of position and, because so many nerves run up the spine, cause great pain.

Movement and posture are two essential, but usually overlooked, aspects of creating an Impact Image. Watch somebody who has learned to stand and move correctly, perhaps through dance, mime or Alexander technique training, and you'll immediately be struck by the powerful silent speech signals perfect posture and harmonious movement create. Such people are as noticeable in the throng of hunched, shuffling men and women as if a spotlight was being trained on them. But you do not need to go to ballet class or stage school to develop an equally impressive and health promoting posture. Here's how to do it alone and at home.

Six steps to the perfect posture

Carry out the following movements at least once a day. The training only takes a couple of minutes. Then practise by carrying the posture on into your daily routine.
1. Stand upright, shoulders relaxed, arms hanging by your side.
2. Unwind your muscles generally. Do not confuse the ramrod stance of a guardsman on parade with good posture.
3. Tuck in your tail to straighten the spine. You'll find this also draws in the stomach.
4. Tighten your buttocks and flatten your abdomen as though

preparing for a blow. This action alone will safeguard you from low back pains while automatically improving your posture.

5. Drop your shoulders, but keep them at right angles to the ground, neither drooping forward nor pulled tensely back.

6. Raise your rib cage by drawing the body upwards slightly, as though you were opening out an accordion, keeping your chin parallel to the floor.

It helps to imagine you are a puppet with strings attached to each ear to provide support. These strings are now pulled evenly upwards. Your head feels like a balloon floating gently above your neck. Learn to carry your head in this position. Avoid allowing it to tilt backwards, as so many people do, since this not only gives a stiff appearance but needlessly strains neck and shoulder muscles.

Practise moving around the room with your body held in this posture. Remain relaxed. There should be no sensation of stress in any of the muscles. If you are moving correctly, the focus of all bodily tensions will be the abdomen. Since this is our natural centre of gravity it can serve as a stable pivot around which other parts of the body move. To help it perform this demanding role, nature has equipped the abdomen with a broad, tough, sheet of muscle – the diaphragm. This enables it to take the strain from the other, longer muscles controlling our limbs. Professional dancers are taught to move from this 'centre' while allowing the remainder of the body to stay relaxed and fluid.

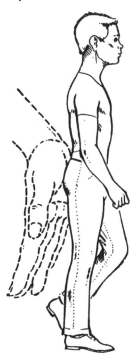

'Imagine that a large hand is applying gentle pressure to your bottom'

57

While walking keep your weight slightly forward and move with a flowing stride, swinging your legs from the hips. Imagine that a large hand is applying gentle pressure to your bottom. Instead of pulling yourself along by lifting the knees too high, which is how the average person walks, push yourself forward from the 'centre' of the body, the abdomen.

When sitting in the office, avoid staying in one position for too long. Change posture regularly and take a mini-break at least once each hour. During each break, roll your shoulders several times, first forward and then back, to relax them. If you are copy-typing or entering data into a computer terminal, try and change the work from right to left and back again every so often to avoid having to look in one direction too long.

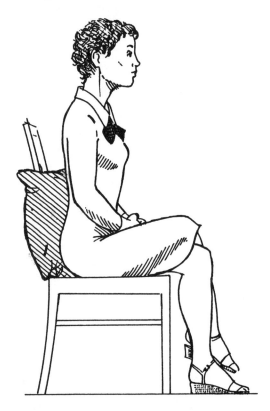

When sitting at home ensure your lower back is fully supported. If necessary place a small cushion between the bottom region of the spine – the lumbar area – and the back of the chair.

If lifting or carrying heavy loads, always keep your spine straight. Bend your knees and lift by straightening them while holding the load as close to the body as possible. If you have to carry heavy bags,

distribute the weight evenly and have one in each hand to provide a balance. If this is impossible, then carry a single heavy bag in one hand for only a short while before swopping over.

Perfect posture and silent speech

The message sent out by poor posture is a generally a negative one. By reducing your overall height you diminish your stature physically and psychologically. Standing and moving correctly adds at least an inch to your height. As we shall see in chapter thirteen, there is good evidence that tall people are regarded as more powerful, dominant, assertive and successful than shorter ones. So making yourself as tall as nature intended helps create an Impact Image. Even if you are on the short side there's no cause to trim further inches off nature's allowance.

As well as maximizing your height, correct posture frees muscles from needless tension, so making all your movements smoother, more fluid and better co-ordinated. This conveys a silent speech message of relaxed confidence and authority, so greatly increasing the sense of presence. Subconsciously we associate purposeful, flowing actions with the three Ds of Determination, Dominance and Directness, all of which create an impression of assurance and honesty. By contrast abrupt, poorly co-ordinated movements – which become more probable when posture is poor – are seen as indicating lack of confidence, uncertainty and even deviousness.

The impact of body shape

During the sixties, American communications guru Marshall McLuhan coined the phrase, 'The medium is the message.' He was talking about TV, but he might equally well have been referring to the body.

I have already looked at some of the associations which are formed in people's minds when they look at different body types. But while tall, slender people – *ectomorphs* – are often viewed as being intellectual, witty and creative, and muscular *mesomorphs* as dominant, cheerful and enthusiastic, overweight *endomorphs* invite mostly negative associations. They are judged to be sluggish, lazy, weaker and less in control. In fact their most positive qualities are considered to be that they are affable, affectionate, tolerant and soft-hearted.

While these are all excellent attributes in their own way, they are unlikely to create a favourable impression in the competitive business world. To make matters worse, overweight people are usually *blamed* for their appearance, even when this stems from problems entirely outside their control. 'Obesity is often associated with laziness or lack of will power,' comments Don Hamachek.

Seeing oneself as overweight is one of the single most potent reasons for low self-esteem. People who regard themselves as even slightly plumper than desirable tend to be far more negative about their appearance than do those who view their weight as normal. In their survey, Professor Cash and his fellow researchers found that only 49 per cent of women and 55 per cent of men who judged themselves to be overweight felt happy about their appearance. By comparison, 91 per cent of the women and 92 per cent of men who judged themselves of normal weight had a positive body image. However women, especially, were often poor at estimating their weight accurately. Underweight women tended to regard themselves as being normal, while normal weight women were more likely than normal weight men to see themselves as being overweight. Women who were overweight classified themselves correctly. This means that women, especially, are prone to see themselves as carrying excess pounds even when their weight is correct. As a result they may diet, or worry, needlessly.

Being underweight can also harm self-image, but this time it is men who are most at risk. The survey found that 83 per cent of women who considered themselves as being underweight had a positive body image, but only 77 per cent of men with below average weight felt happy with their appearance.

While excess weight is unhealthy, what matters so far as silent speech signals are concerned is the effect that a negative body image, arising from dislike of those extra pounds, has on self-esteem. As I have already pointed out, it is impossible to create an Image Impact if you are ashamed of the way you look. It is essential, therefore, to do all you can either to reduce, or increase, your weight to a point at which your appearance causes pleasure rather than pain or to adopt a more positive attitude towards your appearance.

Successful weight loss

There are five key points to watch when losing weight:
1. Avoid crash diets. While they certainly do bring your weight down rapidly, it tends to go back on just as swiftly. This is because you have not changed your pattern of eating. As soon as the diet stops, the pounds reappear.
2. Drink plenty of water when dieting. Dehydration, with its adverse effects on health and the complexion, is far more common than most people realize. This can prove a special problem to people who work in centrally-heated, air-conditioned offices. You need to drink around eight pints of water per day. This is far more than thirst alone demands, which is why waiting to drink until you feel thirsty can lead to dehydration.
3. Never take drugs to help you diet. What matters is not rapid but sustained weight reduction. This can only be achieved by altering bad eating habits.
4. If at first you don't succeed, try another diet. There are dozens of them on the market and it may take time to find one which really appeals to you.
5. Watch out for between-meal snacks. Eat fruit rather than high-calorie chocolate bars. Notice if you eat when stressed or anxious; many people do. Feeding can calm you down, by stimulating a part of the nervous system which slows the body down. Rather than eating your way out of worries, use the relaxation procedure described below.

Measuring your body mass
Before embarking on any kind of a diet, however, make certain you genuinely are overweight. Relying on the height/weight tables published in many diet or exercise books is not a good idea since the figures given are considered unreliable by nutrition experts.

Based on insurance companies' analyses of their longest-lived policy-holders, the first such table was published by the Metropolitan Life Insurance Company in 1959 and revised in 1983 to take account of changes in the mortality statistics. On the original table, for instance, the weight range for a man 5 feet 6 inches tall was 123–156 pounds and for a woman of the same height the range was 115–147 pounds. The revised 1983 version gave figures of 113–163 pounds for men and 120–160 pounds for women. Suddenly a person could be several pounds heavier yet still be said to have an ideal weight.

A better, if slightly more time-consuming and complicated method of assessing your true ideal weight is to calculate something called the Body Mass Index, or BMI for short. Experts at the US National Institute of Ageing regard the BMI as being the most accurate method of determining whether a person is the correct weight for his or her height. Here's how to calculate it – a pocket calculator will make the task easier:

Step 1: multiply your weight in pounds by 703.
Step 2: divide the result by your height in inches.
Step 3: repeat the division by your height in inches.

The final figure is your BMI. A worked example should make the arithmetic easier to follow. Suppose you are 5 feet 8 inches (i.e. 68 inches) tall and weigh 165 pounds. Your BMI calculation is as follows:

Step 1: 165 (weight in pounds) $\times 703 = 115,995$
Step 2: 115,995/68 (height in inches) = 1705.8
Step 3: 1705.8/68 (height in inches) = 25.1

A BMI of 20–25 is regarded as normal. A BMI of 26–30 is on the heavy side while a figure over 30 indicates 'medically significant obesity'. It is a Body Mass Index reached by thirty-four million American citizens.

But being technically at the 'ideal weight' may not prove much of a comfort if you perceive yourself as looking overweight. Here too there is a case for using sensible dieting and reasonable exercise to bring about a more personally pleasing appearance. They can also provide the additional benefits of enhanced well-being, improved stamina and a more energetic, positive outlook.

How to take more exercise
If you don't currently exercise very much start doing so, even if your weight is satisfactory. The gains of regular work-outs are not just in burned up calories and in fitness and greater resistance to illness, but in the sort of impact you make. By firming muscle-tone and improving circulation you'll give yourself a better appearance and enhanced complexion. Improved stamina will help you avoid fatigue during stressful periods of your life.

Aerobic exercise, in which the heart is obliged to work harder for a set period of time – twenty minutes is ideal – also stimulates a positive mood by increasing the production of substances known as endorphines. These are naturally occurring opiates which have an extremely beneficial effect on emotions. So much so that some psychiatrists are now prescribing jogging, cycling or similar aerobic exercise to depressed patients. It often proves even more effective than medication as a means of defeating the blues.

There are many books and tapes available which offer well-structured training programmes designed to cope with all levels of fitness. As a guide to successful aerobics, calculate your maximum pulse-rate by subtracting your age from 220. Then monitor your pulse as you work out.

If you are out of condition check with a doctor before embarking on any exercise programme and be sure to work out at no more than 50 per cent of your maximum pulse. If you are in fair physical shape, then you will need to raise your pulse-rate to 65 per cent of maximum in order to benefit, while somebody in excellent condition should raise the pulse to 75 per cent of maximum. In practical terms this means that a twenty-year-old, with an upper maximum of 200 beats per minute ($220-20 = 200$), should work out as follows:

Unfit: maximum pulse 100 beats per minute (50 per cent of maximum).
Moderate level of fitness: maximum pulse 130 beats per minute (65 per cent of maximum).
High level of fitness: maximum pulse 150 beats per minute (75 per cent of maximum).

Any exercise which raises the heart-rate by the required amount and then keeps it there for twenty minutes can be followed. You do not have to work yourself into an exhausted sweat running or jogging: for many people brisk walking proves perfectly satisfactory. Other excellent aerobic exercises are disco dancing, cycling and fast, continuous swimming. Swimming has the extra advantage of taking the strain off the heart and of working on all the muscle groups. Whatever you decide to do, make an exercise session at least three times a week a part of your regular routine.

Don't, however, be fooled into believing you can eat all you like so long as you take plenty of exercise. As a guide, 3,500 calories equals about one pound of fat. To work off that amount requires some fifteen hours of continuous exercise. Or put it another way: if you eat a bar of chocolate containing 209 calories, you'll have to walk briskly for forty minutes, jog for twenty minutes or swim for twenty-five minutes in order to burn up that extra energy.

Pumping iron – building esteem
Working out with weights is a useful way of strengthening self-esteem for both men and women. In a study by Dr Larry A. Tucker of Auburn

University, 113 male college students attending a weight-training class were compared with 127 others in a personal health class. Those in training used weights and other strength-building equipment twice a week. The remainder heard lectures on health. Before and after the sixteen-week training period, the students all completed assessments which measured self-esteem and attitudes towards their bodies. Prior to the course both groups had very similar psychological profiles. After training those who worked out with weights were found to have a much stronger and more positive self-image. Those showing the greatest improvement were ones who, prior to training, had the most negative feelings about their body. In building up muscles they also boosted their self-image.

The secret of staying relaxed

As we shall see in chapter fourteen, anxiety and tension will almost always betray themselves to the trained eye. But, as we have seen, even untrained observers are usually aware that something is not quite right with your body language, even though you believe the stress is well concealed.

In order to make a positive impression on others it is important to retain control of the situation. And this means, above all else, remaining in command of yourself.

What tends to happen when people feel apprehensive about an encounter is that an increase in physical arousal, the result of the Red Light reflex, is experienced. This may include increased heart-rate, dry mouth or sweaty hands. The bodily changes generate such negative thoughts as 'I can't handle this', leading to further bodily tension and further unhelpful, worrying notions. In some cases this damaging interplay between thoughts and physical sensations can push anxiety over the edge into panic.

To remain relaxed and in control of situations that prove especially tricky or stressful you may need to practise in advance. Proceed as follows:

Find somewhere quiet
Twice a day, for several days prior to the event, sit or lie down comfortably. Loosen any tight clothing, uncross your legs and let your arms hang loosely by your side.

Focus on your body
Now close your eyes lightly and focus on your hands. Imagine them becoming warmer and heavier. Hold this image for a few moments. Include your arms and shoulders. Feel the warmth flowing into your

hands, wrists, arms and shoulders as they become heavier and more deeply relaxed.

Feel yourself sinking further and further into the chair or bed. Notice your body, hands, arms and shoulders growing heavier, warmer and more relaxed. Keep your breathing light and shallow and, each time you breath out, imagine the tensions flowing from your muscles and away into the room on your exhalation.

Next focus on your legs and feet. As before, imagine them becoming heavier and warmer. Picture any stress or tension flowing away from them.

Finally turn your attention to the muscles of the face. These are among the hardest to relax because, from early childhood onwards, we grow used to holding them in a stiff, emotion-concealing mask, which is why so many people suffer tension headaches or pain in the neck and shoulders. Smooth out your brow, keep your eyelids resting lightly together, jaw hanging loose, tongue lying limp in your mouth. Rest your head back against the chair or bed and notice the tension easing away from your face and neck. No tension in your tongue or throat . . . no tension in your jaw . . . no tension in your forehead. Each time you breath out say 'Relax . . .' to yourself.

Soothe your mind
After a few moments picture yourself in some very relaxing setting, maybe lying on a sun-warmed beach, listening to the surf breaking gently on the shore and smelling the sweet scent of tropical blossoms. Or maybe in a beautiful garden, surrounded by flowers and listening to bird-song with a small, clear, stream trickling through the grass. It doesn't matter where you imagine yourself to be so long as the image makes you feel secure, relaxed and content.

Imagine challenging encounters
Allow yourself a few minutes to unwind mentally and physically. Then transport yourself from the tranquil scene to the place where you will encounter that tricky social situation. Conjure as vivid an image as possible of this scene. Try not just to see what will happen, but to hear the sounds associated with it as well. If, for example, you feel anxious about chatting informally to superiors during an office party, you should picture that event in your mind's eye. See the people who will be present, hear the laughter, chatter and click of glasses. In your imagination enter that room, see eyes turning to look at you, voices raised in greeting. Picture yourself relaxed, confident and in control of the situation. Walk over to one of your superiors, extend a hand in greeting. Feel the pressure as you shake hands with him. Imagine making light conversation. See yourself putting into practice the secret language skills I shall describe in a moment.

By mentally rehearsing tricky situations while in a relaxed and receptive mental state, you will find it far easier to handle them confidently and calmly in real life. You can use fantasy training to prepare yourself for any anxiety-provoking encounter.

If you are especially worried about some social situation, carry out this quick relaxation procedure immediately before entering the room. Here's what you should do:

1. Find a quiet, private place. Sit down and deliberately tense ALL your major muscles. Do this as follows: clench your fists tightly and attempt to press the back of your wrists to your shoulders. At the same time . . . shrug your shoulders hard; take and hold a deep breath; flatten your stomach as though anticipating a blow; stretch your legs and point your toes. To tighten the face muscles frown hard, screw up your eyes, clench your teeth and press the tip of your tongue against the roof of the mouth. If you have a firm support behind your head, press backwards to tense the neck muscles.

2. Hold this tension for a slow count to five then release the tension rapidly. Allow your arms to hang limp by your side, your shoulders to droop, your abdominal muscles to flop out. Let your jaw go loose, unfurrow your brow and let the tongue rest limp in your mouth.

3. Take some deep breaths and, as you exhale, feel further tension flowing out from the body.

The whole procedure can be completed in less than thirty seconds but its effect on anxiety is impressive. By deliberately tensing the muscles, you cause a rebound effect which makes them far more relaxed than previously. This increases the threshold at which anxiety will be experienced. We can compare it to a completely filled and half-empty tumbler of water. In the first case it takes only one more drop to cause an overflow, which means that any kind of setback could produce an unmanageable level of anxiety. By emptying out your stress container via rapid relaxation, you are able to tolerate far greater levels of stress without losing control.

Posture, expression and mental attitude

By adjusting the way you walk, stand, sit and look you will not only make your physical presence more striking but also develop a more positive mental attitude. Prove this for yourself by means of the following simple experiment. Stand with your shoulders sagging, spine bent, stomach drooping, arms hanging limply by your sides. Put on a glum expression. Become the image of a dejected, depressed and broken individual. That done, say aloud, 'I feel terrific . . .'

Now change your whole posture. Stand upright. Tilt back your head slightly. Raise your eyes. Draw in your abdomen slightly but not so far that it feels uncomfortable. Smile broadly and shout, 'I feel terrific!'

Which *felt* most positive?

Unless you are a very perverse person indeed, the answer has got to be the second stance.

Our emotions, posture and expressions are intimately linked. Don't wait until you feel happy before you smile; start smiling and the happy feeling will follow. This mood change is more than just a demonstration of the power of positive thought . . .

Smiling helps make us happy

According to psychologist R.B. Zajonc of the University of Michigan at Ann Arbor, there could well be a sound physiological explanation for the link between a happy expression and a positive mental attitude. The human face has on average eighty muscles, although some people lack important ones like the risorius, which extends the angle of the mouth. However the precise purpose of some of these muscles remains a mystery.

What function is served by being able to reflect, with our features, inner emotions? Why, for instance, should we have evolved muscles that can betray fear to an enemy or surprise to a rival? Professor Zajonc suggests that it has to do with creating emotions rather than merely reflecting them. In other words we may smile not *because we feel happy* but in order to *help us feel happier*.

The explanation goes like this. Both face and brain receive blood from the same source, the common carotid artery. As we smile or frown, muscles tighten across the skull, compressing the tiny blood vessels supplying them. This produces small alterations in the volume of blood being supplied, via the common carotid artery, to key regions of the brain. The result is to release or suppress mood-altering chemical messengers. Which means that expressions may not only mirror our feelings but influence them. The result can be greater empathy with those around us. By matching their expressions we are better able to share their emotions and so produce more harmonious relationships.

The theory also explains blushing, a silent speech signal that sufferers would willingly do without. People who blush do so in situations from which they would like to flee but cannot – usually because of social constraints. The excess surge of blood, triggered by the body's adrenalin-powered defence mechanism, is diverted away from the brain – where it would normally be used for aiding us in fighting or fleeing – and into the blood vessels of the face, producing the glowing blush.

Similarly, pallor caused by shock or startle occurs when blood is transferred to the brain from vessels in the facial muscles. It's intriguing to reflect that if the main carotid artery had branched off at the shoulders rather than the neck, we might all have expressed emotions with our arms and blushed with our shoulders.

Support for Zajonc's proposal comes from research by Paul Ekman, professor of psychology at the University of California. Subjects asked to practise pulling happy or sad faces reported that the expressions influenced their mood. Gloomy looks made them depressed while cheerful faces lifted their spirits.

While success can't be guaranteed, if you smile insincerely to cover up anger or hurt, for instance, it's not going to cause you to feel less upset, and there is good reason for supposing that a happy face can boost your mood, not only by triggering the release of 'happy' chemicals in the brain but also by encouraging a relaxed and agreeable response from others. Although, as we shall see later in the book, smiling can be an ambiguous signal, its usual effect is to increase the chances that others will like us.

The golden rules of high self-esteem

While there is no simple recipe for developing strong and positive self-esteem, the following rules will help make for a happier relationship with yourself. Practise each several times a week and you'll be amazed at the boost they give to self-esteem:

1. Make a decision from this moment on that you are going to think, act and speak positively about yourself. Stop running yourself down and start building yourself up. Notice all your good points – in personality and appearance – and write them down.
2. If you start criticizing yourself, then think 'Yellow bumble-bees' or some similar meaningless phrase. That will stop the negative thoughts dead. Then immediately switch to a positive thought. Stop punishing yourself for mistakes made in the past.
3. Let go of any bitterness or resentment you feel towards others. Such negative thoughts will harm you more than them. Bad feelings are a troublesome and pointless burden to carry about. Dump them.
4. After any significant action, whether successful or not, debrief yourself as follows: first consider all the *positive* things you said and did; notice any *positive* outcomes, whether intended or unexpected. Only once you have thought about these aspects of your performance should you think about any *interesting* things

you said or did. These need not necessarily have led to the outcome you desired. But in reflecting on them you may feel they were valid thoughts or actions which you might well repeat on similar occasions in future.

Only after exploring all the *positive* and all the *interesting* features of your performance should you deal with anything *negative*.

Deal with your setbacks, blunders, failures and errors as objectively as possible. NEVER say, 'What a fool' to have done that. Simply notice the mistakes so that you can avoid them the next time. By adopting the PIN (Positive-Interesting-Negative) approach to self-evaluation, you'll be able to build on your attainments and avoid making the same errors twice, without undermining self-esteem.

5. Spend time with people who will help and support you. Avoid negative, overly-critical individuals who engender feelings of gloom and doom. They have undoubtedly got significant personal problems but that is no reason for you to be burdened with their troubles.

6. Prepare a list of things that give you pleasure. They do not have to be large, elaborate or costly. Make a decision to do at least one of them, and preferably more, in the next seven days.

7. Before you fall asleep, repeat *one* of the following affirmations to yourself seven times while lying relaxed and calm. Put your name in the space provided. Use a different affirmation each night for a fortnight then start again.

    a. 'I . . . have a perfect right to happiness and contentment.'
    b. 'I . . . am open to receiving love.'
    c. 'I . . . deserve love just for being alive.'
    d. 'I . . . accept myself totally, I love myself more each day.'
    e. 'I . . . am free and everybody else is free too.'
    f. 'I . . . give myself permission to become a total success.'
    g. 'I . . . am safe with my own energy and power.'
    h. 'I . . . trust my feelings and thoughts.'
    i. 'I . . . can relax and let life flow through me.'
    j. 'I . . . am now willing to give myself all I need.'
    k. 'I . . . am worthy of respect and trust.'
    l. 'I . . . can achieve all I set out to attain.'
    m. 'I . . . love and am loved.'
    n. 'I . . . am willing to give myself all I need.'

Self-esteem and silent speech

I have discussed ways of improving posture, enhancing self-esteem and controlling tension at some length because all send out crucial silent speech messages which otherwise lie beyond our power consciously to control. These are the small, subtle but still potent signals others use when forming an impression about us. By getting these right you will lay down a firm foundation on which more easily manipulated aspects of body language can be built.

Now that you have seen the crucial role played by your own self-image in silent speech, it's time to study the secret language in action. We'll do so by putting an everyday encounter under the microscope to discover the astonishingly intricate and complex non-verbal messages being exchanged during even the most casual of meetings.

CHAPTER EIGHT

Anatomy of an Encounter

*To others we are not ourselves but a performer in their lives
cast for a part we do not even know that we are playing.*

Elizabeth Bibesco, *Haven*, 1951

On the point of entering a crowded room you pause for a moment by the door, searching the party guests for a familiar face. You see a casual acquaintance, catch his eye and cross towards him. Greetings are exchanged. You shake hands, chat for a while, and then move away to talk with somebody else.

During that brief encounter, those fleeting moments of contact, hundreds of non-verbal messages will have been exchanged, and it is these, usually more than any words spoken, which influence the impression you form of one another.

In this and the following chapters we shall explore exactly what goes on during such encounters and discover how to create the most favourable impact, or indeed any other type of impression desired, by means of silent speech.

Meetings and greetings

Every encounter, however brief, can be divided into six stages, and for social success it is essential that you manage each of them correctly. They are:

Stage 1. Initiation
This happens when you are still some distance from the person with whom contact is to be made. Although your whole body is involved, to some extent, in this first stage, the main area of communication is your face, especially the eyes and mouth.

71

Stage 2. Orientation

You walk over and halt beside the other person. Of key significance here is the distance at which you stop and your orientation; that is, whether you are face-to-face, slightly angled or side-by-side. Distance and body angle are important ways of communicating different feelings towards your companion.

Stage 3. Contact

Some form of physical contact is usually made, either a handshake or an embrace. The type of contact chosen, together with your postures, facial expressions, degree of muscular tension and direction of gaze are crucially important here. In my studies, I found that the entire message of this Contact stage could be altered by a change in gaze duration lasting less than a second.

Stage 4. Involvement

As verbal conversation starts, you continue to exchange potent silent speech signals. These non-verbal messages may be used to amplify the words, adding emphasis and meaning. Equally they may, unwittingly, conflict with the spoken language, so producing unease or confusion in the listener.

Stage 5: Disengagement

At some point one or both of you decide the exchange should come to an end. Although the moment of parting is often decided verbally, with someone saying something along the lines of: 'Well, it's been nice chatting. See you around sometime. Bye . . .,' half a minute or more before any such partings are spoken silent speech will have signalled a desire to separate. The main ways in which these silent messages are sent is by use of gaze and body position.

Stage 6: Separation

You move apart and go your own ways. Although there may seem little that can now be done to affect the impression made, an efficiently managed separation is just as important as the previous five stages. In fact my own research suggests that many people who achieve reasonable success in initiating and regulating a dialogue often become less effective during the final seconds of an encounter. And since our memories are best for events which happened most recently, an unsatisfactory disengagement can adversely influence the whole exchange.

In this chapter I shall be exploring the first stage – Initiation – while the remaining stages will be considered in the chapters which follow.

Stage 1: Initiation

With these stages in mind, let's examine that commonplace encounter in more detail to see what silent speech signals were being exchanged as you caught your acquaintance's eye and crossed the room towards him. For the sake of simplicity, I am going to assume an encounter between two males. Female body language follows a similar pattern, although as we shall see in chapter fourteen women tend to be a great deal more sensitive to and aware of the influence of silent speech. They are also more likely to make prolonged and more intimate physical contact during the third stage of the encounter. Even casual acquaintances are more likely to embrace, however fleetingly, than shake hands.

As you advance towards one another, the first silent speech signal usually exchanged is . . .

The eyebrow flash

Microseconds after initial eye-contact, both your eyebrows and the other person's will have lifted and fallen in a movement lasting around one fifth of a second.

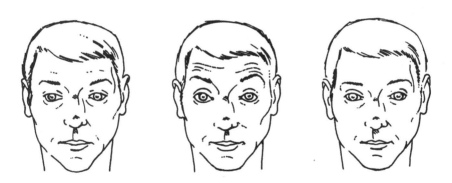

The eyebrow flash has been found in every culture studied.

Called the eyebrow flash, this signal has been observed among Europeans, Balinese, Papuans, Samoans, Bushmen and South American Indians. In fact it appears to be used by virtually every society and social grouping from Bantus to Brahmins and from Afghan tribesmen to New York stockbrokers.

The eyebrow flash also occurs in several species of monkey, so confirming that it is inborn and serves some evolutionary function, rather than being a purely learned response. The purpose seems to be to draw each person's attention to the eyes and face of the other so that clear and unambiguous signals can be exchanged. Used at a distance of between six and twelve feet, its message is one of friendly greeting between people who are on good terms. The eyebrow flash would not be used, for example, between strangers passing in a street. Indeed, to use the eyebrow flash under such circumstances could create bewilderment, anxiety or hostility in the other. Nor is it likely to be used by people who know one another well but are on bad terms. During such encounters, a more usual response is to studiously avoid the eyebrow flash, and often any eye-contact at all, in order to reduce the likelihood of the unwelcome meeting proceeding beyond the first stage. Eyebrow flashes are also used by people giving approval or agreement to others, thanking them, flirting, seeking confirmation, and if starting and/or emphasizing a statement. When combined with a stare and/or a lifting of the head and simultaneous lowering of the eyelids, however, the eyebrow flash can also be used to indicate disapproval or indignation or to admonish the other person.

The only people known deliberately to suppress the eyebrow flash are the Japanese. While they are perfectly capable of exchanging such a signal, it is considered improper and indecent.

Someone who refuses to return an eyebrow flash may be showing a disinclination to become involved with the other person. In these circumstances he responds by rapidly averting his gaze, as if to pretend he hasn't even noticed the signal. But an angry individual eager for a row may also withhold the response, not because he or she wishes to avoid the encounter, but through a desire to make it clear, right from the start, that the meeting is not going to be a friendly one. Instead of averting their gaze, following the refused invitation for a friendly encounter, they maintain a firm, steady eye-contact while the muscles, especially those of the jaw, tighten. You may also find their fists starting to clench slightly, as if in anticipation of physical combat. This is a primitive reaction rather than signalling any actual desire to come to blows, and is found in women as well as men. In women, however, it is often more restrained, sometimes appearing as no more than a slight bending of the fingers or a folding inward of the thumb. Tucking the thumb in when forming a fist is an instinctive means of protecting this vital but vulnerable digit.

Let's look at a typical encounter between an angry male and his victim. John sees Michael, a colleague at work, walking down the office corridor towards him. Being friendly he initiates a greeting using the eyebrow flash. Michael, however, has just been criticized for not completing an urgent report. He blames John for failing to provide him with the necessary information. Michael is eager to let John know just what he thinks of him. He signals this hostility by refusing to engage in a mutual eyebrow flash as they approach. As is always the case with silent speech, a refusal to send an expected signal is, in itself, a powerful message. Before Michael even opens his mouth John anticipates that something has happened to sour their relationship. If Michael is really furious, he will further signal his rage by sustained eye-contact. By stepping up the hostility message several points he alerts John to the fact that a row is brewing.

However a refusal to return your eyebrow flash need not be due to a rejection of that friendly invitation or a sign of impending trouble. Anxious or shy people may fail either to use or respond to the eyebrow flash even when their feelings towards the other person are warm and friendly. As a result they unintentionally create a negative impression before a word is spoken.

Because the eyebrow flash acts subconsciously, few people are even aware of this silent speech signal until it has been pointed out to them. Once you know what to look for, of course, it becomes all too obvious. Some people even feel embarrassment for a while, although this self-consciousness quickly wears off. 'I can always tell people who have reached that stage in your training programme,' a colleague once joked. 'They are the ones walking around with paper bags over their heads!'

But since the eyebrow flash exerts its influence below our normal level of awareness, any refusal to offer or return the signal in situations where such a response would be expected can lead to unease and a negative appraisal.

Susan, a cheerful but very shy art teacher, was branded as 'cold' by staff-room colleagues when she first arrived at a new school. 'She's not a particularly friendly person,' I was told. Susan was, but her body language wasn't. Due to being brought up in an emotionally cold home – her parents seldom held or cuddled her, she recalls – Susan had never learned to use appropriate silent speech signals during encounters. By refusing the eyebrow flash and avoiding gaze she instantly created a sense of coldness and hostility at a first meeting.

Failure to return this signal, for whatever reason, can make the other person feel as hurt and rejected as if you had scornfully and deliberately ignored a hand outstretched in friendship.

RULE TWO FOR SILENT SPEECH SUCCESS

Always initiate the eyebrow flash whenever possible.
Always respond to another's eyebrow flash unless your deliberate intention is to signal hostility.

Judge the distance at which you make the signal carefully. If you raise your eyebrows when too far away the signal may not be noticed. Believing your message has been received, you may then refrain from responding to the other party's eyebrow flash, thus conveying an unintentional message of disapproval or hostility.

If you signal too late – that is, when the distance between you is less than around six feet – the eyebrow flash may be misinterpreted as a signal not of greeting but enquiry. Instead of sending the message, 'Hello, I am delighted to see you . . .' it conveys astonishment or surprise. A typical response to an eyebrow flash made at less than four feet is: 'Is there something wrong with the way I look?' Even when this query is left unspoken it can generate a sense of unease which colours the encounter and creates a negative impression on the receiver.

Uses and abuses of eye-contact

Once eye-contact is made, each person rapidly scans the other's face for further information about attitudes and intentions based on silent speech signals. At the same time both individuals are forming their features into expressions that convey either their true feelings about the meeting or the impression they wish to convey.

How faces are viewed

When we look at somebody's face, particularly for the first time, our eyes scan their features not in a random manner, but according to the systematic pattern illustrated below.

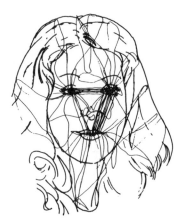

By means of a special camera the pattern of eye-movements used to view a face can be traced.

As you can see our eyes scan the face in a series of triangular movements, first crisscrossing the eyes then travelling down to the mouth.

Research has shown that approximately 75 per cent of the time is devoted to exploring the triangle formed by eyes and mouth, 10 per cent to the forehead and hair, and 5 per cent to the chin, with the remaining 10 per cent devoted to the other features. The average time for scanning the face during the Initiation stage of the greeting is around three seconds.

The power of gaze

Following this brief, but intense, period of eye-contact, gaze is briefly broken, usually by both persons glancing downward. Why downward? Nobody knows for certain, but a likely explanation is that it signals submission, without implying any lack of interest or intention to withdraw from the encounter. The message is, 'I am not going to try and dominate you during this meeting.'

Looking down, or bending the head, has long been used as a gesture of abasement and a sign of subservience in human culture. When a ruler passes his subjects they are expected to bow either their heads or their entire body in recognition of their more lowly status. We kneel or prostrate ourselves in prayer as a symbolic gesture of meekness and obedience to divine authority. As I shall explain in chapters twelve and thirteen, a downward glance – together with other body movements – is used as a sign of submission during courtship and to signal unquestioned acceptance of a superior's right of domination.

Further, when eye-contact is broken in any other direction an impression of distraction or lack of interest may be conveyed. By looking to left or right, you seem to be suddenly paying more attention to something else in the immediate surroundings. Looking upwards is an unusual way of breaking eye-contact during Initiation whose effect is usually to make the other person glance upwards as well, perhaps fearing something is about to fall on them. Even when no head or eye movement follows there is often an increase in bodily tension, indicating that, subconsciously, the individual has become more aroused.

Any eye-break other than downward causes distraction and can even generate a fair amount of discomfort.

Although, as with all these brief and subtle signals, such feelings are invariably experienced below the level of awareness, they powerfully influence our feelings towards each other without either person appreciating how an impression is being created or why we are responding in a particular way.

The absence of a break also causes the other person to feel unease since, as we have seen and will explore more fully in a moment, the intentional or inadvertent message is one of aggression and hostility.

Following a very brief eye-contact break, which seems to serve the same sort of function in silent speech as a comma in a written sentence, mutual gaze is restored and eyes remain locked until contact is established.

The complete pattern of looking during Initiation is as follows:

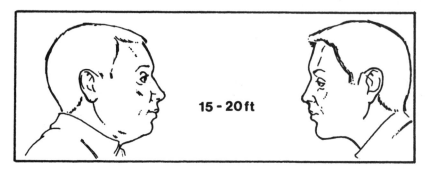

Initial eye-contact.
Approximate distance: 15–20 feet.
Purpose: to establish silent speech contact.

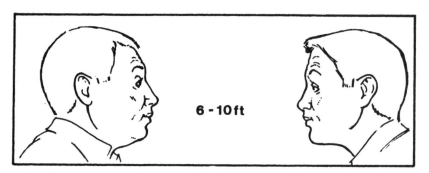

Eyebrow flash.
Approximate Distance: 6–10 feet.
Purpose: to convey friendly intentions.

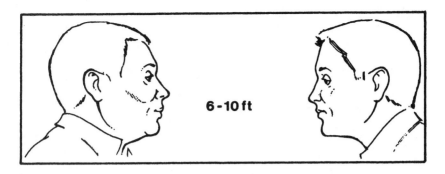

Mutual gaze. Each scans the other's face intently, special attention being paid to the eyes and mouth. This phase lasts around three seconds.

Distance: 6–10 feet.

Purpose: to gain information about the other person's feelings, attitudes, intentions. Body signals can also be read during this scrutiny.

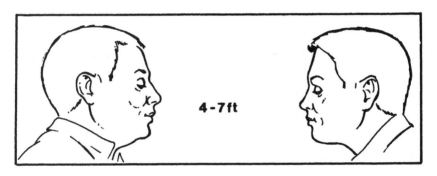

Eye-contact is broken, usually by both glancing downward. A break in any other direction can produce unease.

Distance: 4–7 feet.

Purpose: to reinforce the impression of friendly intentions by signalling mutual submission. The message is, 'I do not intend to dominate you.'

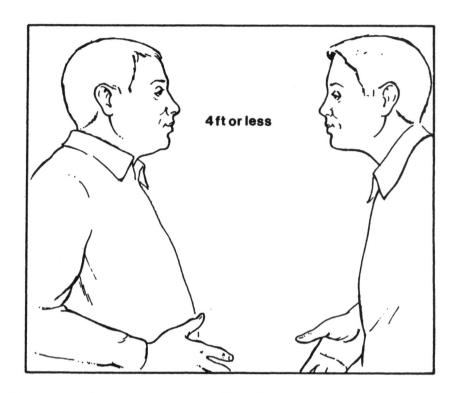

4 ft or less

Eye-contact is restored. Arms and hands start moving into a position
to make physical contact.
Distance: 4 feet or less.
Purpose: to allow accurate positioning with respect to the other
person. To enable hands to be clasped or bodies embraced.

RULE THREE FOR SUCCESSFUL SILENT SPEECH

Always break eye-contact downward, unless it is your deliberate intention to convey a lack of interest in the other person
or to throw them temporarily off balance by a disconcerting
upward eye-break. This has its uses in power-plays which I
shall consider in chapter thirteen.

Why lingering looks make a bad impression

Longer periods of eye-contact at the Initiation stage of the encounter
subtly change the signals being sent. Depending on other silent speech

messages, increased eye-contact can imply hostility or a desire for greater intimacy.

Video recordings of lovers approaching one another, for instance, show mutual gaze is sustained throughout the Initiation stage from the first moment eye-contact is established right the way through to the embrace. These long, lingering glances are a way of communicating mutual adoration.

A loving mother also makes continuous eye-contact with her small child as they greet one another after nursery or playschool. In order to maintain mutual gaze she will also kneel down to bring their faces level. Less affectionate women, by comparison, tend to lean forward rather than kneel down and give much less mutual gaze. Often, in fact, the amount of eye-contact offered more closely resembles that between adult, same sex, friends rather than intimate companions.

Where facial expression and posture convey hostility rather than deep love, prolonged eye-contact during the Initiation stage will be decoded by the other person as further evidence of dislike or disapproval.

As with the unintentionally negative message which stems from a failure to respond to, or initiate, eyebrow flash, an incorrect use of eye-contact during Initiation can have unfortunate consequences. This was one of the problems confronting Millie, a gentle, softly spoken twenty-seven-year-old sales assistant from London who participated in one of my workshops. Once you got to know her, Millie came across as a friendly, warm-hearted woman. But that was not the impression she conveyed to many at first meeting.

After initial contact has been made at my workshops, people are asked to evaluate one another's personalities on various scales. Millie's ratings were low on the scales of friendliness, empathy and warmth, but above average on hostility and assertiveness. Although this was not the view of everybody at the workshop, it was the impression conveyed to more than half. When she saw her scores Millie was shattered. 'But I am so friendly,' she protested. 'I don't feel any hostility to anybody. I want to be liked . . .'

When asked why they had rated Millie as hostile or assertive, nobody could explain why. They just felt that was how she came across at first meeting. A slow-motion recording of Millie's meetings revealed the truth. Unlike Susan, who failed to initiate or respond to the eyebrow flash, Millie sent and returned this initial greeting. But then she made the silent speech blunder that created such a negative impression. Her gaze continued some three times longer than average. Instead of looking for around three seconds when approaching a stranger, she studied their features for between six and eight seconds during the Initiation stage of greeting.

Millie wasn't intending to signal hostility. It was just that she was slightly short-sighted but didn't realize it. Because of this she was unable to obtain sufficient non-verbal information about strangers during the few seconds acceptable at the Initiation stage. Instead of breaking gaze she maintained it almost to the moment that actual physical contact was established during the second greeting stage. This was interpreted by some of those she met as signalling a hostile or aggressive intent. As with long-sighted George, whose inability to use eye-contact effectively I described in chapter four, contact lenses solved the problem and enabled Millie's true personality to shine through.

RULE FOUR FOR SILENT SPEECH SUCCESS

Never normally hold gaze for more than three seconds during the Initiation stage. Look, then break eye-contact briefly. Any violation of this rule can generate a negative impression, even though the person receiving the message is unable to explain the reason for their feelings. The only exception is during a power-play when it is your deliberate intention to disconcert your opponent.

Putting your best face forward

As you may have noticed in the illustration on page 76, the time spent scanning the face is not evenly divided between the left and right side. Dr Darleen Kennedy of Beaver College in Glenside, Pennsylvania has shown that people pay greatest attention to information reaching their right visual field, which means that more time is spent looking at the left side of another person's face.

Dr Kennedy asked students to look at six line drawings of male faces and then, one week later, to pick them out of a pile of twelve illustrations. When making their choice, one third saw only the left side of the drawing, one third the right side and the remainder the whole face. Those who saw just the right side made twice as many mistakes as those able to view either the left half or the complete face. In practice this means people with a 'good' left side are more likely to be remembered than those whose 'best' feature is their right side.

Most people feel they photograph, or look, most attractive when viewed from a particular profile. But what exactly does having a 'good' or 'best' side really mean? Is it mere vanity, or is there some truth in such beliefs?

If you study your own face in a mirror and notice the difference between the edges of your mouth and the corner of each eye, you'll see they are not symmetrical. Eyes and mouth are not parallel. With some people this effect is far more noticeable than others, but nine out of ten individuals will have some asymmetry in these features.

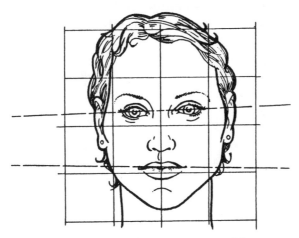

The human face is not symmetrical. Lines projected from eyes and mouth will meet at a point either to the left or right of the face.

If two lines are projected from the eyes and mouth they meet at a point some distance from the face. The significance of this projection point lies in the fact that one of the clues we use in obtaining a sense of perspective is the fact that things close to us appear larger than more distant objects. Artists make use of this effect to produce an illusion of depth on a two-dimensional drawing.

An illusion of depth is created by drawing 'distant' objects smaller.

When we look at a face from any angle other than square on, the most pleasing view is the one in which the greatest distance between the edge of the mouth and the corner of the eye is closest to us, while the smaller distance is further away. This is because the view we see accords with our sense of perspective. Although we are rarely aware of this fact, the impression is still a powerful one. The greater the angle between mouth and eyes the stronger the effect will prove.

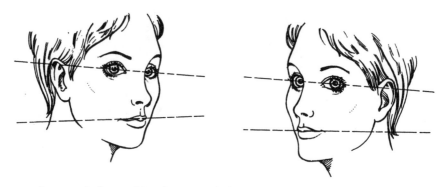

A persons's 'best side' is the one with the greatest distance between the edge of eye and mouth.

Similarly, viewing a face in such a way that the narrow eye corner to mouth edge distance is closest to us, while the greater distance is furthest away, disrupts this rule.

This portrait photograph has been taken from the sitter's 'best' side – showing widest eye-mouth-edge distance.

Portrait photographers and painters generally know about this rule and photograph or paint people from their 'best', i.e. their widest eye-mouth distance, side. You can use the same technique for making your face more memorable. First check whether you are a right or left side projector. Most right-handed people, in fact, project to the right while the majority of left-handed people project left. When talking to somebody, position yourself so that the greater separation is closest to them. In other words if you are a right projector stand on their left side whenever possible. When looking them directly in the face the effect will not, of course, be noticeable. But each time you move into a more profile position the effect will prove subconsciously more pleasing, and more memorable.

The scanning pattern used when studying faces also underlies the importance of lips and mouth as key areas of silent speech communication. In a friendly encounter, lips will usually be formed into a smile. But there are many types of smile. American researcher Dr P. Ekman has identified nineteen of them, and they do not all convey the same message. Some are deliberately deceptive, of course, used to camouflage hostility or apathy. I shall be dealing with ways of detecting the lying smile in chapter fourteen. But even if the smile is genuine, you can tell a great deal about the depth of emotion felt by the sort of smiling employed. And you can vary the signal you are sending out by small, subtle, but highly significant variations in movement of the lips.

The secret language of smiles

Before looking at different types of smile, let's consider why people smile in the first place and what makes this signal so universally accepted as conveying friendly feelings.

Mothers' claims that their babies smile have often been dismissed by doctors, who insist the infant is simply bringing up wind when she twitches her lips in that appealing manner. However, recent research tends to support this popular belief. Even young babies, it seems, use this inborn signal to convey pleasure, delight, excitement or interest. As they grow older, the apparently simple lip movement becomes increasingly complex and difficult to interpret. In both adults and older children a smile can express not only happiness but anxiety, misery, uncertainty or even masked aggression.

'Almost as soon as I started to study "smiling" I found myself in a mass of contradictions,' comments Professor Ray Birdwhistell. 'From the outset the signal value of the smile proved debatable. Even the most preliminary procedures provided data which were difficult to rationalize.'

One of the problems which Ray Birdwhistell and his colleagues from the University of Pennsylvania encountered was the very variable nature of spontaneous smiling. In Peachtree Street, Atlanta, for instance, it was considered perfectly normal for a young woman to smile at strangers. But the same behaviour on Main Street in Buffalo, New York was considered very inappropriate. 'In one part of the country, an unsmiling individual might be queried as to whether he was "angry about something", while in another, the smiling individual might be asked "What's funny?"' comments Professor Birdwhistell. In one area a smile was interpreted as a sign of *pleasure* or *friendliness*, in another as implying *doubt* or *ridicule*.

Crossing a mountain range or even travelling a few miles down a highway could take you from a high-smile zone to a low-smile area. In Birdwhistell's American study, the greatest amount of smiling was found in Atlanta, Louisville, Memphis and Nashville. Middle-class citizens of Ohio, Indiana and Illinois were more likely to smile at one another than people from exactly the same social background living in Maine, Massachusetts and New Hampshire. But these people, in turn, smiled more than western New Yorkers. There was no easy explanation of why this should be, but in many cases it appeared to be due to local social traditions whose origins had long been forgotten.

However, it is clear that children whose parents smile a great deal grow up to smile far more than those raised in a glum, serious-faced family. There are several reasons for this. Children with parents who rarely smile are denied a smiling role model during the early, very impressionable, years of life. It may also be that they are discouraged from smiling, or accused of not taking life seriously enough. Children who smile at times adults consider inappropriate can face strong criticism or even more extreme punishments. I once treated a young boy whose main problem was that he smiled whenever he was scolded. This was an anxiety response, designed to placate angry adults, and he had no intention of being impudent. But that was how it appeared to parents and teachers who, far from being appeased by his smile, regarded it as a clear sign of impertinence and became even angrier and more punitive. A first step to helping him sort out a great many problems in life was to train him to show a suitable expression when being ticked off.

In most social situations, although it must be used with care, the smile is a powerful, and positive, signal. Its potency derives, in part, from its evolutionary history. In mankind's early history the mouth was very much a weapon of attack. Indeed it is ideally suited to fighting, since the tooth enamel is one of the hardest substances known and the teeth are the body's sharpest instrument. Furthermore bites can lead to serious complications, even death, because of the high risk of them causing infection. 'Human bites are more severe than animal bites,' comments Dr Margaret Grossi, deputy commissioner for health in New York City, 'because the human mouth has a wider variety of pathogenic organisms.'

Nor is biting a form of attack mankind left behind with woad and animal skins. In 1980, for example, a total of 1,207 New Yorkers sank their teeth into one another, outnumbering bites from rats, cats and parrots and coming second only to dogs. On average three people a day were bitten, and many more of the less serious bites probably went unreported. The most usual targets are the hands, fingers, arms and shoulders, followed by the face and neck. Police surveys have shown that 75 per cent of bites result from aggression, while accidents during games and sports account for the remainder.

By drawing back his lips in a relaxed manner to reveal closed teeth, a person draws attention to his mouth while signalling friendly intentions. The message is, 'I come in peace. I am not going to bite you.' It was, and is, the facial equivalent of offering your empty hand to demonstrate no weapon is being carried.

We can see an echo of that primitive signal when young children are enjoying mock fights and wrestling with one another in what child psychologists term 'rough-and-tumble play'. Then they clearly signal their non-aggressive intent by keeping the teeth slightly parted and the mouth open and relaxed. This is called a 'play face' and it tells other children that the 'fighting' is all in fun and no violence is intended.

The 'play face' of a happy child engaged in
a rough-and-tumble game at the slide.

Adults use a modified play face during rough and tumble love-making, an important aspect of intimate body language, which I shall discuss in chapter twelve.

The meaning of smiles

You will encounter three main types of friendly smile: simple, upper and broad. These vary from low to high intensity, with higher-intensity smiles communicating a more potent message. In addition you will come across hostile, deceitful and anxious smiles, all of which I shall discuss in chapter fourteen.

Simple smile
These are produced by drawing back and lifting the edges of the mouth. The amount by which the mouth is raised varies the intensity of the smile.

Simple smile – low intensity

A low intensity simple smile reveals uncertainty and a lack of confidence.

A high intensity simple smile is used when the person is friendly but does not know others well.

Here the message is one of uncertainty, hesitation and lack of confidence. There is a desire to make a friendly approach coupled with anxiety about doing so.

Arnold, whose story I recounted in chapter one, used the low-intensity simple smile almost exclusively. This was not, as people assumed, because he was cold and unfriendly, but simply a result of the extreme nervousness he experienced when meeting people. Both smile and gaze usually flicker unsteadily, like a light about to burn itself out. Any response which is seen as being even the slightest bit negative will cause it to switch off almost instantly.

This is a smile to avoid whenever you wish to make a firm, confident impression since the message conveyed is of timidity and a desire not to be noticed. However a low-intensity simple smile can prove helpful in any situation where appearing diffident and unsure of yourself could prove advantageous. When seeking to attract somebody whose body language suggests a certain shyness or diffidence, the low-intensity simple smile can prove far more effective than one conveying a strength and dominance. Why this should be so will be explained in the next chapter.

Simple smile – high intensity
This radiates confidence and warmth, without possessing the impact of an upper or broad smile (see opposite). There is a more pronounced retraction of the sides of the mouth and increased upturn at the edges. Lips are slightly separated so that a small portion of the upper teeth can sometimes be glimpsed. Gaze is steady and the accompanying posture usually relaxed. The intensity can also be increased by slightly narrowing the eyes.

A high-intensity simple smile is the best one to use when meeting people with whom you are friendly, but not on very close terms; for instance a neighbour, distant relative or colleague. Using a more powerful upper or broad smile under these circumstances could cause confusion, since the silent speech message will appear inappropriate to the circumstances. A verbal equivalent would be to exclaim, 'Peter, how nice to see you. What a wonderful surprise. I am pleased to meet you again. This has made my day. I am bowled over with pleasure. What a happy encounter . . .' and so on. A casual friend confronted with such an outpouring of greetings would be bound to wonder whether you were being sarcastic, had taken leave of your senses or had had too much to drink.

The same kind of non-verbal overkill can occur when the wrong smile is employed. Far from creating a more positive impression, it creates a sense of wary unease. Tricia, whose excessive and ineffective use of silent speech I described in chapter one, constantly used high-intensity upper smiles in situations where a simple smile was more appropriate, and broad smiles in circumstances which demanded an upper smile. The result was disconcerting for the person on the receiving end, although – as is usually the case – they were seldom able to explain exactly what feature of her body language disturbed them.

The upper smile

The upper smile derives its name from the fact that the top lip is drawn back far enough to reveal most or all of the upper row of teeth. However the real significance of the upper smile is that the bottom teeth remain covered. To communicate hostility an ape bares its lower fangs, sending the clear message, 'Watch out or you'll be bitten.' Humans too use the uncovering of their lower teeth to signal anger and aggressive intent. By demonstrating that the lower teeth are, like a sheathed sword, not about to be used, the upper smile reassures watchers of the person's peaceful purpose.

When signalling, 'I am pleased to meet you and well disposed,' the smile is produced by retracting the lips, turning them slightly upwards at the edges and partly opening the mouth.

Upper smile – low intensity

A low intensity upper smile communicates moderate pleasure.

A high intensity upper smile conveys pleasure but also good-humoured doubt or amused amazement.

The teeth remain in contact, with only the top portion of the upper row being uncovered. The message being conveyed is a feeling of moderate pleasure at the meeting. You might, for instance, see it when colleagues who work closely together during the year greet one another at the firm's annual party.

Use a low-intensity upper smile whenever you want to create a stronger, friendlier and more confident impression than a high-intensity simple smile can convey. But beware of using it with total strangers at a first meeting, since under those conditions it can strike the wrong note. Second-hand car salesmen who approach a likely buyer radiating a low or – even worse – high-intensity upper smile communicate only their insincerity. The time to use this smile is on a second or third meeting when it sends a positive and believable message.

Upper smile – high intensity
The extra intensity is produced by uncovering more of the teeth, opening the mouth slightly wider and narrowing the gaze by partly closing the eylids. In addition to pleasure, high-intensity upper smiles can be used to communicate good-humoured doubt to amused amazement. To achieve this change in the signal, the lower teeth remain covered with the lower lip curled over them. Still more astonishment or scepticism can be conveyed by resting the upper teeth lightly on the curled lower lip and widening the eyes further. These small differences are capable of communicating a variety of subtle doubting signals, ranging from mild surprise to open disbelief.

This smile is the most frequently faked, either to try and convey a false feeling of pleasure or in response to a photographer's command to 'say cheese'. It is often seen on the faces of celebrities feigning delight at meeting their fans, or bored company executives being presented to the families of their employees.

Use the high-intensity upper smile with great care since, when employed inappropriately, it looks utterly false and will undermine your attempts to convey a positive, confident impression. High-intensity upper smiles should be reserved for close friends or long-term business associates with whom you have a warm relationship.

Broad smile
Both upper and lower teeth are uncovered and the gaze is slightly narrowed. This smile expresses the highest intensity of pleasure, joy and delight. Beyond this lies laughter. The lips are drawn fully back exposing both the upper and lower teeth. These may be closed, in the lower-intensity version of the broad smile, or parted to communicate the greatest possible amusement. This is probably the most infectious type of smile and usually leads to a sharing of enjoyment among a group of people. Such smiles are seldom produced by people on their own. It seems to need the company of others to stimulate the required level of enjoyment.

Broad smiles should only be used in genuinely amusing or entertain-ing circumstances, when laughing and joking with friends or col-

The broad smile expresses the greatest possible pleasure, joy and delight.

leagues, for example, or while playing a good-humoured game. Using a broad smile as a form of greeting is inappropriate and unwise.

RULE FIVE FOR SILENT SPEECH SUCCESS

Use the smile most appropriate to the situation. Smiling inappropriately can create as negative an impression as not smiling at all.

After the smile an encounter usually proceeds smoothly into the second stage of Orientation, during which you position yourself in relation to the other person. Only seconds have passed since initial eye-contact was established but already scores of signals, large and small, subtle and obvious, have been exchanged and impressions have started to form. Your next move is crucial. By coming in too close or standing too far away, by orienting yourself correctly or inappropriately, you can make or break the encounter before a single word has been spoken.

CHAPTER NINE

Close Encounters

Birds and mammals not only have territories which they
occupy and defend against their own kind but they have a
series of uniform distances which they maintain from each
other . . . Man, too, has a uniform way of handling distance
from his fellows.

Edward T. Hall, *Hidden Dimensions*

Within days of arriving in Saudi Arabia, Paul, an oil company
engineer, found himself increasingly uneasy during meetings with his
hosts. The bewildering thing was that he could see no reason for his
disquiet. 'Everybody went out of their way to be friendly,' he recalls,
'but I still felt uncomfortable, even slightly anxious, during encounters
with my Arab colleagues.'

A similar problem was recounted to me by Christina, a Danish-born
magazine editor who emigrated to Australia with her English husband, Mark. Shortly after their arrival the couple joined a Sydney
tennis club and, for a couple of weeks, the atmosphere remained
welcoming and friendly. But before long they started to sense growing
hostility from women club members towards Christina and an
awkward sympathy towards Mark from their husbands. 'Some began
to give me knowing looks at the bar,' Mark recalled, 'while others
would exchange pitying glances whenever I was around.' The mystery
was solved when, in the changing-rooms, a woman angrily accused
blonde-haired, blue-eyed Christina of making sexual advances
towards her spouse. 'And he's by no means the only one,' she stormed.
'You've been flirting disgustingly with every man here!'

Both Paul and Christina had been the unknowing victims of
something anthropologist Edward Hall, a pioneer of non-verbal
communications, termed proxemics: the vital part played by distance
in sending silent speech signals.

Before I explain exactly what made Paul so uneasy and Christina so unpopular, let's explore the role of proxemics in the second, Orientation, stage of your encounter.

After exchanging eyebrow flashes, eye-contact and smiles, you cross the room and come to a halt before your acquaintance. Assuming the distance at which you stopped was your own choice, rather than being dictated by, for instance, the number of guests or the design of the room, what made you choose that precise point rather than one slightly closer or a little further away? Was it chance or something more subtle and significant? All the evidence suggests that the distance at which you halted was no haphazard decision but was determined by a subconscious juggling of six factors:

1. How well the two of you know one another. The warmer your relationship the closer you will stand.
2. Your two personalities. Introverts prefer to maintain a greater distance between themselves and others than extroverts.
3. Your nationality and ethnic background. Cultural norms and expectations exert a tremendous influence over the space we maintain during different encounters.
4. Your ages. People under thirty tend to stand slightly closer to one another than older people. However, when a young person is talking to anybody significantly older than him- or herself greater distance is usually preferred.
5. The nature of the encounter. The friendlier the meeting the closer, physically as well as emotionally, the two people involved will stand.
6. Whether you live in the city or country. As we shall see in a moment, city folk prefer working at closer distances than country dwellers.

Your personal space bubble

Around every man, woman and child there extends a tangible but invisible 'space bubble'. This represents the outer boundaries of our being, the distance at which we prefer to keep others during encounters.

As you can see, although it is popularly described as a bubble, the personal space around you more closely resembles a cylinder at the waist, tapering to a cone around your feet. Unlike most boundaries the outer edges of the bubble are constantly expanding and contracting depending on our relationship with those seeking to enter our territory. Furthermore it applies only to meetings with fellow human beings and not, for instance, to the distance we keep between ourselves and such items of furniture as a desk or table.

Essentially the bubble is a defensive zone which allows us the best chance of survival should a meeting turn out to be more dangerous than anticipated. Not surprisingly, therefore, the better we know somebody, the greater our trust in them and the more intimate the encounter, the smaller our space bubble becomes. When we do not know, like or trust the intruder our bubble widens significantly and we take far greater pains to defend it from invasion.

The nature of the encounter also influences the size of the bubble. When talking formally to a group of people, even when we know them well and are on friendly terms, we need to stand at a greater distance in order to communicate effectively with all of them at the same time.

When dealing with strangers or casual acquaintances in a one-to-one encounter the outer perimeter of the bubble will be determined by two conflicting needs. The first is the necessity to be close enough not only to hear what they are saying but, even more important, to observe their silent speech signals. At the same time we do not wish to be so close to them that we would be put at risk should they suddenly become aggressive and attack us. This means that the final dimen-

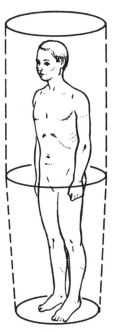

Your personal 'space bubble': the defensive zone we each maintain around our body.

sions of our personal space bubble will depend on the outcome of what is called an approach-avoidance conflict. That is the conflict between the strength of our desire to communicate with them and the intensity of our anxiety over getting into a potentially risky encounter. In arriving at such a judgement we are often biased by the fact that merely being in another person's presence makes us emotionally aroused.

Closeness arouses us

When people are part of a crowd they automatically become more aroused. That is, physical changes, associated with the primitive Red Light reflex or 'fight-flight' survival mechanism, occur. As we saw earlier, the reflex causes your heart to beat faster, blood pressure is raised, sweating increases, the muscles tense. At times of danger to life and limb all these changes make it easier for us to fight or flee more efficiently.

Such arousal is not necessarily perceived by the individuals concerned as a symptom of anxiety. It can equally be viewed as excitement or anger. The precise interpretation of these emotional and bodily changes depends on circumstances. If the situation is one of light-hearted good humour then the arousal will be felt as heightened enjoyment. As a member of the audience for a comedy show, we interpret it as part of having a good time. When the mood is one of frustration or outrage, exactly the same symptoms are likely to be experienced as indications of rage. Which is why a large crowd can change with such terrifying speed from being relaxed and good-humoured to being mindlessly violent. In these circumstances people tend to use one another as models in order to determine how they should behave. If a few start losing their tempers, or deliberately start an agitation, aggression spreads through the crowd with the speed and intensity of a bush fire.

Finally, if the situation is strange or threatening, increased heart-rate, muscle tension and sweating are regarded as indications of fear. We not only run when afraid but make ourselves more fearful by running.

Being watched by others produces exactly the same sort of bodily changes. Which is why playing sports or acting in front of an audience is either far easier or much harder than doing the same things unobserved. When the arousal is interpreted as excitement it produces a superior performance. If perceived as anxiety, however, it undermines ability and reduces our chances of success.

In a rather bizarre study of the effects of other people on masculine anxiety, psychologists secretly observed men using a three-stall urinal. Their personal space bubble was deliberately invaded by a confederate of the experimenters who stood either immediately next to the unsuspecting member of the public or one stall distant. The observers assessed anxiety by the time it took to start urinating. (Passing water is very difficult when anxious since a relaxed state is necessary to operate the sphincter muscles which seal the bladder.)

Results confirmed the experimenters' prediction that when the adjacent stall was occupied urination would be delayed as a result of increased anxiety. It was a dramatic, and some might feel rather indelicate, way of establishing the power of another's presence to trigger the Red Light reflex.

The power of distance

In a pioneering early study of the effects of distance on silent speech, anthropologist Edward T. Hall identified four main body-space dimensions or *Zones*: *Intimate*, *Personal*, *Social* and *Public*. These can be further divided into *Close* and *Far* Zones. Each represents the size of the bubble we try to maintain during different encounters.

By manipulating these distances you can increase the speed with which warm, empathic bonds are formed and deepen the intensity of your relationship. Equally it becomes possible to assert authority more easily, communicate status more swiftly and impress your personality on others more effectively.

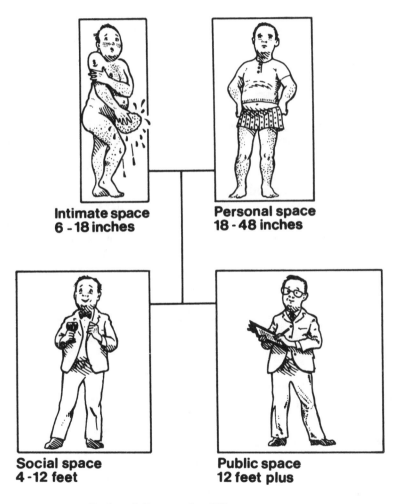

Intimate space
6 - 18 inches

Personal space
18 - 48 inches

Social space
4 - 12 feet

Public space
12 feet plus

Preferred distances for different encounters.

In chapter thirteen I will describe how, by deliberately invading another's personal space or elaborating your own, you are able to disconcert or dominate an opponent during power-plays.

Intimate distance – Close Zone
Distance: 6 inches or less
This distance is reserved for such activities as making love, embracing, comforting and protecting.

Apart from a few special strangers, for instance doctors and dentists, who are given permission to intrude into this Zone, its frontiers remain closed to all but our most intimate companions; literally those 'closest' to us. At this very close range vision is less important than smell and touch as a source of information. The silent speech signals exchanged during such encounters will be described when we investigate love-signs in chapter twelve.

Intimate distance – Far Zone
Distance: 6–18 inches
Into this Zone we allow relatives, spouse, children, parents, lovers and close friends.

Touch is still important. Smell becomes less significant although it still has a role to play, while vision provides us with more information. However, while we are seldom aware of the fact, the images formed are distorted. The range of view is extremely limited and only a small part of it is sharply focused.

Inside this area of clear vision (15°) comes most of the face, but with its features considerably enlarged. Seen from this range the iris of the eye is larger than life-size; so too are the nose, lips, tongue and cheeks. Pores and any blemishes in the skin appear magnified and, therefore, much more obvious. The head, shoulders and sometimes the hand can be glimpsed fuzzily at the edges of vision (30°–180°), where the image is less sharply focused.

For Europeans and North Americans this Zone is crucially important because any invasion by strangers, even with our permission, causes soaring arousal. Depending on the circumstances of the encounter we may interpret these increasing mental and physical tensions as anxiety, irritation, anger or fear.

'At the point where sharp focus is lost,' comments Edward Hall, 'one feels the uncomfortable muscular sensation of being cross-eyed from looking at something too close. The expressions "Get your face *out* of mine," and "He shook his fist *in* my face," apparently express how many Americans perceive their body boundaries.'

Police interrogators frequently make use of the anxiety which an invasion of the Far Intimate Zone produces to break a suspect's

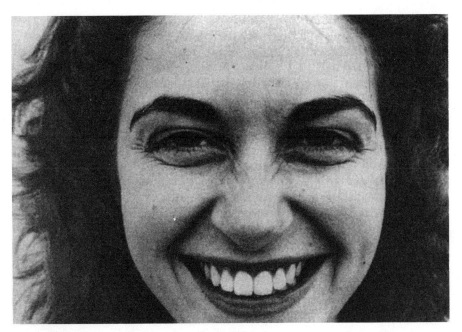

At intimate distance our view of another is limited
and only a small part of the face can be
brought into sharp focus.

resistance. The accused is seated in an armless chair which has been bolted down in the centre of a room. In this position his or her space bubble can be violated from any direction and even several directions at once. As they bellow into their victim's ear, the interrogators press their faces close to his. These bawled questions are a further invasion of personal space since, in Intimate Zone encounters, voices are normally kept low. Such violations of their Intimate Zone will quickly intimidate and disorient all but the most experienced suspects.

A sign I saw recently scrawled in fibre-pen on the dividing window of a New York taxi neatly illustrated this common association between soft words and emotional closeness. 'Please speak loudly, please speak clearly,' it instructed. 'Do not whisper to me. I am not your lover.'

The deliberate invasion of this Zone may also be employed by aggressive superiors to extract information from a reluctant employee or to harass an interviewee, perhaps to find out how well he or she responds to pressure.

Later you will learn how to use deliberate Intimate Zone violations as a means of exerting power over others as well as discovering ways of countering such tactics.

Coping with unavoidable invasions
Living and working in a busy city means that your Intimate Zones will be unintentionally violated by others scores of times a day; when commuting to work in crowded public transport, being jostled on packed pavements or crammed into a crowded elevator, for example. So how do we cope with such regular invasions of the personal bubble?

Sanity and order are preserved by following a clearly defined set of silent speech rules designed to make clear the compulsory nature of close proximity.

The body remains as motionless as possible, and any accidental contact is instantly withdrawn and an apology offered. When the crush of people makes physical contact unavoidable, any parts of the body touching another person are kept under considerable tension. This both limits any casual movements and signals to the other person that the touching is neither intentional nor desired. To relax and move freely under such stressful conditions is to defy a major social taboo. It is a serious breach of one of the most important of many unwritten rules which control behaviour in congested places.

As well as limiting movements of your limbs and torso, you make sure your features remain free from all emotion. Eye-contact, apart from the most flickering of glances, is strenuously avoided. You wear a poker face and keep your gaze fixed firmly on the middle distance, never allowing it to rest on anybody's face for more than the briefest of glances. Speaking to anybody, even a friend, in such circumstances is frowned upon, and if you are reading a newspaper or book it is important to give the impression of being totally absorbed.

'We often hear words like "miserable", "unhappy" and "despondent" to describe people who travel to work in the rush-hour on public transport,' comments body language consultant Alan Pease,' . . . but they are misjudgements on the part of the observer. What the observer sees, in fact, is a group of people adhering to the rules that apply to the unavoidable invasion of their Intimate Zones in a crowded public place.'

Recently I was able to observe how closely packed and semi-naked strangers – two conditions which would normally arouse extreme anxiety – cope with these extreme invasions of their body space. I had taken my young nephew to Orlando's famous Wet and Wild Park, where the attractions include a wave-making machine capable of creating storm-force conditions in a giant pool. As people lay in, sat on or straddled huge rubber rings they would be tossed helplessly – and enjoyably – around the pool. Often the rings collided; there was simply no way of preventing yourself from being flung against your neighbours, and the arms, legs and even bodies of scantily dressed strangers touched, brushed and rubbed together.

I was intrigued to see that the same kind of silent speech rules which keep commuters sane also applied under these very unusual conditions. The surroundings were, of course, extremely important. They provided a licence for semi-nudity, as does any swimming pool or beach. We expect to find people wandering around in bathing costumes, understand the reason for their undress and so no longer feel threatened by it. Even so, people tend to respond to crowded beaches or packed pools by becoming highly territorial. They stake out their claim using towels, mats, books, clothes and other personal possessions. They seek to avoid touching one another by watching where they walk and creating as wide a 'no-man's land' between their own small area and their neighbours as possible. This was occurring all around the pool side at the Wet and Wild Park. But in the wave lagoon such boundaries could hardly be established.

People coped, I discovered, in three main ways. And their strategies provide an interesting insight into the body language rules followed under similar conditions of crowding and unavoidable contact such as dance-floors, night-clubs and sporting events. First, friends and relatives kept together, so creating a small tribal grouping that expanded their territory. Lovers often occupied the same giant rubber ring.

Couples long past the first flush of romance, or perhaps now too large to get together in the same ring, held hands, or in some cases feet, clinging like limpets to one another as their rings bounced and rocked through the waves. Friends would congregate into large collections of rings: the maximum number I saw was eight.

'Tribal groups' formed by friends and relatives to 'defend' their patch of water.

Being in the company of people we know is always a powerful way of reducing anxiety. Police will separate suspects, not just to prevent them from cooking up a story but in order to increase their sense of isolation and fear. If you ever want deliberately to discomfort people, as you might during a power-play, be sure to separate them from colleagues or friends.

RULE SIX FOR SILENT SPEECH SUCCESS

Be careful never to invade another person's Intimate Zone unintentionally. If you do so deliberately, as a manipulative strategy, be aware that you will provoke a powerful increase in arousal.

How this arousal can be used to your advantage will be explained in a moment.

Personal distance – Close Zone
Distance: 18–36 inches
Only close friends can enter this Zone without causing discomfort.

At this distance features no longer look distorted and we can see details of the other person's face clearly, distinguishing such fine details as the length and shape of the eyelashes.

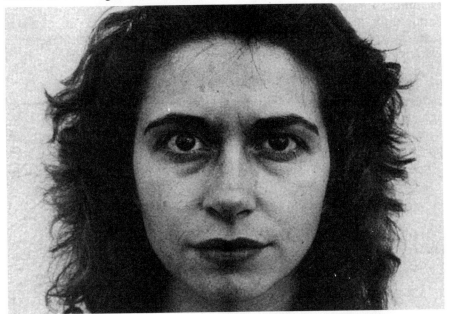

At this distance features are no longer distorted and details of the face can be seen clearly.

As with Intimate Zones, this space should never be invaded without permission. The poet W.H. Auden perfectly captured our powerful desire to protect this Zone from intrusion when he wrote:

> Some thirty inches from my nose
> The frontier of my Person goes,
> And all the untilled air between
> Is private *pagus* or demesne.
> Stranger, unless with bedroom eyes
> I beckon you to fraternize,
> Beware of rudely crossing it:
> I have no gun, but I can spit.

Although they seldom spit, people go to considerable lengths to preserve their Personal Zones. On public transport, in waiting-rooms or restaurants they often use handbags, brief-cases, coats or books to stake out their territory. They also use various barrier signals, such as crossed legs or folded arms, to fend off any unwelcome intrusion of 'their' territory (see chapter thirteen).

Personal distance – Far Zone
Distance: 30–48 inches
Being only just within normal touching range, this Zone is used, literally, to hold another person at 'arm's length'. It is the preferred distance for Western males when talking to casual friends, business acquaintances, neighbours and colleagues with whom we are on good but not close terms.

There is no visual distortion of the features, but sharp focus can be achieved only over a small area of the face, which means we must constantly shift our gaze to make out details, as described in the previous chapter.

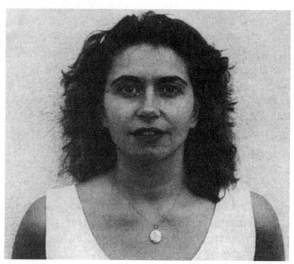

No distortion but gaze must be shifted
to make out details.

When this Zone is invaded by strangers we often seek to maintain distance by edging away, although normally this response is instinctive and unconscious.

Social distance – Close Zone
Distance: 4–7 feet
Touch is impossible. The features no longer appear distorted and both the face and torso can be seen clearly. This Zone is reserved for meetings with strangers and impersonal encounters.

Social distance – Far Zone
Distance: 7–12 feet
Teachers may work at this distance when talking to small groups of students. It is also suitable for meetings, discussions, interviews and similar important but fairly impersonal exchanges.

All those involved are sufficiently close to allow an easy exchange of views and to permit several people to be included in an encounter. Yet at the same time there is no suggestion of intimacy. By deliberately moving from a Close to a Far Social Zone, or using a Social Zone when a Personal one would be expected, you send out a clear message of dislike or disapproval.

Public distance – Close Zone
Distance: 12–25 feet
This is the preferred distance when dealing with strangers. It is sufficiently broad for us to take evasive action if the encounter looks like becoming threatening.

Public distance – Far Zone
Distance: 25 feet plus
The distance at which teachers and lecturers prefer to stand, this is also a Zone which adds prestige and authority to those able to maintain it.

In Theodore H. White's book *The Making of the President 1960* there is an excellent illustration of this commanding use of power. He recounts that when John F. Kennedy's nomination for president became certain, it was reflected in the greater deference paid to him by advisers. As Kennedy entered the room, 'The others . . . surged forward on impulse to join him. Then they halted. A distance of perhaps thirty feet separated them from him, but it was impassable. They stood apart, these older men of long-established power, and watched him . . . no one could pass the little open distance between him and them uninvited, because there was this thin separation about him, and the knowledge they were there not as his patrons but as his clients.'

In chapter thirteen I shall explain how, by manipulating Public Zones, you can enhance your prestige and status during power-plays.

Personal zones and close encounters

The difficulties which faced Paul in the Middle East and Christina in Australia had to do with confusions between Personal and Social Zones.

Paul flew to Saudi Arabia unaware that Arab males prefer to use Close *Personal* Zone (eighteen to thirty-six inches) in situations where the Western man would regard a Close *Social* Zone (four feet plus) as appropriate. By standing at a distance which, to Paul, signalled an unacceptable degree of intimacy they made him feel confused and uncomfortable. Paul is far from unusual in his discomfort. So common is this culture clash problem that some firms who do business in such 'close proximity' countries as the Middle and Far East train staff to behave in a relaxed and friendly manner even when their personal space is apparently being violated.

In one study which explored the value of such training, a group of English students were taught to use Arab silent speech signals, including interpersonal distance preferences. They and an untrained group then talked to Arabs for five minutes and were rated according to the impression they had made. The results showed conclusively that training led to increased liking, warmth and positive evaluation. In every case they were preferred by the Arabs.

A similar difficulty can occur when Americans, who prefer to maintain a Personal Zone of eighteen to forty-eight inches between themselves and acquaintances, meet the Japanese, whose Personal Zone can be as narrow as twelve inches. As the Japanese moves forwards to reduce what is, for him, an unacceptably wide bubble space, the American steps back to keep him at a comfortable distance. As a result they can manoeuvre around the room performing what body language psychologists have rather uncharitably termed the cocktail party two-step.

You can use this as the basis of an amusing game to enliven any dull party. It works like this. Find somebody who needs a wide Personal Zone. You can identify them by simply observing the extent to which they shift position to maintain their desired distance when chatting with other guests. Engage them in casual conversation and, while doing so, gradually decrease the distance between you. Their almost certain response will be to take a step backwards. The object of the game is to see how far around the room you can manoeuvre the unfortunate guest before he or she – it is safest to play this with a same-sex partner – becomes so disconcerted that the conversation is brought to an abrupt close!

Women tend to be far less concerned when same-sex strangers invade their Far Personal Zones, perhaps because girls are brought up to be less fearful of physical intimacy than boys. But they usually respond strongly, and negatively, to a similar invasion by a man.

When a woman invades a male Personal Zone she had better beware. For whether or not the intrusion is intentional the powerful message conveyed by greater physical proximity is a desire for more intimacy. It was this unintended signal that gave Christina her undeserved reputation as a man-chaser among Australian tennis club wives: Europeans feel comfortable with an Intimate Zone whose Far Zone boundaries are eighteen inches from their body. Australians, on the other hand, extend the outer limits of their Intimate Zone to twenty-five inches. As a result, when Christina positioned herself at what would have been an acceptable distance for a Personal Zone in Denmark, she sent out a strong silent speech message of a sexual advance. And this was how the signals were interpreted by both the men and their outraged wives. To make matters worse Danes make much greater use of eye-contact than Australians, and this too can indicate sexual interest, as we shall see in chapter twelve. The result was that Christina's innocent, but culturally inappropriate, body language branded her a husband-chaser.

City zones vs country zones

Differences are also found in the personal space needs of people who live in the city and the country. By observing how close two people stand when shaking hands you can often deduce whether they live in a major urban area or the countryside. Those who live in the cities work within a Personal Zone of eighteen inches, which allows them to shake hands easily without taking up too much space. In the country, where there is less competition for space, people's Personal Zones may be as wide as forty inches, which means they have to stretch and lean forward slightly when shaking hands. The more sparsely populated the area from which they come, the wider the distance at which they will make contact.

Such knowledge could help you enjoy success when meeting somebody whose home is in a remote part of the country. If you extend your hand when you are eighteen inches away the other person may well feel threatened and defensive. By adapting to his preferred Personal Zone and shaking hands at a greater distance you can immediately win his confidence.

The same rule applies when dealing with people who are used to a far narrower Personal Zone. Here if you shake hands at what, for you, would be an acceptable distance they may interpret your distance from them as a sign of dislike or lack of interest. By moving in closer before extending your hand you can match their culturally determined space needs and so generate more positive feelings. The only way to determine an individual's space needs in various situations is by close observation before making any approach. As we have seen, there are many factors which can influence a personal preference. But in general the following nationalities can be characterized as preferring a closer or more distant encounter on first meeting:

Preferred distances	Nationalities
Close	Arabs
	Japanese
	South Americans
	French
	Greeks
	Black North Americans/Hispanics
	Italians
	Spaniards
Moderate	British
	Swedish
	Swiss
	Germans
	Austrians
Far	White North Americans
	Australians
	New Zealanders

As you can see, the distance at which you halt before extending your hand can play a significant role in the effect your presence produces on the other person. It can, without your even being aware of the fact, arouse anxiety or anger, provoke feelings of hostility or empathy. And all before a word has been spoken.

RULE SEVEN FOR SUCCESSFUL SILENT SPEECH

Make sure you are working at the correct distance to achieve the results you require. Take into account individual and cultural differences, as well as the nature of the relationship. Learn to work at a variety of distances without feeling alienated or uneasy. The more flexible you can be in manipulating another person's various Zones the greater control you will be able to exert over the encounter.

When to break the rules

So far we have looked at the negative effects of violating Personal or Intimate Zones. But there are some situations when you can greatly enhance the impression you make by intentionally invading the other person's space. These are encounters in which you offer the other person a large number of rewards. These could be verbal – for instance praise and encouragement – or non-verbal – smiling a lot and giving the correct amount of eye-contact. Under these circumstances the invasion is likely to make you seem more friendly and agreeable than you would be if the Zone violation had not occurred.

In an experiment by William Leipold, students were given personality tests to discover whether they were introverts or extroverts. You will recall that introverts tend to keep people at a greater distance than extroverts. They were then called into an office where they were praised, criticized or given a neutral comment. In the critical encounter they were deliberately upset by being told their grades were extremely poor and accused of not working hard enough. In the praise situation they were warmly congratulated on their good work. The neutral remark consisted of asking them how they felt about the course. The students were then sent into another room, in which was an interviewer, and asked to sit down. Students who had been praised chose to sit closer to the interviewer than those who had been criticized. Ones who had received a neutral comment positioned their chairs midway between the two extremes. But under all conditions introverted students sat further away from the interviewer.

In a similar experiment conducted by Judee Burgoon, experimenters manipulated the mood and behaviour of sales staff by intentionally violating their Personal Zones. In what was termed the 'high reward' condition they presented themselves as a well-to-do couple interested in luxury furnishings where 'price was no object'. They were smartly dressed and well spoken. In the 'low reward' condition they appeared as shabbily dressed students looking for a cheap TV to be bought on credit. The personal distance violations consisted of first establishing the sales person's preferred Personal Zone and then deliberately violating it, either by halving or doubling the initial distance. The encounters were observed and recorded by psychologists posing as other shoppers. After five minutes the customers asked the sales person if they could use the store's telephone.

In the high reward condition, sales staff showed the greatest interest when their Personal Zones were violated by the customers halving the distance between them. When they increased the distance, interest declined. Female shoppers received more smiles in both violation conditions.

When the shoppers were poorly dressed and of seemingly low status, however, Personal Zone violations were differently received. As distance reduced, tension increased and the sales person gave more indications of stress and fewer signs of liking.

Requests to use the telephone were more likely to be refused when low status female shoppers violated their Personal Space. However both high and low status male shoppers were more likely to be allowed to use the store phone after violating the Personal Zone by moving closer.

RULE EIGHT FOR SILENT SPEECH SUCCESS

Under certain circumstances deliberately violating someone's Personal Space can enhance mutual liking. But only do so if you are rewarding the person with verbal praise and/or warm, encouraging silent speech signals. Under these conditions closing the distance between you will enhance their liking, interest and willingness to co-operate with you.

The best approach is to start the encounter at a distance which meets their Body Zone expectations and decrease the distance between you once some rapport has been established.

The importance of position

So far we have only looked at distance, without taking into account a second, but no less significant, aspect of body space: the position adopted in relation to the other person. In theory this could be anywhere along the boundary line illustrated below.

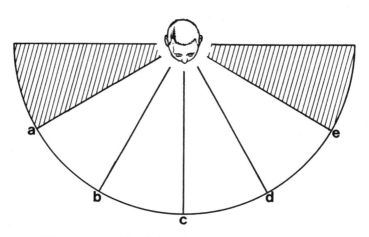

Where you could and should stand during an encounter.

The extremes are clearly unsuitable for lengthy encounters since to maintain eye-contact and see one another's face signals, the heads have to be kept uncomfortably turned. Most encounters, therefore, occur between points A and E on the drawing.

Whether you choose to position yourself to the other's left or right should be determined not by chance but after taking into account your 'best' side (see pages 84–5), which means you will either be standing between A and C or E and C.

But which position offers the greatest chance of silent speech success?

The answer will depend on (1) the sex of your companion and (2) how well you already know that person. Studies have shown that men will position themselves between B and C or C and D when talking to somebody they know and like. In other words they feel happiest with a frontal position. Women, on the other hand, prefer a more adjacent position when talking to friends, which means between A and B or D and E.

But these positions are reserved for friends or people with whom they are on good terms. What happens if a stranger occupies the same position? Research shows that it creates antagonism and dislike.

A possible explanation for these differences could lie in Western child-rearing practices. Boys, who are encouraged to be highly competitive, are especially sensitive to silent speech signals indicating competition. And, as we shall see when looking at power-plays in chapter thirteen, a facing position is one most usually adopted in situations where males are competing rather than co-operating.

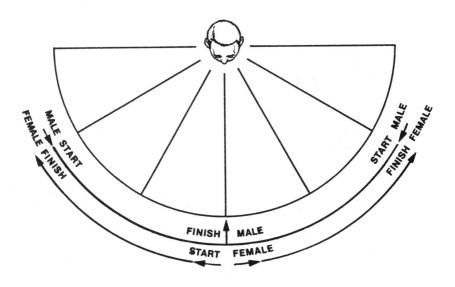

Women, on the other hand, are encouraged to co-operate and so favour an adjacent position in friendly encounters. If a stranger occupies this position, however, they feel under threat since it provokes subconscious thoughts of an intimate encounter.

Favoured position for two males at first encounter.

These differences can lead to considerable confusion between the sexes. A woman who wants to appear friendly to an unknown male may find that an eyeball to eyeball approach, which is non-threatening for her, produces alarm and consternation. Equally a male who tries to get to know a strange female by sitting beside her in what is for him a non-threatening manner arouses dislike or downright hostility.

RULE NINE FOR SILENT SPEECH SUCCESS

Never stand directly opposite an unknown male or adjacent to an unfamiliar female. With a man start at a more side-on position and gradually work your way around to a more frontal one.

With a woman, adopt the opposite approach by starting the encounter in a frontal position and then moving slowly to a more adjacent one.

This rule will not only safeguard you against unwittingly arousing negative feelings but will actually assist you in generating a positive mood. As, over the course of the meeting, you gently shift position, feelings of warmth and liking will be increased. This happens when, subconsciously, the other person has to decide why, although you – a relative stranger – are now occupying a position reserved for friends, he or she does not feel intruded upon. The – once again subconscious – conclusion reached is that you must be a friendly, warm person with whom they feel an immediate sense of empathy and ease.

When people are seated
In this chapter I have considered distance and position from the viewpoint of people standing and talking. But the same general rules apply if you are both seated, although here the type of seats provided may constrain your ability to manipulate these two critical factors for silent speech success.

In a study by Byrne and his colleagues, male and female students working in a university library had their personal space invaded by a stranger in one of two ways. Sometimes the person sat opposite them at the table, sometimes beside them. After five minutes they left and the students were then questioned about their impression of that individual. The questions were designed to explore the students' moods, their attraction towards the stranger and their motivations for being in the library and choosing to sit at 'their' table. In addition the students were asked what they thought of the library as a work-place. The findings were striking. When the stranger had sat directly opposite men, he was evaluated in very negative terms. However male students were much less affected by strangers taking a seat beside them. Women responded in exactly the opposite way. They found side by side invasions far more stressful and worrying than across-the-table encounters. However they were not disturbed by face-to-face violations of their Personal Space. The experiment was repeated using both male and female intruders without the results being affected.

113

Further confirmation of the findings came from the way in which male and female students tried to mark out their territory with books, bags and so forth. Males created barriers primarily between themselves and facing seats, while women placed possessions on the chair beside them. You can check this for yourself in libraries or restaurants where men and women are reading or dining alone.

Here are four further rules when people are sitting down:

RULE TEN FOR SILENT SPEECH SUCCESS

Never stand when somebody else is sitting, unless it is your intention to dominate or intimidate them. Height is a powerful dominance signal (see chapter thirteen).

RULE ELEVEN FOR SILENT SPEECH SUCCESS

Avoid, if possible, deep arm-chairs which compel you to sit well back in them, since this will limit your ability to send out a number of important posture signals.

RULE TWELVE FOR SILENT SPEECH SUCCESS

When chairs can be moved, the rules for personal distance described above apply, although you can get away with sitting closer to another person than you could if standing. This is because the chair increases our sense of security, especially when its arms provide a physical barrier between us and other people.

RULE THIRTEEN FOR SILENT SPEECH SUCCESS

Avoid sitting immediately *beside* a female stranger or *in front of* a male stranger. Whenever possible follow the movements described above by starting the encounter sitting adjacent to a man and facing a woman.

If you have followed the rules of silent speech a good foundation for success will have been established. But the next few minutes are still critical: now you move into the Contact stage of your encounter by reaching out to shake hands.

CHAPTER TEN

The Hidden Power of Your Handshake

The greatest sense in our body is our touch sense . . . it gives
us our knowledge of depth or thickness and form; we feel,
we love and hate, are touchy and are touched through the
touch corpuscles of the skin.

J. Lionel Taylor, *The Stages of Human Life*

The initial interview had gone fine. Philip's track record was impressive, his manner calm, confident and relaxed. The job was virtually his. Until the moment he shook hands with the company chairman. In that one, brief moment of touch, Philip's hopes of employment vanished. 'It was like clasping a dead fish,' the chairman recalled with a grimace. 'The worst, dampest, weakest and most disgusting handshake I've ever encountered. And this was somebody applying for a job in a department where he'd be shaking hands with clients many times a day. He'd have cost us a fortune in lost business.'

We've probably all experienced the 'wet fish' grasp and almost certainly formed a negative impression of that person the moment our hands came together. Most of us have also suffered, literally, at the hands of iron-grip merchants who consider any handshake which fails to break a few metacarpals the sign of a wimp. But between these extremes there lie a host of silent speech signals which can be communicated by the apparently simple act of shaking hands. They range from a strong warning of intended dominance to an unequivocal signal of surrender. The language of the handshake is, in fact, as subtle and complex as the ritual of the ancient Chinese courts. It is also as powerful. By using it correctly during that first moment of physical contact you can, in less than five seconds, confirm an already favourable impression or do much to correct an initially unfavourable one.

A handshake is one of the Emblems used in the vocabulary of silent speech (see chapter 3, page 20). But although it is the most widely used form of greeting in Western society, shaking hands is by no means a universal signal. Many traditional Arabs greet one another by kissing beards; Bantus clasp hands then raise them slowly into the air before disengaging; Eskimos rub noses. Such contacts are called 'tie-signs', a category of non-verbal signals used to indicate, or establish, special bonds between people. Researchers have identified more than 450 different tie-signs, although many are extremely uncommon or used only in specialized encounters, such as between a doctor and her patient. Others are found in courtship rituals and during love-making. The handshake, however, heads the list of the fourteen most frequently used tie-signs.

The handshake provides us with direct and immediate information about another person. As Dr August Coppola points out, 'There are no poses, no lies, nothing static . . . Since our only way of knowing each other is to sense the slightest movements, it seems impossible for people to mask their reactions, for the very attempt to do so would be sensed as a hesitation or restraint within the touch relation.'

The history of the handshake

Why do people in Europe, America and many other parts of the world shake hands when they meet?

The original, ancient purpose was to demonstrate that you were unarmed. By showing your dominant, i.e. weapon-carrying, hand empty of any weapon your friendly intentions were made clear. The military salute developed for a similar reason.

During Roman times shaking hands was used not as a friendly greeting – which was expressed by grasping forearms – but as a pledge of honour. And it was in this situation that the handshake was first employed in more modern times. At the start of the Industrial Revolution, some 150 years ago, the custom arose of 'sealing agreements' and 'making deals' by means of a handshake. Business people still refer to 'shaking hands on a deal'. As industrialization spread, the handshake lost its special commercial significance and developed into a social courtesy used when greeting and, very often, parting from others.

The hand that shakes the hand

The human hand is an extremely complex and robust device. It's been calculated that the fingers bend and stretch at least twenty-five million

116

times during the average lifetime. Thanks to this combination of resilience and flexibility it is capable of communicating a wide range of messages, despite the fact that an average handshake lasts only some five seconds, during which the hands will be pumped four or five times. The philosopher Immanuel Kant called the hand the 'visible part of the brain', while Dr Bronowski referred to it as 'the cutting edge of the mind'. Not surprisingly, therefore, it provides an accurate reflection of thoughts and feelings occurring below the level of awareness.

The handshake most likely to convey an impression of confidence and high self-esteem is firm and dry, applying a strong but not excessive pressure steadily for the time the contact lasts. This applies to both sexes, although women are expected to use less pressure than men.

During the course of a handshake, information is conveyed in six ways:

1. The appearance of the hand: the length and shape of the palm, fingers and nails together with their cleanliness.
2. The texture of the grip: whether the hand is soft and delicate or hard and horny.
3. The degree of dryness or dampness.
4. The amount of pressure used: ranging from overly strong to insufficiently firm.
5. The time spent in contact with the other person: by increasing or decreasing the time spent shaking hands from the average five seconds, the meaning of the handshake is significantly changed.
6. The style of grip: this is something I shall describe in a moment.

The amount of eye-contact you offer while shaking hands, your facial expression, whether or not your free hand makes contact with another part of the other person's body, your posture and degree of bodily tension will all play their part in determining the handshake's ultimate message.

The appearance of your hand

Jagged, chewed and dirty nails create a uniformly unfavourable impression in anyone applying for a job demanding more brain than brawn. Torn nails are one of the most widely recognized indications of nervousness, while dirt beneath even well-trimmed nails raises doubts about the owner's self-esteem and desire to make a favourable impression. 'I have a fetish for cleanliness which encompasses clean fingernails . . .' the CEO of a major multinational company told me recently. 'People who take a pride in their appearance, in my book, will also take a pride in their work.'

I shall be discussing ways of improving the look of one's hands in chapter fifteen.

The texture of your hand

During the Russian Civil War, roadblocks were set up by the opposing White and Red forces at which a brutally simple check was carried out to decide a traveller's social class. It consisted of a handshake. Having the soft hands of a non-manual worker was sufficient reason to be hurried before a firing squad if you were a member of the bourgeoisie unfortunate enough to be stopped at a Bolshevik barricade. Similarly, possessing the hard, horny hands of a worker might condemn you to execution at the hands of the Tsar's supporters.

Today the texture of another's hand when shaking it still conveys a message which can mean the difference between making a favourable and an unfavourable, if no longer fatal, impression. Most noticeable to the touch are conflicts between a person's occupation and his or her skin texture. A musician or surgeon whose palm and fingers were covered with hard, calloused skin would provoke as much surprise and curiosity as a farm-worker whose hands were pale, soft and delicately textured. The simple rule is that the feel of your hand should be congruent with the image you are seeking to convey. In some instances a slight degree of roughness in the hand of a professional man can create a favourable impression. It conveys a sense of practicality, a feeling that you are not just an ideas person but one capable of making things happen. In other circumstances even a slight feel of calloused skin could create a negative response.

The moistness of your handshake

One of the surest signs of anxiety is a moist hand caused by sweating. Examine the surface of your hand and you will see three types of lines: creases caused by the way the hand moves – flexure lines; small wrinkles which multiply with age and are due to a loss of elasticity in the skin; tension lines and papillary ridges which give us our finger-prints. The first two are important so far as appearance and texture are concerned. The third are involved with moistness. When we sweat they swell in order to improve our grip. This reflects a curious feature of hand sweating. All our other sweat glands respond to temperature changes, producing more moisture as the temperature rises in order to keep us cool. The papillary sweat glands, alone, become moist in response to stress, tension and anxiety. They are a part of the Red Light reflex. At night, no matter how hot your body feels, your hands will stay free of sweat. This fact is used by lie-detector operators and clinical psychologists to measure anxiety-triggered changes in bodily arousal.

What typically happens is that the subject is wired to a simple electronic device known as an ESR, or Electro-Dermal Skin Resistance meter. This puts a tiny quantity of electrical current into the hand by means of electrodes attached either to two fingers or across the palm.

118

As the subject becomes more aroused, the increase in sweating makes their skin a better conductor of electricity and the resistance falls. When they relax resistance increases. The ESR monitors these variations in resistance and provides an output in the form of a pointer moving across a dial or a sound which rises and falls with resistance changes.

Dr Desmond Morris recounts how, during the Cuban Missile Crisis when the world was poised on the brink of nuclear war, laboratory experiments into hand sweating had to be temporarily abandoned. 'The general increase in stress raised the sweating rate to an extent that made it impossible to get a "relaxed" reading from any of the subjects being tested,' he reports. 'Such is the sensitivity of the human hand.'

Another person's hand can be an equally sensitive detector of arousal, since moist hands are almost always an indication of arousal. Even when the effect operates on the other person at a subconscious level, as it frequently does, the overall effect is to convey a negative impression.

To avoid betraying your tensions it is advisable discreetly to wipe your palm before shaking hands. An alternative method for ensuring a dry handshake, but one which requires a little practice, is to master the art of hand-warming by conscious effort. Here's how it works:

When we become tense, our hand not only starts to sweat more, but also grows colder. This is because the Red Light reflex diverts blood away from the capillaries in the dermis, the cells directly beneath the outer layer of skin, and sends it to the muscles in preparation for fighting or fleeing: which is why people go pale when shocked or scared. The removal of blood helps to produce the cold, clammy sensation of many handshakes.

By sending blood back to the capillaries of dermis, you will not only warm and dry your hand but also feel more physically relaxed.

Practise two or three times a day, if possible using some kind of biofeedback device to check that you really are warming the hand successfully. The cheapest method is to purchase a small alcohol (not clinical) thermometer and attach it to one finger. Electrical thermometers which work by means of a heat sensitive resistor called a thermistor can also be obtained from specialist biofeedback suppliers and even some electronics stores. They are more expensive but easier to use and offer greater sensitivity.

How to mentally hand-warm
Try each of these three procedures. All work well, but you may find one easier to perform and better suited to your particular needs.

Hand-warming method one: Focus on your dominant hand (i.e. right hand if right-handed) and simply imagine it getting warmer and warmer. For many people this is sufficient to produce a change of two or three degrees and ensure a warm, dry handshake. The amount of time taken varies with practice, but once you have perfected the skill it can be achieved in just a few seconds.

Hand-warming method two: Picture holding your hand in front of a blazing fire or plunging it into a bowl of comfortably warm water.

Hand-warming method three: If creating a mental image proves hard, simply hold the palm close to your cheek. This is a hot spot and you should be able to feel the warmth. Imagine that this is being transferred from your face to your hand.

The pressure you use

Men with an excessively strong handshake probably picked up this bad habit from fathers who insisted that the bone-crusher was a truly 'manly' handshake. Women whose grip pressure is minimal were probably warned by their mothers that anything stronger is unfeminine.

Bone-crushers and limp-rag handshakes aside, there is no single right or wrong pressure. It all depends on the impression you want to create in a particular situation. As a general guide, however, the firmer the grip the greater the suggestion of a desire to dominate. This could be an unwise signal to send if, for instance, you were applying for a job. Gripping your prospective employer's hand too firmly will convey a silent speech threat and could cost you the job by making you appear hostile or aggressive.

When you want to convince a colleague, or subordinate, of the strength of your personality and determination to achieve your ambitions then a firm, dominant grip could prove extremely effective, especially if used in the dominant style described below.

To signal co-operation, trust and empathy match the pressure you employ to that used by the other person. Equal pressure should always be employed with the 'friendly' handshake described below.

Slightly reduced pressure can be safely employed with the 'submissive' grasp (see below), but never allow the hand to feel excessively limp.

Contact time

As with pressure, timing is a matter of great subtlety. In my research, variations in the duration of contact as slight as a second could, under certain circumstances, entirely alter the message being sent.

In general a handshake which is briefer than is expected or considered appropriate to the situation conveys a lack of enthusiasm, interest, warmth or empathy. A handshake lasting slightly longer than expected communicates interest, attention, enthusiasm and a desire to co-operate. However when the length increases only slightly, a positive message can become a very negative one, as the person whose

120

hand is being tightly held starts feeling trapped. This sense of being engulfed by and imprisoned in the other's handshake is intensified when a dominance grasp (see below) is employed and/or the pressure is felt to be excessive. In order to ensure that your slightly longer than normal clasp sends out a favourable message it is essential to frame the handshake with four other silent speech signals: (1) eye-contact (2) smile (3) adequate but not excessive grip pressure (4) a slightly leaning forward posture.

A prolonged handshake is often used in conjunction with the 'glove' grasp (see below) or some form of embrace. The one most often used between males is to clasp the other's elbow, forearm or shoulder with the opposite hand. This can convey great warmth and empathy, but it needs to be used with considerable caution. The only times it can be safely used is with an old friend being greeted after a longish absence or a colleague whom you are saluting on some special occasion, such as a retirement presentation or award. When employed inappropriately the message conveyed is unpleasant and extremely damaging to your chances of making a favourable impression.

The amount of eye-contact given while shaking hands, the facial expression and whether or not the free hand is used to make contact with other parts of the person's body all add to or detract from the message of the handshake. These are points which I shall discuss in later chapters.

To explore the effects of different combinations of pressure and clasp duration, a male and female shook hands with a large group of men and women who were unknown to them, deliberately varying the amount of time they clasped the others' hands and the strength of their grip. The people whose hands had been shaken were then asked to assess the shaker's personality.

The shortest handshake lasted just two seconds, the average five seconds and the most prolonged nine seconds.

The type of pressure used and the duration of the handshake together produce very particular effects, as shown below.

Pressure	Duration		
	Too short	Correct	Too long
Soft	Effect 1	Effect 2	Effect 3
Firm	Effect 4	Effect 5	Effect 6
Very firm	Effect 7	Effect 8	Effect 9

Effect 1: Very negative impression conveyed when used by either sex. The man was viewed as having a passive, weak, effeminate, unassertive and disagreeable personality. Females were regarded as weak, hopeless and helpless by the majority of both male and female subjects.

Effect 2: A generally unfavourable impression is made on both sexes, with men finding it slightly more disagreeable than women. A male shaking hands in this way was seen as lacking assertiveness and ambition, being passive and overly submissive. The woman was considered docile, unambitious and lacking individuality.

Effect 3: This combination also created a generally unfavourable impression, although subjects were less able to explain why they had made this judgement. The man was considered insincere, cold and calculating; the woman cunning, dominant and manipulative.

Effect 4: Both the man and the woman tended to be viewed as somewhat hostile, uncaring and insensitive. This was especially so in the case of the woman, perhaps because people expect women to be warmer, less impatient and more empathic.

Effect 5: Created a positive impression in both sexes and proved to be the ideal combination for the majority of encounters with strangers. Both sexes viewed the man as friendly, straightforward, warm, co-operative and empathic when shaking hands. The woman was regarded as being more than usually dominant and assertive by other women, and ambitious, career-minded but slightly lacking in femininity by men.

Effect 6: This handshake produced a somewhat negative appraisal, especially when given by a woman. Both sexes associated it with an overly dominant and somewhat aggressive individual. The man was viewed as determined and ambitious to the point of being ruthless. He was also considered to be successful and achieving. Women were regarded by both sexes as strong, authoritative and emotionally controlled.

Effect 7: Both the man and the woman were considered impatient, driving, insensitive and brusque. It created an especially negative impression when used by the woman, who was viewed as cold, domineering, ruthless and hostile, especially by other women.

Effect 8: The handshake created a positive impression when used by the male but a less favourable one when employed by the woman. The man was considered assertive, successful, self-assured, confident and striving, although likely to be uncaring and overly assertive. The woman was viewed as threatening by males and excessively aggressive by other females.

Effect 9: The handshake created a negative impression when used by both sexes. Some subjects reported feeling intimidated. Women who gave this handshake to other women were seen as disagreeable and lacking in femininity. Males too felt somewhat dominated and some commented privately that the woman was probably a lesbian. When men gave this type of handshake to other males they were viewed as hostile and aggressive.

How does your handshake rate?

Most people are blissfully unaware not only of the positive or negative impression their handshake can convey but also of the type of handshake they offer others. Without becoming obsessional about it, knowing how others rate your grasp is extremely helpful for effective Impression Management. To do this, ask friends and relatives to score you on the following scales:

5	4	3	2	1
Very dry				Very moist

5	4	3	2	1
Very firm				Very limp

5	4	3	2	1
Strong grasp				Faltering grasp

5	4	3	2	1
Grasp too long				Grasp too brief

Do not rely on the impression of just one or two people, but use a selection and then take the average. Remember that their impression of your handshake will, to some extent, be a reflection of their own. If their own hand is very dry, even a small amount of moisture on your own could give them an impression of excessive dampness. Similarly should they have an extremely powerful grip, your perfectly normal handshake may seem too weak. By averaging out a number of ratings you can arrive at a consensus. To analyze your handshake take into account both your total score and ratings of 5 or 1 on any of the five scales.

Score
20–17: Your handshake could well be too much of a good thing for many people in most situations. It conveys an impression of dominance rather than friendliness. This is fine when you want to assert your authority (see chapter thirteen to learn how you can use handshaking as a power-play strategy), but unsatisfactory in most social encounters.

16–10: An excellent handshake for the majority of social situations. It conveys strength and self-assurance without making the other person feel threatened or dominated. But be prepared to make a more assertive handshake in some types of power-plays.

9–4: Your handshake probably gives a rather unfavourable impression. Take steps to improve the first moment of contact.

Styles of handshaking

As important as how you shake hands is the *way* the other person's hand is shaken. By using different types of grip the message is significantly changed. What sort of handshake you decide to use must depend on the sort of impression you wish to convey. As I mentioned above, there are three possible messages: I am going to attempt to dominate you . . . I seek to co-operate with you on equal terms . . . I am prepared to submit to you . . . .

The dominant style
If you wish to tell the other person in effect 'I am taking charge', turn your hand so that the palm faces downward while shaking hands.

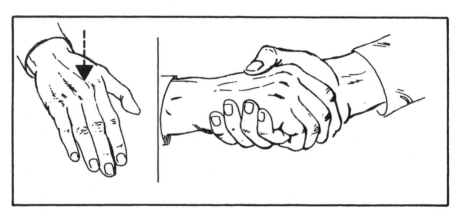

The Great Man Grip.

To convey this message your hand need not be precisely parallel with the ground, but simply pointed downward in relation to the other person's hand.

In a study of successful senior managers, the majority were found to employ this dominant handgrip. Where two equally assertive and powerful people meet, there is often a struggle to gain supremacy during the handshake. The outcome is usually a vertical palm contact, the 'man to man' tie-sign.

In chapter thirteen I shall be describing a simple counter to the Great Man Grip which not only enables you to turn the tables on the other person but automatically places him or her in a subordinate position.

The co-operative style

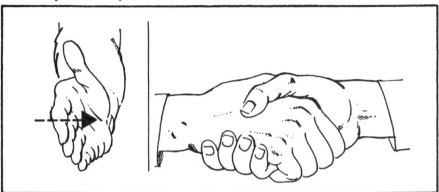

The 'Let's Get Together' Grip.

This handshake should be applied with a pressure equal to that of your companion where you desire to communicate full equality. However by slightly increasing either the pressure applied or the duration of the grasp, you can subtly indicate that while it is an equal partnership, your rule will be slightly more equal than his. It implies that should there be a showdown or dispute, your view can be expected to prevail. The response to this increase in pressure or duration should be noted with care. When the other reacts by increasing his or her pressure, do not expect an easy victory in the struggle for dominance. However, where more pressure on your part is tolerated without any increase in the other's grasp, that person will probably submit to your demands with little more than the occasional token protest.

If an attempt to prolong the handshake is permitted, then, once again, your will has been allowed to prevail. This probably means he or she is prepared to allow you to take the initiative in other matters as well. When the response is to draw away, your attempts at dominance are being resisted. But notice how it is done. If briskly and confidently you can expect an open fight should your views conflict. A tentative, perhaps ineffective, attempt to pull away means the other person is more likely to resist you indirectly and covertly.

The submissive style
If you wish to convey your willingness to subordinate yourself to the other's will, offer your hand with the palm facing upwards – the mirror image of the dominant signal.

The Give-in Grip.

This is the appropriate handshake when dealing with a dominant employer whom you wish to placate by signalling your readiness to act on his, or her, orders. Under these circumstances responding to a Great Man Grip by adopting the same style silently signals an intention to contest his position. Whether or not such a message is to your advantage depends on the situation, but it generally proves unhelpful. A more subtle way of submitting, which conveys the sense of surrendering from a position of strength rather than giving in out of weakness, is to combine the Give-in Grip with slightly stronger than normal pressure at the first moment of shaking hands. Then, as the other person applies pressure, allow your own grip to relax slightly – never to the point where your handshake becomes weak and limp, but down to a Co-operation Grip level. This is especially effective when dealing with a dominant superior, since strength generally respects strength and despises weakness.

If you immediately submit, the other person has no sense of having imposed his or her superior will and may, therefore, feel cheated. You are likely to be looked on as insignificant and not a force to be reckoned with. By resisting before resigning, the strength of your character and determination is subconsciously communicated. The other feels a greater sense of achievement and is more likely to respect and take notice of you in the future.

You must not automatically assume that if a person uses the Give-in Grip he or she intends to signal submission. There may be a medical reason, such as arthritis, for presenting the hand in this way. There are also certain professionals, such as surgeons, concert pianists and artists, who employ a slightly limp, palm-upwards grasp as a means of protecting their hands from damage. Finally, such a handshake is widely used in Islamic countries where it represents a cultural tradition rather than reflecting any weakness of character. Islamic women greeting Europeans will almost always use the 'Dead Fish' Grip. In fact a sharp, firm, hand-squeeze may well be a sexual advance.

In addition to these three basic grips there are various modifications. Used correctly they can intensify a message of warmth, sincerity and the desire for friendship. But handle them with care, since if employed inappropriately the results can be extremely negative.

The Glove

Both your hands are used to cover and submerge the other's hand. This type of handshake is much favoured by politicians wishing to impress voters with their positive virtues. When used in this way it almost always has just the opposite effect, arousing grave doubts and deep suspicions. *Never* use the Glove at a first meeting; only after a warm relationship has already developed. Employed in this way it can help to enhance your impact.

The Double Hand Touch

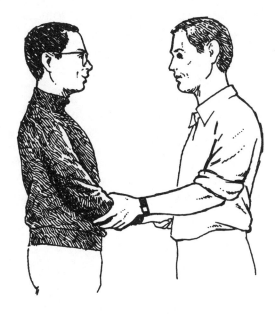

To intensify the impression of warmth and empathy still further, move the left hand (for a right-handed person) up the arm. But proceed with caution: the higher up the arm the left hand moves, the more intimate the gesture becomes since you are starting to invade the other's body space. I shall describe the uses and abuses of body space later in this chapter.

The Wrist Grasp

This should only be used with somebody with whom you are already on warm, personal terms, such as a best friend or relative.

The Shoulder Grip

As the left hand travels further up the other's arm, the degree of intimacy implied increases considerably. The grasp must only be used with people with whom you share a strong emotional tie.

As you can see, the seemingly simple and straightforward handshake turns out to be an extremely powerful but complex silent speech signal. Now that you know how it can be used to best advantage in various situations your ability to manage the impression made at initial contact should be far better.

The Shoulder Grip.

129

RULE FOURTEEN FOR SILENT SPEECH SUCCESS

Keep your hand dry – under all circumstances.

Keep the pressure you apply moderate – under most circumstances.

Hold the other's hand for around six seconds – under most circumstances.

RULE FIFTEEN FOR SILENT SPEECH SUCCESS

To convey dominance use the Great Man Grip, stronger than normal pressure and slightly longer than usual grasp.

To convey friendship and a desire for co-operation use the Get Together Grip, moderate pressure and normal grasp time. If you want to add a little assertiveness to your signal then apply slightly greater pressure. If you want to enhance the friendship aspect, maintain moderate pressure but hold for slightly longer. While doing so smile, have a relaxed facial expression, maintain eye-contact throughout the handshake and lean forward slightly.

To signal submission, employ the Give-in Grip. Grasp and duration should be normal.

CHAPTER ELEVEN

Successful Self-selling

The deepest principle in human nature is the craving to be appreciated.

Dale Carnegie

Many years ago I attended a Judy Garland concert at the Hollywood Bowl. She performed much of her act on a stage extending into the audience. Not long after the concert started it began to rain. For the spectators the choice was either to leave, or to stay and get drenched. Judy Garland could easily have taken shelter by walking off the apron. Instead she stayed, and sang and was soaked along with thousands of her fans. Despite the torrential downpour nobody moved from the auditorium and she finished to one of the longest, loudest and most enthusiastic standing ovations I have ever heard. We were applauding her singing, of course, and her energy, and her enthusiasm and personality. But just as much, I believe, that audience was saying, 'Thank you for making everyone present feel special, privileged and appreciated.' By her action she had demonstrated how much she liked her audience. And when we are liked by somebody the normal, human reaction is to like them back.

And that's really the secret of how to be liked and admired by others. You make people feel good about you by helping them feel good about themselves.

'The desire for a feeling of importance', commented Dale Carnegie in his self-help classic *How to Make Friends and Influence People*, 'is one of the chief distinguishing differences between mankind and the animals.'

Here is a short but powerful psychological assessment which can *either* provide you with fascinating insights into your personality and character *or* tell you a great deal about your best friend. But you must choose, because it cannot do both. If you want to find out about yourself tick any of the A statements which apply. If you want to learn more about your best friend tick the B statements.

Personality insight test

I would describe myself/best friend as . . . (remember, tick A for your own personality assessments, B if you want to find out about your best friend):

A Romantic
B Honest
A Intelligent
B Warm
A Humorous
B Devious
A Concerned
B Articulate
A Fun-loving
B Fast-talking
A Creative
B Light-hearted

Now I have a confession to make. The test assesses nothing at all – directly. What matters is whether you decided to evaluate your own personality and character by ticking the six (A) statements, or your friend by ticking the (B) statements. If you decided to find out about yourself, then you are in good company. Eighty-seven per cent of all those offered this assessment decide they are more interested in learning about themselves than in discovering more about another person.

It's not surprising. We are, after all, the most important person we know. When the New York Telephone Company analyzed people's phone calls they found that the single most frequently used word was the personal pronoun 'I'. It occurred nearly 4,000 times in 500 conversations.

There is nothing which fascinates most of us more than ourselves. Which means that when people take an interest in us, we become far more interested in them.

During the fourth, Involvement, stage of any encounter, in which your goal is to create the most favourable impression, the key to success is communicating a genuine interest in the other person; to make him or her feel important, valued and appreciated. One way is by saying the right things, of course. But this is only partially effective. After all we expect people to be pleasant and polite. If their flattery becomes excessive we quickly doubt their sincerity and form a negative impression of their honesty. 'What', we wonder, 'is that

132

person really thinking – or saying – about me behind my back.' By communicating your interest by means of effective silent speech this risk is reduced. People are far more distrusting of the spoken word than they are of correctly used body language. As we know, a great deal of the influence exerted by silent speech occurs below the level of normal awareness. This means they become favourably impressed at a deep, subconscious level.

To communicate your interest you will be using five types of signals: gaze, facial expression, posture, gesture and touch.

Look – listen – learn

Earlier in the book I mentioned that common memory problem, recalling people's names after a first meeting. 'I'm introduced to somebody and two minutes later I've forgotten who they are,' is a common complaint. As I explained, such instant forgetfulness has nothing to do with a defective memory. It's simply that being primarily concerned with the impression we are making on someone, there's no time to think about the impact he or she is having on us. You can instantly improve your memory for names simply by listening carefully when first introduced. At the same time study the other person carefully – but not so intently that your keen gaze is mistaken for a hostility message. While looking at them, silently repeat their name a few times. While chatting, try introducing their name into the conversation occasionally. It will pay you big dividends.

We all feel flattered when somebody met fleetingly and some while ago remembers our name. The extremely favourable effect this has was well described by Thomas J. Peters and Robert H. Waterman in their best-selling analysis of American corporate performance *In Search of Excellence*. Late one evening the two arrived at the Washington Hotel in search of a bed for the night. They had stayed there, briefly, some time before. 'To our astonishment the concierge looked up, smiled, called us by name, and asked how we were,' they noted. 'She remembered our names! We knew in a flash why in the space of a brief year the Four Seasons had become the "place to stay" in the District and was a rare first-year holder of the venerated four-star rating.'

So remember people's names and use them. It is the *most important verbal message* you will ever use.

The power of anchoring

You can create an even more lasting and positive impact by 'anchoring' the positive emotion which your use of the name evokes.

Anchoring is a simple but potent silent speech signal which involves briefly touching the other person as his or her name is uttered. While saying the name when shaking hands works up to a point, the effect is even more powerful if an additional touch is used. A typical encounter is illustrated below:

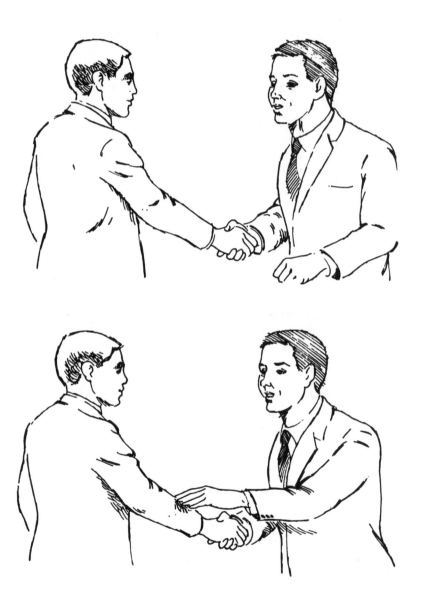

Anchoring in action. First arouse a positive emotion then 'anchor' that feeling with a light touch to the other's forearm.

As you can see in the second drawing, one man is giving the other a light touch on the forearm. The impact of this second, brief, contact derives from the fact that you have aroused positive feelings by your friendly greeting and recall of the other person's first name. This makes him or her feel important, appreciated and special. As you repeat the name and lightly touch his or her arm, that feeling is linked, or anchored, to your presence. Which means that on a subsequent meeting you can reactivate a similarly warm response by use of the same light touch. The sequence is as follows: Arouse positive emotion . . . anchor with light touch . . . good feelings are now linked to that touch. At a later meeting, reactivation of the initial – favourable – impression creates this sequence: Light touch . . . positive feelings aroused . . . positive feelings associated with your presence.

This is a similar response to that demonstrated by the Russian physiologist Ivan Pavlov when he conditioned dogs to salivate at the ringing of a bell by linking the sound of the bell with the prospect of being fed.

The handshake works less well as an anchor because it's something we do so often and with such a wide range of people, some of them liked and admired, others probably disliked or even despised, that no particularly warm emotion attaches to the action. The anchoring touch, by being unusual, serves as a far more powerful trigger. But be careful about where and how the other person is touched by following the advice given below. For the anchor to work successfully it cannot be used in isolation from the rest of the message you are sending. Having your name remembered by somebody who is silently signalling a negative emotion, such as anger, anxiety, depression or indifference, is hardly likely to make you feel good about yourself. In fact quite the opposite is likely.

Now let's explore the five components of effective Impression Management during the Involvement stage in detail:

Gaze

'He speaketh not,' said the poet Henry Longfellow, 'and yet there lies a conversation in his eyes.' We have already seen some of the ways in which such a conversation can occur. Now we must explore the impact created by where, when and for how long you gaze at another.

People are constantly making important deductions about a companion's intentions, honesty and personality through that person's use of gaze. Downward glances, for example, are perceived as a sign of modesty, wide eyes are associated with wonder, frankness, terror or naïvety. We speak of people being able to 'kill with a glance', having 'shifty eyes' or an 'icy stare'.

135

While many of these assumptions have little scientific evidence to support them, there is no doubting the importance of gaze in successful silent speech. Which is why it is essential to avoid placing barriers between your eyes and the outside world. Any type of spectacles, but particularly dark glasses or, even worse, mirror glasses, create a negative impression which it may be very hard to overcome. Where there is a vision problem, wearing glasses may be unavoidable, although as George and Millie discovered to their benefit, contact lenses are always a better choice so far as silent speech is concerned.

Unless your eyes have abnormally heightened sensitivity to light, the only reason for wearing dark glasses indoors is to convey the impression of remaining aloof and detached from your surroundings. Reactions to people wearing dark glasses are uniformly negative. They are evaluated as threatening, because being unable to see their eyes makes people feel they are being stared at by someone possibly cold, remote and devious. Even tinted optical glasses arouse suspicions of insincerity, deceit and lack of empathy.

People who wear dark glasses during a stressful encounter may be unintentionally betraying a high level of anxiety. As I explained earlier in the book, when people become aroused or anxious their pupils automatically dilate, allowing in more light and creating a need for dark glasses to compensate for the eyes' greater sensitivity. So do not assume that your opponent in the dark shades is trying to look mysterious and detached. He or she could well be on the point of panic.

The effect of wearing spectacles

According to the American humorist Dorothy Parker, 'Men seldom make passes at girls who wear glasses.' While this is an obvious exaggeration, there is no doubt that glasses can both trigger stereotyped assumptions about the wearer and act as a barrier to ready intimacy.

Glasses create an impression of authority and intellect rather than warmth and empathy, which makes them ideal for situations in which you want to dominate or impress others by your intelligence but an obstacle to success in many social or intimate situations.

If you are obliged to wear spectacles, consider using them to make a favourable impression at work or in any situations where it will pay to be seen as especially bright, but change to contact lenses when socializing.

Selecting frames which complement your appearance is also important. I shall be describing the best choice for differently shaped faces in chapter fifteen.

Unless there are medical reasons for wearing them, avoid tinted, dark or reflecting glasses. If you want to be seen as warm and empathic wear contact lenses rather than spectacles to correct vision defects.

Men and women gaze differently

Many studies have shown that women use gaze to a far greater extent than men. They look at others more often and hold their eye-contact for longer periods. In one experiment male and female students were interviewed by somebody who maintained eye-contact throughout the exchange, and the extent to which the interviewee returned this gaze was observed through a one-way mirror. Females were found to look more at the interviewer than males when speaking, while listening and during the informal discussions which follow. This may be due to the fact that women tend to listen more attentively than men, and attentive looking is usually associated with more careful listening. But women dislike being gazed at more than men, especially when males are doing the looking. In this situation the majority of women, unless they possess above average self-confidence, quickly glance away.

Some feminist writers have suggested these sex differences in gaze are due to women suffering from a sense of inferiority in male-dominated society: 'Eye-contact is a sure indication of status,' comments Rita Mae Brown. 'Most (female) non-feminists lower the eyes or look to the side, returning a gaze furtively, even more furtively with men. Feminists use more eye-level contact than non-feminists and lesbian-feminists sometimes hold their eyes so level in conversation that it unnerves other non-lesbian women, since this sort of eye-contact is considered predatory among heterosexuals.'*

This passage illustrates how an unexpectedly long gaze is perceived as a threat, an aspect of silent speech which we shall consider later in the book. But the situation is complicated by the fact that although women tend to break eye-contact quickly, they return the gaze just as rapidly. The sequence is: Gaze – rapidly look away – return gaze – look away – return gaze. This pattern of looking, rarely found in men,

---

*Rita Mae Brown, 'The Good Fairy', Quest (1974), No. 1. 62.

may be repeated half a dozen times during encounters lasting less than thirty seconds.

'For many women, in many real-life situations,' comments N.M. Henley in her book *Body Politics*, 'visual information may be a prize furtively caught in stolen glances when men have turned their gaze momentarily, or when men are occupied with each other or with other matters. The image of the female gossip peeping out of windows from behind draperies may suggest something about the dis-ease with which women are expected to intrude visually upon their world.'

Men dislike being gazed at, especially by other males, although not to the same extent as women. In one study, male and female experimenters stared at men and women for some three seconds, and observed whether or not their gaze was returned. When a male experimenter made eye-contact with other men, 80 per cent of them averted their gaze immediately. When gazed at by a woman only 40 per cent did so.

Among animals, prolonged staring is a signal of aggression. Studying gorillas through binoculars, for example, is extremely hazardous since they are very likely to interpret your interest as an especially formidable stare and instantly attack.

When studying young children in playgroups I frequently saw dominant children compelling others to hand over a toy, give up a game or surrender a favourite place at the head of the table merely by fixing them with a long, penetrating stare. The same effect carries through to adulthood, as a novel study by three Stanford University psychologists revealed. Mounted on motorscooters they stared, from a distance of around five feet, at motorists waiting for a red traffic light to change. The immediate response of the startled drivers was to avert their gaze and, according to the report in the *Journal of Personality and Social Psychology*, to begin to indulge in a variety of apparently nervous activities such as fumbling with their clothing or radio, revving up the engines of their cars, glancing frequently at the traffic light or initiating animated conversation with their passengers.

The degree of anxiety aroused was assessed by the speed with which the drivers pulled away as soon as the light changed green. In almost every case, however amiable the experimenter appeared, steady gaze was enough to get motorists of both sexes pressing the pedal to the metal and leaving rubber on the road in their haste to escape. Stared-at motorists left the lights almost two seconds faster than average. To check that it was the gaze which aroused anxiety and not simply unusual behaviour, an experimenter was stationed at the street corner with a hammer and instructions to start tapping the pavement whenever a car drew up at the lights, but not to look at the driver. Although bizarre, this activity did not produce any abnormally rapid departures.

138

This illustrates the powerful nature of prolonged gaze and its importance in silently psyching-out an opponent during non-verbal power-plays.

You can also learn a great deal about another person through their use of gaze. Not only from how often they give eye-contact and how long the gaze is held, but also from the way in which eye-contact is broken, whether upwards or downwards, to right or to left. These clues, which I shall describe in detail in chapter fourteen, can provide important indications as to their personality, their trustworthiness and even the way they are using their memories.

How to give effective eye-contact

Here you need to know three things: where to gaze, how long to gaze and when to gaze.

Where to gaze
This varies according to the type of encounter. During business meetings the eyes normally focus on a triangle formed by lines drawn across the bridge of the nose and down the edges of each eye.

 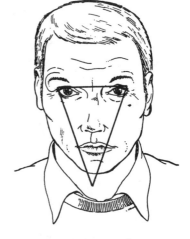

The gaze triangle for business encounters.   *The gaze triangle for social encounters.*

Fixing your gaze in this area conveys interest, intensity, seriousness and self-confidence.

In a relaxed, friendly encounter your gaze should shift downward to take in the nose, lips and chin.

This communicates interest and a desire to get to know the other person better, perhaps even intimately.

How long to gaze
Business and formal encounters If you are a man dealing with another male, maintain eye-contact only for between 60 and 70 per cent of the time. Anything less is liable to be interpreted as a sign of shiftiness, unease or a lack of confidence. Longer gaze, however, will be interpreted as aggressive.

If you are a male dealing with a woman, reduce eye-contact slightly, to around 50 per cent of the exchange. But be very careful not to allow your gaze to drop below the business target triangle since, as we shall see in a moment, this implies a desire for greater intimacy.

If you are a woman dealing with a man and wish to assert yourself in the situation, use eye-contact around 70 per cent of the time. Should you wish to silently signal a compliant or submissive attitude, reduce the duration of gaze to about 50 per cent. Be aware, however, that the longer period of eye-contact will communicate a strong, dominant and self-confidant personality which some men may find disturbing and stressful. Whether or not this state of mind is one you would welcome, or wish to avoid, depends on the purpose behind your encounter. Where the important thing is to assert authority then the longer gaze is obviously necessary. If you are more interested in winning co-operation, it may be prudent to reduce the degree of dominance somewhat.

If you are a woman talking to another woman, then maintain eye-contact for around 70 per cent of the time. This should not normally arouse any discomfort. Be careful, however, to keep your eyes on the target triangle. Women who are unused to dealing with assertive, confident females and/or have doubts about their sexuality could interpret the longer gaze as a threat or sexual invitation, especially when the gaze falls lower on the face.
Social and informal encounters Here the amount of gaze you give depends on what you hope to get from the encounter. If you wish it to remain on a friendly but non-intimate basis, follow the advice above for business meetings. Should you be interested in developing a more intimate relationship then increase the gaze duration and allow your eyes to sweep the other's face and body, down to the crotch area, from time to time.

Beware of cultural differences
The rules above apply when two northern Westerners are addressing each other, but there are wide cultural differences in the amount of gaze considered acceptable and these must be carefully born in mind.

As Michael Argyle points out, 'Too much gaze was regarded as superior, disrespectful, threatening, or insulting by Africans, Asians and Indians. Too little gaze was interpreted as not paying attention and impolite, especially by Arabs and South Americans; too little gaze was also seen as insincere, dishonest or shy by subjects from a variety of cultures.' The Navaho Indians, for example, are trained not to look directly at another person while talking. Among the Wituto and Bororo Indians of South America, both speaker and listener will fix their gaze on some nearby object when conversing, and tribal story-tellers turn their backs on the audience. A man from the Luo tribe of Kenya and his mother-in-law must turn their backs on one another while speaking, while Nigerians are taught that it is ill-mannered to look into the eyes of a superior while addressing him.

When dealing with a Japanese, avoid gazing at the face at all but look instead at the neck. This national aversion to gaze may result from experiences during early infancy. Japanese babies are carried on the mother's back a great deal and so have little training in giving and returning eye-contact. Other groups which prefer short periods of gaze are Asians, Indians, Pakistanis and Northern Europeans. High gaze groups include southern Europeans, Arabs and Latin Americans.

When to gaze
To create maximum rapport, be sure to offer eye-contact whenever the other person *starts* talking. This reassures him or her that you are paying attention and also subtly flatters by conveying that what is being said has considerable interest for you. Continue to make eye-contact, using any pause in their flow of speech to break eye-contact. Look away briefly just before replying, since this sends a message of a thoughtful and considered response. Return gaze while speaking, using natural pauses in your dialogue to shift gaze momentarily. When you have reached the end of your remarks, glance downward to clearly signal your desire for a response from them.

Remember that the greater attention and interest you can convey by means of appropriately used gaze, the more other people will believe you like them and the more liking they will show you in return.

Gaze and job interviews

If a potential employer gives you frequent eye-contact during a job interview then there's an excellent chance of your being offered the position. Where gaze is linked to smile and frequent head movements then the job is virtually guaranteed. Ray Forbes of the business department at the University of Wales Institutes of Science and Technology and Dr Paul Jackson of Sheffield's Applied Psychology

Unit found that successful applicants received twice as much direct looking, three times more smiling and twice as much head-nodding as unsuccessful ones.

Manipulating gaze

By controlling the amount of eye-contact another person gives you, and manipulating the moment at which such gaze is offered, it becomes possible to manage not only the impression made but whatever aspects of that encounter you wish to be best remembered. Here's how it is done:

If the other person is offering you what appears to be insufficient gaze it may be because he or she is shy, anxious, hostile or uninterested. In any event the first step is to *reduce* the amount of eye-contact you give, while at the same time ensuring those periods of gaze you do offer are returned. By reducing gaze initially, you can put a timid or nervous person at ease while making it less likely that an aggressive individual is going to interpret your gaze as a threatening signal. It may also help to step back slightly, so allowing the other person more personal space. This can have a dramatic effect in reducing both anger and anxiety. Then, while gazing at the other person, use a hand or finger gesture to draw attention to your eyes. This can be done simply by gesticulating with either hand as though to illustrate some point you have just made.

Use a hand or finger to draw the other's attention to your eyes.

Alternatively, and more conveniently when the exchange is taking place in cramped conditions, simply point one finger at either eye by touching the side of your nose or gently rubbing your cheek.

Touching the side of the nose can also be used to control the other person's gaze.

The eyes have a particular affinity for any type of movement – after all in primitive man anything that moved could pose a threat – and so are drawn upwards with the rising finger to meet your gaze. As eye-contact is established you must say and do something to create a favourable impression. This could be a warm smile and using that person's name in an agreeable context. For instance, 'I really do admire the way you've decorated this room, it shows such good taste.'

Research shows that after three days we can only remember around 10 per cent of anything we are told. By using gaze as part of your routine Impression Management procedures, you can ensure that the small proportion recalled is most favourable to you. Months after an original meeting the person will still remember some pleasant comment you made. And even when the precise nature of your remark is forgotten, an agreeable feeling lingers. On subsequent meetings that person will be much more inclined to view you in a friendly light.

The head-tilt

This is an extremely powerful silent speech signal which is virtually guaranteed to create a favourable impression or win co-operation. It involves combining the eye-contact with a smile and sideways tilt of the head.

I found that willingness to assist with a simple but time-consuming task – accompanying an apparently lost tourist to an address two blocks away – increased by 200 per cent when the favour was combined with this potent non-verbal message. You can also use the inclined head to increase feelings of empathy and warmth on a first meeting. When used at the start of the Involvement stage it creates an extremely favourable impression.

The head-tilt signal can also be used to win the co-operation of young children, since it almost always causes the youngster to whom it is sent to comply with the sender's wishes.

RULE SEVENTEEN FOR SUCCESSFUL SILENT SPEECH

Use a head-tilt, together with eye-contact and a warm smile, on first meeting to increase the warmth and impact of your presence. Use the same gesture whenever you are asking for help or co-operation.

Gaze direction and written presentations

One of the problems about making a presentation from written material is that it greatly reduces eye-contact. Argyle and Graham found that mutual gaze fell from 77 per cent to 6.4 per cent when subjects were asked to plan a European holiday with a map placed between them. Eighty per cent of the time was spent staring at the map. Even a vague outline of a map was looked at for 70 per cent of the time. This means that your opportunities for Impression Management through gaze manipulation are limited. Unless, that is, you take advantage of a potent silent speech signal called the 'power-lift'.

Imagine you are attempting to interest somebody in a sales brochure and naturally wish them to pay very special attention to the most favourable aspects of the goods or services on offer. Here is how to proceed. Follow the printed lines of text with a pen or pencil until you come to a point you especially want to be remembered. At this moment, slowly raise the pen until it points to the corner of your eye – right eye if you are right-handed, left eye if left-handed. The other's gaze will lift with the point of your pen until eye-contact is established. At this point repeat the key part of the proposal.

Power-lifts are especially effective in fixing the information *you* wish to be retained in the other person's memory.

Research has shown that around 80 per cent of information about the world reaches us via our eyes, 10 per cent through the ears and the

The power-lift used to manipulate another person's attention during written presentations.

remainder from other senses. This means that during a written presentation the amount of information absorbed through your verbal message can drop as low as 10 per cent when what is being viewed is unrelated to the content of your speech, but never rises much above 30 per cent even when both the spoken and printed messages coincide. By using the power-lift to compel eye-contact and then repeating the key factor from your presentation, you can increase recall for that specific message to 85 per cent or better.

Using gaze with a large group

When talking, whether formally or informally, to a group of people it is essential to move your gaze so that each receives some eye-contact and, therefore, feels included in your presentation. Notice how professional entertainers regularly take in their entire audience, from stalls to gallery, in order that nobody feels excluded.

The inability to provide eye-contact with an audience is one of the major drawbacks of reading from a script. Working from cards or brief notes is a far more effective method of delivery. Recently politicians have taken to using a so-called 'sincerity machine' to get around this very problem. This is a teleprompter which projects the speech on to transparent perspex screens placed either side of the podium. The words, which are invisible to the audience, can easily be seen and read while the speaker gives the impression of spontaneity. The speaker can also look from side to side, so – literally – taking in the whole audience. Before technology came to our aid the only alternative was to memorize an entire talk.

Autocues have, of course, been used in TV for many years, allowing newsreaders and presenters to follow their script when staring straight into the camera lens and out of the viewer's set. But it is only much more recently that politicians have realized that a much greater impact can be achieved through a combination of silent and spoken speech.

With practice, however, even script-bound orators like Margaret Thatcher can use some non-verbal signals. As Max Atkinson points out in *Our Masters' Voices*, 'Like most speakers who seldom stray from their prepared scripts, Mrs Thatcher continually moves her head up and down from lectern to audience and back again . . . the timing and direction of her glances are remarkably rhythmic, and go through a cycle of movements that keep recurring at very regular intervals and in much the same order . . . the usual pattern involves about three glances to the left followed by one to the right, and the sheer regularity of these movements may be one of the factors which has contributed to the view held in some quarters that her public-speaking style has a tendency to be rather monotonous.'

146

Speaking from behind a podium, also necessary when reading out a script, blocks some other silent speech signals as well, such as 'Illustrators' which can be used with good effect to emphasize points, underscore major ideas and maintain a rhythm that helps to cue an audience when to applaud. These are points which I shall discuss in detail later in the book.

RULE EIGHTEEN FOR SUCCESSFUL SILENT SPEECH

When speaking to a group ensure your gaze includes them all. Avoid reading from a script if possible. Either memorize what you wish to say or use brief notes.

Learning to use eye-contact

If you are rather shy and unassertive, you may find it very hard to employ gaze during Impression Management. In this case train yourself in its effective use by doing the following:

1. Relax as much as possible. The hand-warming procedure described in the previous chapter will help you do so quickly and unobtrusively.
2. Plan some topics in advance. It helps take the edge off nervousness if you have prepared for a conversation.
3. While speaking, stand or sit comfortably. If standing balance your weight evenly.
4. Anxious people often fix their gaze too far down the face in an attempt to avoid eye-contact. This conveys a negative impression. You can improve your ability to focus on the target triangles by using beforehand this simple exercise which raises eye level and provides a boost to one's confidence:

   Stretch your arms up high, open your mouth wide and tilt your head back so that you are staring at the ceiling. Now slowly lower your arms, close your mouth and tuck in your chin. Allow your gaze to follow the movement down, but stop when your head stops moving. You are now looking 'down your nose'. As you tilt your head back to the normal position your eyes will be correctly aligned for gazing at the target triangle. By doing so you will communicate confidence, interest and involvement.

The power of touch

I have already mentioned one use of touch – to anchor and then reactivate warm and positive feelings towards you. Correctly used, touch can enhance the impression you make in other ways as well. But be careful: when employed inappropriately it can rapidly undermine any favourable impression you have already made.

Studies have shown that, as with gaze, the sexes differ significantly in their response to touch. Women find a touch from an unknown male disagreeable, but men feel as comfortable being touched by a woman stranger as by a woman friend. Women touch one another on the arm, hand or back more than men and hug each other more frequently, but shake hands far less than males. 'Such touches', report psychologists Richard Heslin and Tari Alper, 'are highly pleasant to men regardless of their acquaintanceship with the woman, but they are only pleasant for women when the toucher is a close male friend.'

Touch can also be a way of conveying status. Superiors are more likely to touch a subordinate than the other way around, and older people are more likely to initiate touch with a young person than vice versa.

Touching, when used correctly as part of an overall silent speech message, can give you three positive benefits: (1) In the right setting it makes people feel more positive both towards you and their surroundings. (2) In a situation where you are comforting or offering sympathy, touching will help another person to talk, especially about themselves. (3) It increases your influence over others. People will more readily comply with your requests or grant you favours. In one study, people borrowing from a library had their hand lightly brushed by the librarian as she issued the book. Outside they were stopped and asked to complete an evaluation of the service offered by that library. Those who had been touched responded more favourably on all the questions asked.

There are two main reasons why touch has this effect. The first is that because it violates – however slightly – a social norm, it conveys the feeling that the person's need is genuine. Secondly, it communicates trust and liking on the part of the person doing the touching. It also subconsciously raises the status of the person who touches while slightly reducing that of the touched, so making compliance more likely.

Where to touch

Safe areas for each sex in different sorts of non-intimate relations are shown opposite.

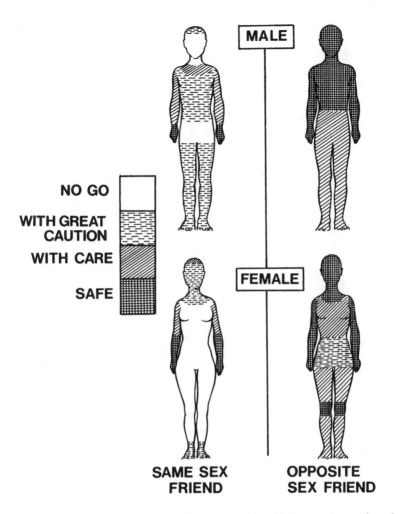

NO GO

WITH GREAT CAUTION

WITH CARE

SAFE

MALE

FEMALE

SAME SEX FRIEND

OPPOSITE SEX FRIEND

The 'safe' places to touch with a (i) same sex friend (ii) opposite sex friend (iii) same sex stranger (iv) opposite sex stranger.

How to touch

This depends on your relationship with the other person. The better you know them, the firmer and more intense your touch can be. With a stranger, however, especially another male if you are a man, be very careful how you use touching. The safest rule to follow is to confine yourself to one brief, light, tap on the arm immediately following a handshake in order to anchor a good impression. Women can afford to be slightly more tactile with both sexes at first meeting, and will convey a better impression by making their touch firmer and slightly longer lasting. But again the touch should be confined to the arm.

When people are better known your touch can be more obvious and of longer duration, but males should always be wary of offering too much touch, especially in public, to other men. Subordinates should be especially careful when touching superiors because of the conflict in status which may be communicated. Often it is safest to disguise your purpose by asking to borrow some object such as a pen, or requesting a light. As you return the pen or cup your hands around the cigarette lighter, it is usually quite easy to brush hands with the other person. Even this fleeting and apparently accidental contact can significantly enhance the impression you make.

The part played by posture

As you stand chatting, your posture can convey either warmth and openness or a refusal to become involved. We have already seen that a forwards-leaning stance combined with smiling, eye-contact and a relaxed posture communicate empathy, interest and liking. This can be further enhanced by an open-arm posture which conveys warmth and acceptance.

Folded or closed arms, on the other hand, communicate rejection, passivity and shyness.

However your choice of posture should also be determined, to some extent, by how the other person is standing or sitting, for there is a useful way of subconsciously enhancing the other person's liking for you by mirroring their stance.

Mirroring

Also known as *postural echoing*, this involves copying the other person's posture. If their arms are folded, yours should be as well. When they lean back, so should you. Mirroring comes naturally to people who know one another intimately. Watch a long-married couple, for instance, and you'll see how closely they mirror one another's movements, gestures and postures.

In the photographs below, the two men are unconsciously copying one another's posture and gestures as they engage in a friendly conversation.

By deliberately mirroring another's body language you greatly increase empathy. When used correctly, mirroring is one of the most

150

rapid and reliable means of developing rapport and winning another's confidence. With only a little practice you will find it comes so naturally that, after a while, the response is spontaneous. During negotiations I have found it increases the chances of agreement by up to 50 per cent, while during sales presentations it can double your chances of making a favourable impression.

Parting

With the exchange at an end, you reach the final stages of the encounter – Disengagement and Separation. The only point to watch here is to make the ending quick but smooth. The worst possible way to finish is little by little, going away a short distance and then returning, bidding farewell several times only to come back for another brief discussion or a final word.

If you are saying goodbye to a business colleague after a meeting in your office, then walk him or her at least as far as the door. When you want to emphasize the value placed on your relationship, it's worthwhile escorting him as far as the elevator or even the car. By going out of your way, you intensify the feelings of acceptance and empathy.

A final handshake is also worth while: you should always initiate it. This provides an opportunity for some final anchoring, thus reinforcing the positive feelings established during the encounter. It also allows you to maintain control of the last moments of the exchange, so subtly communicating a sense of having been in command of the situation throughout.

A neat conclusion to the encounter is especially important because of an aspect of human memory called the primary and recency effect. This means we remember most clearly what we heard first and last. Which means that the moment of parting tends to linger long after the content of the exchange has been forgotten.

CHAPTER TWELVE

Love-signs

Love makes mutes of those who habitually speak most
fluently.

Madeleine de Scudery, 'De l'amour', seventeenth century

The next time you are having a drink with someone special and want
to know if he or she finds you attractive, try this simple experiment.
After drinking, casually place your glass close to theirs. If it is allowed
to remain there, you are being welcomed into their personal space, an
invitation which strongly suggests an interest in developing the
relationship further. If, however, their glass is moved out of the way
the chances are your advances are being spurned.

The way in which people respond to invasions of their personal
bubble is one of the surest love-signs in the repertoire of silent speech.
Which is why, under inappropriate conditions, trespassing on somebody's Intimate Zone may be interpreted as sexually threatening.

I had a good example of the anxiety such a signal can create when
appearing on the Terry Wogan television programme. While we were
sitting side by side on a studio couch he asked how to tell if somebody
was attracted to you. I mentioned a desire for physical closeness as one
of the surest signs and, while talking, edged a few inches nearer to him.
He immediately slid to the far side of the sofa, widening the distance
between us.

'Only demonstrating,' I explained.

'I've been in show business a long time,' he joked, suggesting he
interpreted the invasion of his personal sofa space in terms of a sexual
advance.

Manipulating distance in order to demonstrate your attraction for
somebody can prove a hazardous manoeuvre. Before doing so it is
essential to read another's body language carefully, and perhaps to test
their response by initially invading their personal space with some

inanimate object, such as the glass, a newspaper, paper or book. If this advance guard meets with a favourable reception then you can follow up your advantage.

Courtship, whose evolutionary purpose is getting close in order to mate, depends to a considerable extent on silent speech signals. 'To woo someone we might send and receive more than a thousand courtship signals,' explains Dr David Givens, a University of Washington anthropologist and expert in non-verbal communication. But even with the help of silent speech getting together can be tricky. 'Animals seem to have a natural aversion to the laying-on of paws or whatever with a stranger,' he comments. 'It's adaptive. If you aren't wary, you're liable to be eaten, or chased away or bumped off.'

Ten steps to intimacy

Studies have identified ten silent speech steps leading from first advances to coitus.

Step 1: Eyeing the body. We saw in the previous chapter how, when a formal encounter becomes more friendly, gaze drops from the upper business target triangle to take in the lower parts of the face and upper parts of the body, the 'social triangle' of expressions.

Be alert for this shift, which sometimes involves the other person changing his or her stance, moving back slightly in order to take in more of your face.

Step 2: Eyeing the eyes. As intimacy increases so does the amount of mutual eye-contact, resulting in those long, soulful, looks so eloquently described by romantic novelists. A refusal to return gaze in a situation of potential intimacy is a clear sign that the other person is uncertain or uninterested.

Step 3: Hand touches hand. Unlike the formalized handshake, this contact is usually light but lingering. It may be disguised by some apparently innocent action, such as placing one hand beneath your partner's elbow to guide him or her through a crowded restaurant, offering a cigarette and brushing fingers in doing so, or helping to put on a coat.

Step 4: Hand touches shoulder. Once again this message can be hidden within some socially acceptable gesture. Up to this point each individual can withdraw from the encounter without either suffering too much lost pride. The person who has made the advance may feel disappointed, but not overly rejected. Both can pretend that no advance was made. But the next step involves a definite commitment. Once this silent speech Rubicon has been crossed there can be no going back without suffering a severe blow to one's pride.

Step 5: Arm encircles waist. By bringing the hand closer to the genitals the encircling arm signals a desire for far greater intimacy. If this is accepted then the couple usually move quickly to the next step . . .

Step 6: Mouth touches mouth. The kiss is a uniquely human non-verbal signal and one which, when intense, leads to sexual arousal by both partners.

Kissing is what non-verbal communication specialists term a Relic Signal. That is a throwback to mankind's prehistoric past when mothers would feed their babies, as many animals still do, by regurgitating food into their mouths.

During the human kiss, especially in deep kissing as a couple explore one another's mouths with their tongues, chemical information is exchanged via the saliva, and the roles of smell and taste become important.

Step 7: Hand caresses head. While embracing the couple explore one another's face and hair. This is especially significant because it indicates great trust between the couple. Because our heads are extremely vulnerable, only those we feel close to and at ease with can touch them without vigorous protest.

Step 8: Hand fondles body. The couple begin to explore each other's bodies, either through the clothes or probing beneath them. The fondling, stroking, touching and caressing produce strong sexual arousal and, given the right circumstances, this pre-copulatory stage is very likely to lead to intercourse.

This couple, with eyes only for each other, have reached step 8 intimacy as their hands caress each other's body.

Step 9: Mouth caresses body.
Step 10: Hand caresses genitals.

After this the only remaining step, apart from ending the encounter, is genital-to-genital contact.

From step 8 onwards, close proximity means that most body language is ineffective since at this distance the eye can no longer sharply focus face or body, so that much of the visual information on which we usually rely for interpreting silent speech is lost. For this reason a couple who have reached step 8 – sometimes earlier – will often close their eyes. Eliminating useless and distracting visual information allows them to concentrate more fully on their senses of temperature and smell, two seldom-appreciated but vital aspects of intimate silent speech.

The heat of passion

The core temperature of a normal, healthy human is 37 degrees centigrade (98.4°F), but skin temperature is always lower than this and varies according to our emotional state. As I explained in earlier chapters, when we are anxious or afraid this peripheral temperature drops as blood is sent to the muscles. If we are relaxed or sexually aroused, the blood flows back from the muscles to capillaries in the skin, so increasing its temperature. During the more intimate stages of a passionate encounter, the presence or absence of this rise in body heat sends an important message to our companions. People who are emotionally cold are also likely to be physically cold. Anxiety prevents the return of warm blood to the skin, so leaving them cooler to the touch, a signal interpreted – usually correctly – as dislike, lack of interest, distaste or disapproval. When a man or woman is described as 'hot stuff' or we speak of a 'warm embrace' it may well be almost literally true. As they become more passionate such people really do get very hot and their partner reads this – correctly – as revealing their emotional state as well.

The sweet smell of sexcess

In 1572, a royal ball was being held in the Louvre to celebrate the marriage of Marie de Cleves to the Prince de Condet. The sixteen-year-old bride, who was said to have great beauty, 'having danced for a long time and feeling slightly overcome by the heat of the ballroom, went into a dressing room where one of the Queen's maids helped her to change into a clean chemise.' The Duke of Aragon, who came by chance into the room after the young princess had left, picked up the discarded chemise and used it to wipe his face. 'From that moment on,' noted a contemporary writer, 'the Prince conceived the most violent passion for her.'

This story is far from fanciful. The way in which our sense of smell has evolved means that odour is one of the most potent silent speech signals two people can exchange. Nerves carrying the messages of smell are wired directly into a part of the brain called the olfactory bulb, and it is from this bulb that regions responsible for the highest levels of human thought – the cerebral hemispheres – evolved. Because these impulses arrive in a region of the brain responsible for memory, for example, we tend to recall memories linked to smells far more accurately, and over much greater periods, than those associated with sight, sound or touch.

'Odours act powerfully upon the nervous system,' commented the seventeenth-century writer Johannes Muller. 'They prepare it for all pleasurable sensations, they communicate to it that slight disturbance or commotion which appears as if inseparable from the emotions of delight, all of which may be accounted for by their exercising a special action upon those organs whence originated the most rapturous pleasure of which our nature is susceptible.'

The role of smell in love signals was noted by Aristotle three centuries before the birth of Christ. In Roman times aromatic baths and massages with sweet-scented unguents were a regular prelude to love-making. Civet and ambergris were popular among the leisured philanderers of Imperial Rome, who used aromatic spices to scent their breath. The value of vanilla as an aphrodisiac is demonstrated by the fact that the name of this spice is a diminutive of the Latin *vagina*.

Not only is our sense of smell powerful in terms of the emotions evoked, it is also extremely sensitive. Receptors in the nose can detect the presence of a substance called ethylmercapton, which is present in rotting meat, in amounts of less than a 400-billionth of a gram.

Each person possesses a smell signature as unique as his or her fingerprint. This results from the action of bacteria on an oily substance, sebum, secreted by the sebaceous glands in our skin. Because of the large number of fatty acids the body produces and individual differences in our skin's acidity or alkalinity and temperature, no two people ever produce exactly the same odour. The final smell signature consists of these oil secretions, blended perhaps with odours of food, drink, perfume, aftershave, deodorants, cigarette smoke and smells absorbed from our surroundings.

Can body smell be deliberately used as a means of increasing attraction? The perfume industry certainly believes it can, and there is both anecdotal and some laboratory evidence to support such a claim. Richard Kraft-Ebbing, the German sexologist, for instance, described how 'A voluptuous young peasant man told me he had seduced quite a

157

considerable number of chaste girls without difficulty by wiping his armpits with a handkerchief while dancing, and then using this handkerchief to wipe the face of his dancing partner.'

One substance sometimes used in perfumes which is claimed to increase sexual allure is androstenediol, which is chemically related to the male sex hormone testosterone produced in the testes. Psychologist Michael Kirk-Smith tested its potency by asking subjects to evaluate portrait photographs, some of which had been sprayed with androstenediol. He found that both men and women rated photographs of women which contained the perfume as more attractive. However it had less influence on judgements about the relative attractiveness of males. Dr David Nenton, a leading British researcher, found that women in the middle of their monthly cycle reacted more strongly to the odour.

To explore the effects of perfume on male judgements about female attractiveness, Dr Robert Baron of Purdue University asked ninety-four males to take part in an experiment which, he explained, was investigating the influence of 'first impressions' on character assessment. The men were then divided into four groups. The first met and chatted briefly with a female assistant who wore jeans, a sweater and perfume. The second group spent a similar time with a woman wearing skirt, blouse, stockings and the same brand of perfume. The third and fourth groups met a girl who was dressed either formally or informally but wore no perfume.

The results showed that perfume alone did not make a woman appear any more attractive. Differences were only found when both scent and the manner of dress were taken into consideration. The girl who had perfume and wore skirt, blouse and stockings was regarded as cold and unromantic. When perfume was associated with casual dress, jeans and a floppy jumper, however, it was perceived as warm and romantic.

Baron then varied the experiment by having half his subjects deliberately angered by either a male or female collaborator while the other half had a pleasant encounter. Some of his confederates wore perfume, others did not. After the first meeting, the subjects were allowed an opportunity to be verbally aggressive towards the confederate.

When the collaborator was a male, wearing a perfume increased the level of aggression against him by subjects who had previously been provoked, but lowered the level of aggression by those subjects who had not been previously angered. When the collaborator was a woman, however, perfume increased the level of verbal aggression whether or not the subjects had previously been provoked.

The results suggest that wearing perfume greatly increases the risk of a woman becoming the victim of aggression by males and makes a male more at risk from males who are already upset. For the best results, a woman should use a perfume with casual clothes but not when dressed more formally, unless she wishes to create a sense of remoteness and emotional coldness.

Responses to natural body odour vary greatly according to culture and familiarity. Entering a stranger's home one is immediately bombarded by a host of strange odours, to which the householders are usually oblivious. 'In the northern European tradition most Americans have cut themselves off from . . . olfaction,' comments Edward Hall. 'Our cities lack both olfactory and visual variety.'

Arabs attach far greater importance to natural body odours, believing that it is possible to read character and personality from them. During encounters many Arabs will deliberately inhale another's breath, something most Westerners are careful to avoid. So much value is attached to a person's smell that, when arranging a marriage, the broker sometimes asks to smell the prospective bride. If she does not 'smell nice' he may reject her, not primarily because her odour might prove offensive to the bridegroom, but because a girl who smells bad is thought to have a hostile or discontented disposition.

So far as an aid to courtship is concerned the case for wearing expensive perfume remains unproven. In some circumstances it may help but, as David Benton points out, 'Sexual attraction relies on many factors including personality, social skills, past experiences and the present situation. If everything else is suitable then an odour may make a small difference but the product of an aerosol spray is unlikely to be the predominant influence and compensate for other failings.'

The best advice seems to be to use any perfume sparingly and to allow natural body odour to work for you by not disguising or covering it with man-made products. Such odour should not, of course, be so overwhelming as to prove offensive. Remember the nose is our most delicate sense organ and a little smell goes a very long way.

Attracting attention

To explore flirting in public, Dr Monica Moore of the University of Missouri-St Louis and her colleagues spent more than a hundred hours studying two hundred unaccompanied white women, aged between approximately eighteen and thirty-five, in singles bars. They found that females usually made the first move in attracting attention, using one of fifty-two different kinds of behaviour. These fell into three main categories: movements of the face or head, gestures and posture changes. The signals included smiling, skirt hitching, pouting and knee touching. The most common were smiles, surveying the room, keeping time to the music, leaning forwards towards a male – sometimes brushing his body with her hand or breast – a head toss, pouting, brushing back the hair and a gaze lasting three seconds or longer. All were extremely effective, bringing attention from the man to whom they were directed within fifteen seconds.

However the extent of flirting behaviour depends very much on setting. While Moore and her co-workers saw an average of seventy such acts in the singles bar, they fell to nineteen in the university snack bar, ten in the library and five at a women's centre meeting.

'Those women who signalled most often were also those who were most often approached by men,' Moore reports. Which underlines a key fact about love-signs. You have to give in order to receive. But it doesn't matter whether the attention-seeking signals are sent out by males or females. In fact women sending out the right silent speech signals to strange men are likely to enjoy greater success than males signalling to unfamiliar females.

The first date

Psychologists studying dating among American adolescents have identified what they call a 'courtship' dance leading from first meeting to intercourse. For the courting to be successful the man must wait for an appropriate signal from his partner before moving to the next step of the dance. When the boy holds the girl's hand, for example, he must wait until she presses his hand – a signal to continue with the courtship dance – before attempting the next step, which is entwining his fingers with hers.

Partners label one another 'slow' or 'fast' depending on how they move through this dance. Those who skip a few steps or reverse their order are considered 'fast'. If one fails to respond to a 'go' signal or takes action to prevent the next step occurring, he or she is regarded as 'slow'. For example, the male is only allowed to approach the woman's breasts after the first kiss. She may then block his hand by placing her upper arm against her body. Courtship dance protocol forbids approaching the breast from the front, and the boy does not really expect to be allowed to touch her breasts until after considerable kissing.

The courtship dance – sending the right signals

Tom was the envy of all his male colleagues at the office because he seemed to have no trouble at all in finding attractive women partners. Often within minutes of arriving at a party he would be deep in conversation with a woman who subsequently accompanied him

160

home. How did he do it and can any interested man, or women, emulate his success? The agreeable answer is that such encounters should prove no problem at all, provided the right silent speech signals are sent out.

Courtship signals – males

The first step is to attract attention to yourself so that eye-contact can be made. There are various ways of doing this, most involving a form of self-grooming such as adjusting your tie, fiddling with the collar, rearranging cuff-links, flicking dust from your sleeve or shoulder, smoothing your hair.

Once the other's attention has been caught the next step is the correct use of eye-contact and facial expression. As we have seen, women tend to be somewhat averse to the stares of unknown males, so avoid a long, lingering look at this stage in the ritual. An initial gaze of around three seconds is appropriate under most circumstances. Expression and posture should remain relaxed and friendly. Do not smile immediately on making eye-contact. A far more effective combination of signals is to delay smiling until after eye-contact is established. The message conveyed by this slight hesitation is, 'I was only being polite at first . . . but now I've taken a good look . . . wow!'

Use a low-intensity smile (see page 88) about one second after making eye-contact. Continue to gaze for a further two seconds, then break eye-contact by looking *downward* to either right or left. The significance of using a downward rather than a horizontal left or right eye-break will be explained in chapter fourteen. Gaze should be almost immediately re-established, this time with a high-intensity simple smile (see page 88) and an eyebrow flash. Continue to smile and gaze for a couple more seconds before making an approach.

The most effective sequence of eye and face movements, together with an approximate timescale, is as follows:

Gaze/smile/gaze/break gaze/ return gaze/smile/approach.
1 sec.......2...3.......4...............5.......7........8.........10

This approach tends to work best, our studies show, with warm, intelligent and sexually unassertive women, from men who are dressed either formally or casually, but not in an aggressively masculine way. The silent speech signal can be translated as: 'I am confident, friendly, warm, with high self-esteem and sexually experienced. I am also interested in you.'

Should you desire to convey a more macho image, the signals can be altered slightly in order to communicate a vigorous and aggressive message. Eye-contact should be longer and the smile either made less intense or avoided entirely. Posture should be less relaxed and more

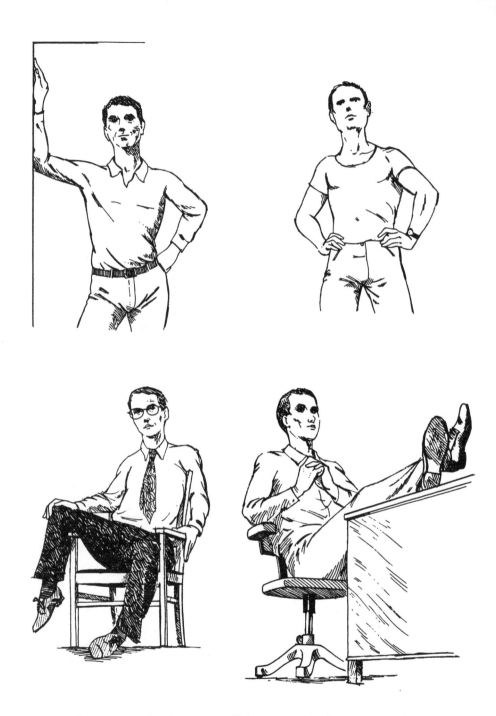

Four ways to dominate space: (i) leaning against doorpost or wall; (ii) hands on hips; (iii) spreading in a chair; (iv) controlling both chair and desk. All convey confidence.

dominant. One way of signalling dominance is to 'take possession' of part of the room or furniture, so expanding the territory to which claim is laid.

As we shall see in the next chapter, command of space is one of the main ways humans communicate status.

Aggressive sexuality can be communicated by any hand gesture which draws attention to the genital area. For instance . . .

The cowpoke posture
One or both thumbs hooked into a belt, with the downward pointing fingers framing the groin, is one obvious signal.

The leg massage
Lightly stroking either the outer or, less often, the inner thigh.

The leg spread
Spreading the legs wide to offer a crotch display when leaning against the wall or seated in a chair.

While all these messages are a great deal cruder than the subtle signals described earlier, they can – so I am reliably informed – prove highly effective in certain situations. It depends on whether the woman of your choice appreciates the caveman approach. In each case the silent speech message is one of great sexual and social confidence with the implication that any woman

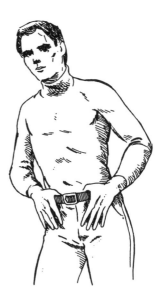

The cowpoke posture.

should feel honoured to be approached so obviously by such a hunky guy.

Not surprisingly, when this performance comes with heavy gold chains, muscled chests and hair curling through a partly unbuttoned denim top, many females find it a total turn-off. Others, although considering the tactics crude and unromantic, are, despite themselves, attracted by the raw masculinity and sexual dominance which these signals convey. It is, of course, necessary for the man to live up to the promise of his body language if the encounter is not to end as an embarrassing fiasco.

Courtship signals – females

As Monica Moore's research showed, women have a far wider and more subtle repertoire of courtship signals than men: over fifty, as against twenty-eight for men, were identified in our studies. Here are ten of the most common for men to watch out for. They have been rated on an attraction scale from 1–10: the higher the score the greater the interest implied. These ratings are based on the responses of a randomly selected sample of five hundred British and American males.

Region: head and neck
Hair toss: The head is flicked to one side, briskly moving the hair over one shoulder or away from the face. The length of the hair is unimportant. *Attraction rating*: 5.

The hair toss.

The open lips.

Open lips: Some researchers view this as an attempt to mimic female genitals. Cosmetics or saliva used to moisten the lips increases the intensity of the invitation. Pin-up photographers instruct models to lick their lips immediately prior to taking a picture for this very reason. *Attraction rating*: 7 (dry lips) 10 (moist lips).

The sideways glance.

The preening gesture.

Eye-contact: Used as in male courtship signals. Women who are sufficiently self-assured to use gaze at all tend to be much less inhibited about it than men. This is presumably because, as we have seen, males respond far more positively to eye-contact from a woman than most females do when gazed at by a man. *Attraction rating*: 8.

Sideways glance: This too is a variation on the 'look, break gaze, return gaze' sequence which proves so powerful when used by men. The action is to look at the man through partially closed eyelids but drop the gaze a moment after it has been noticed. *Attraction rating*: 9.

Region: hands and arms
Exposing the wrists: The woman slowly uncovers her wrist and displays her palm to the man in whom she is interested. This silent speech signal is easiest to send when smoking, which may be one reason why many women find the cigarette such an invaluable social tool. *Attraction rating*: 5.

Grooming: A preening gesture, which is often followed by a head toss. The woman massages neck or head with one hand. This has the effect of raising the breast on one side of the body and intensifying cleavage. It also exposes the armpit which, even when shaved, has erotic significance as a mimic of the genital area. *Attraction rating*: 4.

165

Playing with any cylindrical object.

Playing with any cylindrical object such as a pencil, pen or cigarette is often a reflection of subconscious desires, but it may simply mean the woman is feeling sexually interested rather than attracted to any particular male. *Attraction rating*: 1.

The knee point.

Region: Legs
The pointing knee: The woman sits with one leg tucked under the other, her knee pointing at the male who has attracted her. Any interested male who sees this clear signal should immediately return eye-contact. *Attraction rating*: 8.

166

Open legs, when sitting or standing, indicate a general sexual interest and not necessarily attraction towards any male in particular. However males looking for a pick-up can use this as one indication that it might be worth while sending a few courtship signals in that female's direction. *Attraction rating: 5.*

Entwined legs are used to draw attention to the limbs while conveying an impression of high muscle tone. This mimics the muscle tone seen in sexually aroused people of both sexes. *Attraction rating: 9.*

Open legs.

Entwined legs.

Crossing and uncrossing the legs while being watched by an interested male is a strong attraction signal, especially when the woman simultaneously strokes or rubs her thigh. *Attraction rating*: 10.

Crossing and uncrossing legs.

Shoe play: Fiddling or playing with one shoe while seated in a relaxed position mimics phallic thrusts and can be a strong sign of attraction. Equally, it may simply represent the displacement of strong, but not specifically directed, sexual drive. *Attraction rating*: 4.

Shoe play.

Put-offs to come-ons

At any point during a silent speech exchange, one of those involved may decide to stop the courtship dance and change partners. If, of course, they were never interested in the first place, initial attempts to communicate attraction would simply have been ignored. This may be done by refusing eye-contact, turning away or even sending out positively discouraging messages by frowning, glaring or glowering.

By observing and being sensitive to put-offs during your come-ons, it becomes possible either to avoid wasting time in courting an embarrassing rejection or, if you are interested in saving the situation, to switch tactics.

Both sexes send out two main types of put-off when wishing to discourage further non-verbal advances: *blocks* and *barriers*. In the descriptions below I have given each a rating indicating the degree of rejection it implies. As with attraction, they are scaled from 1 (slightly defensive) to 10 (very rejecting).

Body blocks
These are attempts to shut out the unwelcome message by interposing some physical object between yourself and the other person. In a railway carriage, for instance, a passenger unwilling to continue a conversation with a stranger will raise her newspaper or book between them. Dark glasses are often worn for this purpose. Parts of the body can also be used as blocking agents. Autistic children, who loathe being looked at, will block by hiding their face behind their hands.

Blocking is often seen during stressful business meetings and negotiations when an overwrought individual covers his eyes with one or both hands. Blocks are normally used to pre-empt a courtship display but can also appear some way into the encounter, perhaps because one of those present becomes suddenly upset or embarrassed by the exchange. At a recent party I watched an older man and attractive young woman embarking on a courtship dance at a distance of some six feet across the floor. All was going well until the man suddenly blocked by averting his gaze and hastily lifting a large wine glass to his lips. The reason for this sudden blocking became apparent a moment later, when the man's wife appeared from the crowd around a buffet table.

Although blocking often marks the end of an exchange, there are occasions when it is actually a come-on rather than a put-off. This happens when a young woman pretends to be coy and hard to get. While giggling with mock embarrassment, she will partly cover her eyes and turn away. But these pseudo-blocks are easily identified by their brief duration and by the fact that all the other body signals are positive and welcoming.

169

An 'end of the road' block will usually involve, in addition to the blocking gesture itself, tense posture, blank or hostile expression and little body movement. When this is sent the turn-off rating is 100 per cent. It is a red light warning you to go no further.

If, however, the block is accompanied by a relaxed body, friendly or at least neutral expression and some movement of the hands, arms or body then it serves more as an amber light: the silent speech signal is proceed but use caution. Men should lower the intensity of their signals. If they have been sending out aggressive, sexually dominant messages then it will help to switch to a more subtle approach. Reduce the amount of eye-contact slightly and send out some appeasement signals by looking instead of merely glancing down as you break gaze. A relaxed posture is also important, since increased bodily tension can trigger the primitive Red Light reflex preparing the other person to fight or flee. If you are standing to one side of the woman, adjust to a more full-face position.

Women who receive this signal should first check whether there is some reason, other than a rejection of their advances, for the block. The appearance of the man's partner or a gossipy friend are fairly common reasons for blocking. Equally the man may have spotted another higher status male, who he has reason to believe is emotionally involved with the woman and who is now heading in her direction.

If there seems to be no such explanation for the block consider whether you may have been coming on too powerfully. Many men find a sexually assertive woman anxiety arousing and would sooner look for a potentially more submissive and less demanding partner. When an open-leg display is being used, for instance, it could help to change to an entwined leg posture or simply place one's legs demurely side by side.

Barriers

These are usually less defensive than blocks. They translate into spoken language as, 'Convince me that you should remain . . .' instead of, 'Go away, I don't want you.' The most widely used barriers involve folding the arms or crossing the legs. But within these apparently simple movements there is a range of important variations.

Barrier signals of all types have been found to significantly reduce the amount of information being allowed through to the brain. In one American study, two groups of university students attended the same lecture. One group was told to listen while seated with arms and legs uncrossed, while the second kept their arms tightly folded across their chests throughout. When tested on their attitude towards and knowledge of the lecture, those who had used a folded-arm barrier were not only far more critical of the lecturer, but remembered nearly 40 per cent less information. We'll begin by looking at the arm barrier, starting with the full fold. As with attraction signals, these have been rated on a scale of rejection ranging from 1, very slight, through to 10, for a total turn-down:

Standard fold: Conveys a defensive, negative attitude, and reveals uncertainty and insecurity. The person disagrees with what is being said or done. If you notice this during a business presentation it is time to change tactics.

The standard arm fold.

The stress of being in a public place is demonstrated by these arm-fold barrier signals.

171

When used as a response to a sexual *come-on* it represents a challenge, but not an insurmountable obstacle to success. Once again the best approach is to slow down, and maybe even take a few non-verbal steps back. You have been pressing too hard and the object of your attentions is getting worried, fed-up or insulted. *Rejection rating:* 6.

The fist fold.   The arm clasp.

Fist fold: The message is a stronger and more daunting one. The person is not merely defensive but aggressive. You will have to work that much harder to break down the barrier. Or give up the attempt to attract as a bad job. *Rejection rating:* 9.

Arm clasp: Here the shoulders are gripped firmly, sometimes to the extent that blood is drained from the knuckles. It represents either extreme anxiety over the situation or great anger. *Rejection rating:* 10.

With the full fold, you need to break the barrier before it will be possible to achieve any further progress. The quickest way to do this in a social situation is to offer the person a glass, cigarette or something to eat. As soon as the barrier is down, seize your opportunity for removing the cause of their negative feelings. At a business meeting a cup of coffee, document or pen can be used to the same end.

Alex, the insurance salesman whose brilliant use of body language I described in chapter one, used to keep a variety of cards up his sleeves for breaking down barrier signals. These included photographs of his wife and children, for use with married prospects, ·his Labrador dog –

for animal-loving prospects – and his boat, for sailing enthusiasts. He also had an antique pocket-watch which he would hand over for inspection and an electronic credit card-sized diary. 'But it doesn't matter what you use,' he explained, 'so long as it's sufficiently interesting for the person to want to reach out and take it. By doing so the arm barrier is automatically destroyed.'

Partial blocks

These are less daunting than full blocks, because they signal not so much rejection as a lack of confidence on the other person's part.

One view is that this gesture has a comforting effect on insecure people because it echoes the experience of having their hand held when a child.

When this signal is seen in a courtship dance, the more effective counter-response is to reduce the amount of self-confidence you are communicating. Remember people feel most comfortable in exchanges with those whose level of self-esteem matches their own. If you have been sending out signals of great self-assurance, a less confident individual may begin to feel threatened. When the barrier is seen in a business discussion, then identify what aspect of your proposals may be creating uncertainty and do whatever is necessary to set the other party's mind at rest. *Rejection rating: 2.*

A partial block signal.

Leg barriers

As with arm barriers it is important to read these in context. For instance the standing leg-cross illustrated on the next page is the usual position adopted by Europeans, Australians and New Zealanders when forced to sit in uncomfortable chairs for any length of time. Americans, by comparison, tend to cross their legs slightly differently.

The standard leg cross.

The American version of the leg cross.

In many situations neither indicates a negative attitude. If, however, a person switches to this position after you have started to send out come-on signals and combines the barrier with other silent speech messages of displeasure, such as folded arms and a blank or hostile expression, you will need to change strategies. If seated beside the person on a couch, for instance, increase the distance between you – to reduce any feeling of personal space violation – and offer a head-tilt and smile. *Rejection rating:* 4.

Hand-locked legs

Here the hands are used to draw the leg into the body and lock it there.

This represents an extremely defensive and negative attitude. Your message is not being at all well received and the best advice is probably to stop wasting time and find a more amenable partner.

In a business encounter, read the sign as evidence of a stubborn, probably highly opinionated individual who is going to fight you every inch of the way unless you take great care and act with considerable skill. I shall be discussing ways of getting around such people in the next chapter. *Rejection rating:* 10.

The hand-locked legs.

Standing leg cross

Finally we have crossed legs in a standing position.

This is a typical posture when people are introduced to a group for the first time and are uncertain how to proceed. If you see it in response to come-on signals, you are certainly proceeding too fast. Back off for a while and allow the person to get used to the situation before proceeding. It doesn't mean they are repulsing your advances; merely that more time is needed to analyze the situation.

One method for breaking out of this impasse is to suggest you both move to another part of the room. Use a plausible excuse such as, 'Shall we go where it's less crowded . . .' or, 'let's move away from the music.' This obliges the person to uncross their legs. Offering something to eat or drink similarly

The standing leg cross.

compels the arms to unlock, at which point you are in a position to press home your advantage. *Rejection rating: 5.*

It pays to be sensitive to the numerous signals used during courtship. These love-signs of silent speech are often far more important than words in developing intimacy.

Observe and act on blocks or barriers. These should never be ignored or negative feelings will build to a point where you cannot control them. If noticed and dealt with early on, however, it is often possible to remove the cause of the anxiety or hostility they reveal.

Courtship is a complex dance of silent signals which many men, especially, find difficult. They misread signals from those to whom they are attracted and send out confused, conflicting or inappropriate messages of their own. But at least human males are not in the hazardous position of the wolf spider, whose courtship, like ours, is heavily dependent on silent speech signals. If he sends out the wrong kind of message to his partner there's no second chance. She eats him!

CHAPTER THIRTEEN

Power-plays

One man is no more than another if he does no more than another.

Cervantes, *Don Quixote*

A middle-aged company director was carefully reversing his Rolls-Royce into a narrow parking space when a young man in a battered Mini nipped into the gap. Locking his car, he remarked with a grin, 'Sorry, Grandad. The world belongs to the young and the quick.' Without a word the businessman continued reversing, pushing the Mini sideways and depositing its battered remains on the pavement. He then locked the Rolls and handed his business card to the horrified youth. 'No doubt your insurance company will contact me,' he remarked calmly. 'And you're wrong, by the way. It belongs to the strong and the rich.'

It's an anecdote which perfectly illustrates the role of territory in power-plays. For the most important way to communicate your dominance over others is through the control of valuable space. Closely related to this is the extent to which you can dictate how other people spend their time. That is your ability to determine not only where another person shall be, but when he must be there and how long he has to stay. The higher your status and the greater your power the more territory and time you command. The tyrant has absolute authority over his slaves' every waking moment. He can specify where they must go, what they must do and how long has to be spent on the task. Prison guards exert a similar power of time and place over inmates.

Depending on his status, an employee has greater or lesser ability to regulate either the time and/or place of work. The boss may work from home, take three-hour lunches and play golf whenever the mood takes him. The production-line employee enjoys no such concessions.

In some companies even the time allowed for going to the lavatory may be strictly controlled.

> ### RULE NINETEEN FOR SILENT SPEECH SUCCESS
>
> The secret of a successful power-play depends on your ability to control the other person's time and space.

Planning your power-play

Before you can decide what power-play tactics will prove most effective, two decisions must be made. First you must ask yourself, 'What kind of impression do I need to make to achieve my purpose in this encounter?' In other words are your goals best served by being dominant, co-operative or submissive?

Within this framework there can be many variations. You might wish, for example, to be both assertive and placatory; to co-operate from a position of strength rather than equality; or to submit only after being dominant.

To decide which approach is appropriate you must, of course, have a clear idea of the desired outcome. Embarking on a power-play without establishing firm goals is like going hunting by blasting away blindfold in the hope of hitting something edible. Once the purpose is decided you must next ask yourself, 'What status does the other person enjoy and how do I compare?' There are *two* answers to this question. The first is his genuine status within an organization: that individual's place in the hierarchy, his position in the pecking order. Secondly, there is perceived status. How important, irrespective of actual position, does that individual believe himself to be?

I shall be explaining how to identify genuine status and distinguish it from self-importance in the next chapter.

As a rule of thumb a domination power-play is only going to prove effective provided your status is higher than that of your opponent. This rule needs some qualification. Status here means *within the same arena*. If your status is derived from authority in a different area of expertise, it may be possible to dominate somebody of higher status. A doctor, even a junior one, could take control of a government minister's time and space by despatching him to hospital if he had suffered a medical emergency.

In most cases where there is an unfavourable difference between your own status and the other person's you must use power-plays designed to win co-operation and prevent yourself from being domi-

178

nated. Where the other's real status is equal to your own, you may use either domination or co-operation strategies, but should avoid showing submission since this upsets the status balance in the other person's favour.

So far as real importance is concerned, you cannot always rely on job title. As anyone familiar with the Machiavellian nature of big business knows, awkward but unfireable executives are frequently shunted off into some quiet backwater where they can do no harm, placated by some high-falutin but meaningless rank. Which means that while the title on the calling card, notepaper and office door can be a starting point when deciding true status, it's often more reliable to rely on other sources of information.

The most helpful place to begin this exploration of power-play silent speech, therefore, is by considering the six ways true status can be determined from non-verbal clues.

1. Space and status

During the past decade New York developer Donald Trump has bought many landmark buildings around Fifth Avenue and Central Park, transforming them into money machines named after himself. Starting with a $200,000 trust fund set up by his builder father, he has accumulated a fortune estimated at $3 billion. One of his properties, on the site of Bonwit Teller's former art deco department store and now called Trump Tower, is a bronze glass and red marble testimony to the potency of space in conferring prestige and status. Entering the building from Fifth Avenue, visitors are confronted by a soaring atrium, complete with a giant waterfall.

Trump Tower provides the perfect illustration of the close relationship between scarce space and high status. Territory nobody much wants does not, of course, provide much prestige. Owning one hundred square miles of desert is obviously a lot less impressive than having title to one square mile of Manhattan.

The use of space to confer status can be seen in many old churches, where social class rather than piety determined the seating arrangements. For the priest there was an elaborately carved pulpit which, by raising him above his congregation, ensured he was both physically and symbolically the focus of attention. Somewhat taller than the pulpit, however, and often elaborately decorated with carvings, a canopy and coat of arms, were the spacious pews occupied by the lord of the manor and his family. These faced the pulpit across the heads of commoners crowding narrow benches in the body of the church.

Architect Duncan Joiner comments that, 'Not only is the place for these important people set aside physically from the places for ordinary people, but the form and decoration of the box further emphasizes its difference from the other seating places in the room and

Trump Tower on New York's Fifth Avenue epitomizes the extravagant use of space to communicate status.

the social differences between its occupants and the occupants of the room generally.'

In any major organization, being given a larger working area is as sure a sign of favour as losing space – by being moved to a smaller office or having one's office partitioned to provide a bigger office for another executive – is an indication of disfavour. In *Blind Ambition*, John Dean, counsel to President Nixon, comments that in the White House, 'Success and failure could be seen in the size, decor and location of offices. Anyone who moved to a smaller office was on the way down. If a carpenter, cabinetmaker or wallpaper hanger was busy in someone's office this was a sure sign he was on the rise . . . movers busied themselves with the continuous shuffling of furniture from one office to another as people moved in, up, down or out. We learned to read office changes as an index of the internal bureaucratic power struggles.' He claims that even a newcomer was able to detect minute changes in status by monitoring such manoeuvres. He recalls how one senior staffer comforted himself over the loss of a private bathroom, taken to provide extra space for Henry Kissinger, with the thought that, 'I'm glad to know the place I used to shit in will be Henry's office.' Dean remarks that this man was the only person in the White House not to care about having his office area reduced in size. And that was probably because he was planning to leave anyway. For the rest of the staff such matters were of paramount importance.

Not even academic institutions are free from this struggle for status through the control of space. One anonymous faculty member from a major American university recalls his experiences on his department's Space Committee:

'I found the first few meetings . . . to be rather mystifying – it seemed that we were making maps of the department's space in the building and colouring it in four different colours . . . it was only gradually that it dawned on me that I was taking part in no mere exercise but rather in the renegotiation of treaties in a newly reorganized department in the manner of Truman, Churchill and Stalin at Potsdam, and with a comparable degree of emotion on the part of all concerned parties. The arguments had relatively little to do with who really needed the space and more to do with feelings about how much space they had in the past, how much they had been promised, and how much they deserved – the assignment of offices, laboratories, and the like was taken as central to their status and worth as human beings.'

2. Height and status

Tall men have an inborn advantage when it comes to status. Because they naturally occupy more space they are also viewed as being more powerful and dominant. Between 1900 and 1968, for example, the successful candidate in the US presidential race was *always* the taller of the two. More recently Nixon, Ford and Carter were all above average height. The effect is less powerful where women are concerned, possibly because greater height leads both sexes to evaluate them as being rather unfeminine and somewhat more threatening.

The association between height and power has its origins in childhood, when we are surrounded by taller, larger and stronger adults who have absolute authority over us.

If you are on the short side do not assume that this means an automatic loss of status. A lack of stature can be compensated for by controlling space in other ways, for instance through gaining power and possessions. Merely being seen as having a high status will add inches to your perceived height. This was demonstrated by an ingenious experiment in which a speaker was introduced to different groups of undergraduates in one of five different ways. The first group were told he was a university student; the second, a demonstrator in psychology; the third, a lecturer in psychology; the fourth, a senior lecturer in psychology; while the last group were informed he was a professor of psychology at Cambridge University. After his talk, the students were asked for an estimate of his height to the nearest inch. As his academic standing increased so did their perception of his height. The professor was seen as being a full five inches taller than the student!

As someone unkindly, but accurately, remarked about the late billionaire shipping magnate Aristotle Onassis, 'He was a short man — until he stood on his wallet.'

3. Possessions and status

The slogan on a best-selling US T-shirt reads, 'The person with the most toys has won!' A more accurate message would be, 'The person with the biggest toys is boss.' These include large and costly cars, impressive homes set in rolling green acres or apartments in the most exclusive city neighbourhoods, and big, well-positioned offices with expensive furnishings.

On seeing the president's Oval Office in the White House, John Dean felt awed by the sheer size of the fittings. 'I could feel the importance of the office as I took it all in,' he recalled in *Blind Ambition*: 'My attention was caught by the conspicuous rug and the huge desk . . . Two Presidents, maybe four, could have worked at it without disturbing each other.'

4. Location and status

In the White House, office location was as significant as its size and decor. Those with the highest status were closest to the president.

It is the same in any major organization. The greater an employee's importance, the closer his or her office will be to the seat of power and the more favoured its position within the building.

In tall city buildings the best position is high up, where the air is cleaner, traffic noise less intrusive and views more spectacular, and in a corner position so that picture windows can offer breathtaking vistas in two directions. While such views are agreeable in themselves, they also confer status by the fact that a pleasant outlook is a scarce resource in most cities. The less favoured a person's office location, and the further removed from decision-making centres, the lower his or her status, prestige and importance to the company.

5. Privacy and status

Superiors are, within limits, able to violate the privacy and personal space of those lower in the pecking order with impunity. The boss can stroll unannounced into his underling's office at whim – an invasion of space which is usually denied subordinates. He can also touch those lower in the hierarchy, for instance by placing an arm on their shoulder, without asking permission – an act of familiarity which would be poorly received if initiated by a low-status individual.

The more privacy a person enjoys the higher their status. CEOs usually have private bathrooms, senior executives elegant but shared facilities, while the remaining employees must make do with a far less exclusive washroom. In many companies ambitious managers view the 'key to the executive washroom' the same way soldiers regard a field commission.

A stretch limousine signals status by occupying expensive space.

For high-status individuals there are many other privacy perks, such as private dining-rooms, the peaceful surroundings of VIP lounges and first-class travel, executive jets and limousines with smoked-glass windows to whisk them through congested city streets. Their office sanctuaries are guarded by secretaries and receptionists whose job is to keep unwanted visitors at a distance. By contrast lower-status employees have much less privacy. Junior managers may be obliged to share a room, while assistants and secretaries must put up with the noise and lack of privacy afforded by a general office.

In *Rooms With No View*, a collection of essays about women in the media, one anonymous writer described working conditions in a TV network's advertising department:

'The Spot Sales Department has sixteen male salesmen and sixteen female sales assistants. The salesmen hustle television spots (sixty-, thirty- and ten-second commerical breaks) to advertisers. They sit in individual windowed offices. The women are crowded (all sixteen of them) on to the outer-office floor. The noise of sixteen typewriters, telephones, and voices on that outer floor is almost deafening.'

6. Time and status

The higher your status the greater your ability to control the time of a large number of people. You can fix appointments to suit your convenience and keep people waiting.

'Your position in the waiting hierarchy often determines your importance,' comments Robert Levine, professor of psychology at California State University, Fresno. 'The longer the line, the more important the person becomes. The value of financial consultants, attorneys or performers is enhanced by the simple fact that they are booked up well in advance ... the least accessible are sometimes elevated to saviour-like dimensions.'

In American universities there is a widely accepted but unwritten rule which says that before they can leave students must wait ten minutes for an assistant lecturer who turns up late to take a class, twenty minutes for an assistant professor and thirty minutes for a full professor. When this was put to the test in a study by psychologists James Halpern and Kathryn Isaacs, it was found to have wide application.

These, then, are the six main ways in which status, and with it the ability to dominate others and avoid being dominated by them, is achieved.

Power-plays

In any encounter you will wish to do one or more of the following: *Dominate*, *Submit* or *Co-operate*.

A dominant encounter is known as a zero-sum game, a term derived from games such as poker where one player's gain is another's loss. In zero-sum games there are always winners and losers.

During submissive encounters the other's gain is your *apparent* loss. I say apparent since the only good reason for voluntarily submitting is as a means of gaining an even greater reward later on. The strategy is similar to a chess player allowing minor pieces to be taken while planning the cunning trap that will checkmate his opponent's king.

You might also act submissively to placate a high status individual who has power over your future.

Co-operative or non-zero games are those in which both parties gain something from the exchange and leave the negotiating table satisfied. During a co-operative game it may be necessary to dominate the proceedings at times and be submissive on other occasions. In other words you must approach the encounter in a flexible frame of mind.

While the words spoken will, of course, play an important part in the course of any such exchanges, the non-verbal element is, in many ways, more important. As I have stressed throughout this book, silent speech has the ability to emphasize, underline and amplify what is said. Equally it can, when used inappropriately, greatly undermine even a strong position by weakening or contradicting the spoken word. By reading others right you can also, as I shall explain in the next chapter, discover deeper meanings to certain expressions and identify deceptions, whether deliberate or otherwise.

In this chapter I am going to deal in most detail with power-plays in which you either seek to dominate the other person or are countering their own attempts at domination. This is because we have already considered many of the silent speech signals involved in co-operative or submissive encounters in previous chapters.

The desire to dominate

You will wish to be dominant when . . .
1. negotiating or dealing from a position of weakness;
2. doing so may yield greater concessions or other gains;
3. the other person's reliability or motivations are in doubt and you wish to ensure compliance by instilling fear;
4. it is necessary clearly to establish your authority in order to prevent disputes at a later date.

The last strategy (4) is often a wise one to follow when appointed to manage a team. It follows the logic of the teacher who, on starting to teach a new class, would always single out and severely chastise the biggest boy in the class for no reason other than to demonstrate his ability to rule with a rod of iron. He would then feel free to operate a far more liberal regime without fearing a loss of control. If you start out being dominant it is always possible to become co-operative later. If you start out allowing yourself to be dominated, regaining dominance, or even achieving co-operation on terms of equality, becomes far more difficult.

Others, of course, will seek to dominate you for exactly the same reasons. They are most likely to make such attempts if you . . .

1. show any willingness to submit on unfavourable terms to yourself. They will often test you during a first meeting to identify any vulnerable areas;
2. are in a position of weakness – whether financial, physical or emotional;
3. are a woman dealing with a male;
4. are a younger person dealing with an older one;
5. are a supplicant seeking a favour.

It is essential NEVER to appear submissive at a first meeting, NEVER to betray a weakness. ALWAYS act with assurance and disguise requests for favours as mutually beneficial opportunities.

People with little genuine status but an exaggerated sense of their own importance frequently attempt to dominate others in order to bolster their egos and disguise from themselves their lack of power. Into this category come the legions of petty bureaucrats, minor functionaries and self-important low-grade officials whose sole purpose seems to be making life as difficult and tiresome for other people as possible.

Dominating by controlling space

You can reduce the risk of being dominated by making a confident impression from the first moments of your encounter. I have already discussed, in chapter seven, the importance of adopting the right posture. This not only makes you appear more self-assured but also adds to your height, so enhancing perceived status. The way you walk into a room is also an important silent speech signal. In *Down and Out In Paris and London* George Orwell describes a man who could never be mistaken for anything other than a vagrant:

'One would have known him for a tramp a hundred yards away. There was something in his drifting style of walk, and the way he had of hunching his shoulders forward, essentially abject. Seeing him walk, you felt instinctively that he would sooner take a blow than give one.'

A professional wrestler once told me the vital importance of walking correctly when making your way back to the dressing-room after an unpopular victory in the fight. Enraged spectators have been known to inflict more injuries on fighters than they are ever going to receive in the fight. But such risks can be averted by walking correctly: 'The majority of people are cowards. When you leave the ring the essential thing is to move very slowly. Speed up and they'll go for you. Walk slow and you become a giant.'

So move calmly, coolly and deliberately. Without appearing diffident or lacking in enthusiasm, take your time entering the office and sitting down. This does not mean going so slowly you give the impression of being indecisive or hesitant. Rather you should walk with the calm confidence of a monarch surveying his domain.

Hurrying not only betrays nervousness but makes you appear furtive and of low status.

Who mostly runs around an office? The GOFFAS, scurrying about as they Go For coffee, carry messages, buy sandwiches, collect stationery or deliver documents.

Who are the GOFFAS? A company's most junior, least important and lowest-status-of-all employees. So don't allow yourself to be confused with them. Walk like the rightful owner of that territory does, with pride and assurance.

There's another benefit from proceeding with a measured pace. Hurrying increases your level of bodily arousal, so making you more at risk from the Red Light reflex. We not only run *because* we are afraid, we are fearful *because* we run. You can further reduce any anxiety the encounter may be generating by following the acronym WASP: Wait – Absorb – Slowly Proceed.

In a domination attempt, the other person may show signs of becoming impatient or make some other attempt to hurry you along. Resist. Give in to this tactic and you've already placed yourself in a submissive posture. One counter-strategy is to pause and admire some aspect of the decor, perhaps comment on a painting or remark on the view. Out of politeness the other person is obliged to take the time to respond to your comments, and this automatically slows the proceedings.

Walk slowly, walk deliberately and walk tall. Take the time to review your surroundings. Adopt the manner of a proprietor, not the furtive air of somebody who doesn't really belong there. Imagine you own the place and move accordingly. Never allow yourself to be hurried.

The power handshake

In chapter ten I described how it is possible to communicate dominance by means of a downward pressure. To take command of the proceedings from the first moment of contact you should use this handshake. If, however, it is used against you, then the control that person is attempting to exert has to be countered immediately to avoid leaving an impression – even a subconscious one – that you are prepared to relinquish authority over the meeting. But attempting to neutralize the handshake by turning the other's hand back into the submissive position presents two major difficulties. First, it is very hard to achieve and second, your intention is obvious. Instead, use this counter-move to turn the tables on your would-be dominator: on being presented with a dominant handshake (palm face downward), move your left foot forward as you reach to take it.

Now move your right leg forward and, while doing so, shift to the other's left and invade his or her personal space. Finally bring your left leg over to your right to complete the manoeuvre.

By doing this you achieve two important advantages. Firstly the other's dominant handshake is smoothly transformed into either a co-operative one or, by extending the move slightly, into a submissive one. Second, your deliberate invasion of his personal space increases the other's anxiety and sets him at a further disadvantage.

An effective counter to this move is to tense your muscles and, by transforming your arm into a stiff rod, prevent it from being turned. If you meet such resistance it is unwise to continue or the handshake may turn into some kind of bizarre wrestling match. There are two ways of responding, and the choice depends on the nature of the encounter.

The first is to disengage immediately but to prolong eye-contact for a moment while doing so. This conveys the message that you are well aware of what has been happening and are simply refusing to rise to the bait. Far from appearing as an act of surrender, this can actually

Counter the dominant handshake by invading the other's personal space. Move your right leg forward . . .

. . . and shift to the other's left.

strengthen your position and weaken his by conveying an air of superiority on your part. His strategy in offering a dominant handshake is transformed into a childish and unsuccessful act of attempted one-upmanship.

The alternative on seeing a hand proffered in a dominant position, but combined with a tense body, is to grasp the other's wrist and shake hands by placing your palm against the back of the person's hand.

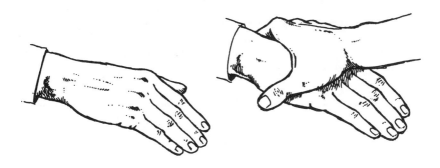

An alternative, but riskier, counter to the offer of a dominant handshake is to grasp the other's wrist.

This counter must be used with care, however, since it causes a degree of embarrassment which may only increase feelings of hostility towards you.

The power gaze

As we have seen, gaze which is only slightly longer than normal conveys a hostility signal, even when combined with a non-threatening expression. Make use of this during a domination power-play to increase the other's unease. Simply hold your gaze for two or three seconds longer than normal every now and again. As I mentioned earlier, eye-contact is normally broken by looking to left, right or down. Never break your gaze downward during a dominance power-play since it implies submission. You may, however, occasionally break contact by glancing upwards. Because this is an unusual, and therefore unexpected, manoeuvre its effect can be disconcerting. Once again your object is to throw the other person off his or her guard in order to achieve some advantage.

Countering the power gaze

Mutual gaze obviously takes two. If you refuse to play, the other person's attempts at prolonged eye-contact will be immediately thwarted. So avoid allowing yourself to become transfixed by their stare. Recognize the tactic for what it is and simply look away the moment you start feeling uncomfortable. However remember never to break your gaze downward, for the reason given above, but always to left or right. If your goals are best served by attempting to dominate the other in return, then utilize the same power gaze yourself.

RULE TWENTY-ONE FOR SILENT SPEECH SUCCESS

Use prolonged gaze to disconcert others. But refuse to return a prolonged eye-contact. Break gaze either left or right but never downward.

Sitting down – the power seat or punishment chair

In some offices where power-plays are taken seriously and used with deliberate intention rather than haphazardly and usually unintentionally, as is often the case, there may be a special 'punishment' chair. This will have been chosen and positioned with great precision in order to undermine the occupant's self-confidence and capacity for dominating the situation to the greatest possible extent.

Sometimes the chair is sufficiently uncomfortable to deter people from outstaying their welcome. It seems to be a variation on the famous Larsen chair, a seat intentionally designed to exert a disagreeable pressure on the back when used for more than a few minutes. Its purpose was to prevent people occupying the seat for too long in places such as fast-food restaurants, where a rapid turn-around is required. On other occasions, however, especially in luxuriously-appointed offices, the chair will prove dangerously deep, low and comfortable. The trouble is that one usually subsides into a posture from which it is not only extremely difficult to get up but also hard to make any further movement at all. To make matters worse the seat is often fairly low, placing you below the other person so that you have to stare upwards at him. As you will recall from chapter nine, loss of height and limited body movement make it far harder to remain dominant. Furthermore, the 'visitor's chair' is often placed at a distance from the desk so that, seated behind this barrier, the occupant of the office can control space more effectively. It may also be positioned in such a way that a bright light, from a nearby table-lamp or the window, shines directly into the face. This is a commonly-used strategy in so-called 'stress' interviews, where the purpose is to disconcert the unfortunate applicant in the belief that this provides insight into how he or she copes under pressure.

Be on your guard for both these ploys. Avoid them by declining to sit in an overly comfortable chair which threatens to undermine your control over the situation. Instead choose a less hazardous seat which can then be positioned in the most favourable position to dominate the proceedings (see below).

Where to sit – in an office

As we saw in chapter nine, there is ample evidence that the choice of seating position can exert a powerful effect on the nature of the encounter. One of the earliest studies, conducted by Robert Sommer, focused on conversations between people seated around a hospital cafeteria table.

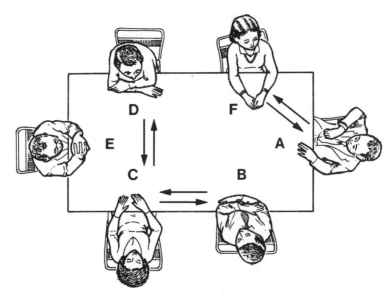

Where to sit in an office.

Sommers found that individuals F and A were twice as likely to talk to one another as C and B, while they in turn were three times more likely to converse than C and D. No conversations were recorded for the remaining positions.

So choose your chair with care. If offered one which places you significantly lower than the other person, or which might prove hard to get out of, politely decline it – perhaps on the grounds of having a bad back. Choose a chair without arm-rests if possible – they offer far greater freedom for gesture – and when available one which allows you to sit as upright as possible. This ensures that your height is fully exploited, so making it easier to command space.

Selecting the seat often enables you to move it to a more favourable position. This could be away from the path of direct sunlight or into a better orientation with regard to the other person. For confrontations select a face-to-face position, but if you intend to try and win co-operation a right-angle orientation is the most effective.

The best seat in a restaurant

Try to reserve a table close to the wall. Those around the centre of the room are extremely distracting, with other diners and waiters constantly passing behind each chair. If possible book a corner location and then take the corner seat. The advantage is that you command an excellent view of everything that is going on. Whether your guest sits facing you or at right angles, *you* will occupy most of his field of vision. Furthermore because a wall, or walls, form a backdrop, your silent speech signals are going to be easy to see and therefore more influential.

Only if there is absolutely no alternative should you agree to sit side-by-side, since silent speech signals are very hard to read in this position. You'll find it harder to read his body language and equally difficult to communicate non-verbally.

RULE TWENTY-TWO FOR SILENT SPEECH SUCCESS

Whenever possible choose where and how you sit. Select a chair without sides, which is easy to get out of and puts you at the same height as the other person. Avoid the trap of the deep but confining 'punishment' chair.

Space invasions while standing

We have already seen the importance of maintaining a personal space around us, and the tensions created when this private domain is invaded. By deliberately trespassing on another's space you can often gain a slight advantage. But remember that this particular silent speech tactic can be a two-edged sword. You are liable to become just as uneasy when invading the other person's space as they are made by your trespass.

Countering standing space invasions

If your space is being deliberately invaded as part of a power-play then you can do one of two things. Provided you can cope with the invasion, and this becomes fairly easy with a little practice, not only permit space invasion but make a modest advance yourself. This restores your advantage since unless the other person is able to cope with the unease such close proximity creates, he will be obliged to withdraw.

If you find it hard to tolerate such an intrusion into your personal bubble, then side-step to increase the distance. Never take a step back to restore the desired space since this is a signal of submission: monarchs frequently demand that their subjects walk backwards from their presence. Move either to left or right, then turn slightly so that the other person is obliged to move in response. This gives you the silent speech advantage.

Space invasions in the office

To dominate another person's office space you need to identify the different zones it contains. The key factor is the location of the desk, since this divides every office into a public and private zone, as illustrated below. The public zone is one in which visitors are received; the private zone is regarded by the occupier as very much his or her private territory.

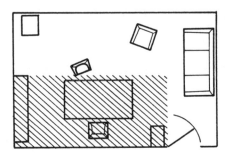

The public and private zones in an office.

Within the public zone, boundaries are marked out by the position of chairs in relation to the desk. Both distance and orientation to the desk are significant. The better-known the visitor, and the higher his or her status, the closer to the desk he will be invited to sit.

Notice especially the direction in which the occupant is sitting. While seated at the desk does he or she look out of the window or face the door? A desk turned so that the owner looks out of, rather than into, the office indicates the highest status. It means that the security system for checking callers is regarded as so reliable there is no chance of an unwanted visitor slipping past.

Although room size and shape obviously influence the positioning of furniture, most offices approximate to one of the six lay-outs shown below, first identified by Duncan Joiner. The private zones within each have been shaded.

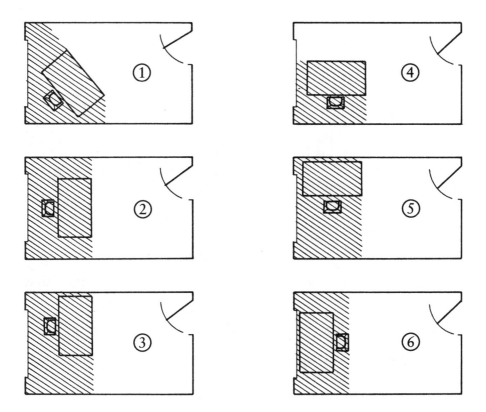

1. The desk forms a diagonal barrier across the corner of one room, facing the door.
2. The desk faces the door and creates a barrier across the width of the room.
3. The desk forms a barrier across the room, but allows for greater space at one side.
4. The room is open on the door end, with the desk forming a barrier within the room.
5. The desk, pushed against one wall, no longer offers a barrier of any kind.
6. The occupant looks out of the window rather than in towards the door.

The first lay-out defines private and public zones most distinctly, while the last makes the least distinction between the two areas. Arrangements 1 to 4 are intended for *formal interactions*, that is encounters which take place across a desk with the owner ensconced in his, or her, private zone and the visitor strictly confined to the public zone.

In a study of 132 offices, Duncan Joiner found most were arranged so that the occupants could see both the door and a window, while maintaining distinct public and private zones in their offices. However since the windows were almost always far larger than the door, the decision to sit where the entrance could be seen was considered significant. 'Being able to see the door from one's working position implies a readiness for interaction,' he comments, 'and the fact that a large proportion of the sample adopted this kind of seating position, suggests that to be able to see who is coming into the room, and to be instantly prepared for them – that is, to have one's *front* correctly displayed – is possibly more important than being able to glance out of the window.'

By *front* Joiner means the self-image the occupant wishes to present to callers in order to stage-manage the impression they get of his or her status, skills and abilities.

The desire to create and establish a clear identity is so basic to human nature that some psychologists rate it as more important than an individual's desire for stimulation and security. The office and its lay-out are, therefore, an extension of the occupant's personality, and points to consider when assessing that person's true status (see chapter fourteen).

To dominate the occupant invade his private domain, either immediately on entering the office or after a few moments and on some plausible pretext. You might, for instance, employ the 'please read this paper' tactic. Here you pass a document over the desk, then, on the pretext of wishing to clarify certain points, move to a position where you can read the paper. This invariably allows you to intrude into the occupant's private zone. Such an intrusion generally makes the other person uneasy, thus increasing their tension and offering you a psychological advantage.

If that seems too stressful, you can obtain a less significant but still worthwhile advantage by invading the private zone with some personal possessions such as your notebook, pencil or cigarette packet which is positioned so that it intrudes into the occupant's domain. Few people are bold enough to push it away, so you can gain a small victory at little risk.

Repelling space invaders

Only tolerate a space invasion if you wish to co-operate from a position of weakness or allow yourself to be dominated. When your private zone is intruded upon you must take prompt and decisive counter-measures. Since you can hardly push the invader back into the office's public zone, some subterfuge must be employed.

Avoid moving away yourself. It's the equivalent of a military retreat. Prevention is better than cure for this silent speech tactic, so ensure chairs are too heavy or difficult to be easily moved, or that entry to your private zone is blocked by small items of furniture such as a low table or waste-paper basket. Even the most dominant of intruders generally draws the line at shifting furnishings in order to invade your territory.

If invasion has occurred, use some strategy to manoeuvre the invader back to the public zone. One tactic is to offer coffee and then, when it arrives, to instruct your secretary to place it on a table in the public zone. A document serves the same purpose. Alternatively you could ask the person to move on the pretext of getting a report from a filing cabinet or drawer. What matters is that the invasion be repelled as promptly and decisively as possible. While the visitor is allowed to occupy your private territory you remain at a significant disadvantage.

Counter invasions from personal possessions by responding in kind. Cover that object with some item of your own, such as papers, a magazine or file. If the person notices or comments, simply remove your article and return their own to them, perhaps with some comment like, 'Sorry, I didn't notice it.' By forcing a retreat you retain the advantage.

Dominating space

Convey dominance by fully occupying the space available. Don't cower in a corner or huddle meekly into your seat – spread yourself. If seated, lean back in your chair and place both hands behind your head. This gesture is frequently used by lawyers and doctors to emphasize their superiority over clients and patients. It signals perfect confidence and high self-esteem. The message is, 'I am in total control of the situation. Leave everything to me.' Studies have shown that managers use it 75 per cent of the time with subordinates but less than 5 per cent of the time with superiors.

Hands behind the head reveals great self-confidence.

A second potent dominance gesture is 'steepling'. Fingers and thumbs are spread and pressed together with palms separated. Like the 'arms behind head' signal it conveys superiority and confidence, but it is more likely to be used by people whose use of gesture is otherwise restricted. The height at which the steeple is made tends to be lower when listening than speaking, although women have been found to use a lower steeple than men under both conditions.

Steepling with the fingers.

When standing, adopt a relaxed stance with your legs slightly apart. This not only gives you better balance but also 'plants' you more firmly on the ground, symbolizing your possession of the territory. Given a free choice, move into the other person's territory.

Countering space spread

The correct response to a 'hands behind head' silent speech signal depends on whether you want to transform the meeting into a co-operative one or to match power-play for power-play in a struggle for dominance. In the first case, break the posture by handing the other person some paper to read, or compel him to adopt a different posture by any other appropriate distraction. If you are content to match the dominance which this gesture implies, simply copy it. While such a response may sound and feel slightly childish, the clear silent speech message is that you consider yourself just as smart, confident and dominant as the other person.

Steepling should simply be observed, together with the body language which immediately proceeded it. If you are a salesman then a series of positive silent speech signals, such as nods of encouragement, smiles and an interested expression just prior to steepling means that the gesture can be taken as a clear 'buy sign' and you should immediately close the deal. If, however, the silent speech signals which led up to steepling were mostly negative – frowns, refusal to give eye-contact, irritated expression and so on – make no attempt to close. Instead backtrack in an attempt to identify the cause of your prospect's lack of enthusiasm for the proposal.

RULE TWENTY-THREE FOR SILENT SPEECH SUCCESS

Your ability to dominate others can often be enhanced by a deliberate invasion of their personal space.

Dominating by controlling time

If you have it in your power to keep the other person waiting then *always* do so. Forget about punctuality being the politeness of kings. Deliberately delaying an appointment is an excellent domination strategy, for two reasons. First it implies that you are extremely busy. This makes your time appear more valuable and your allocation of some of this precious resource to your visitor an act of greater generosity. The result is that he or she feels *more* indebted to you, and therefore more submissive – recall that being a supplicant makes domination more probable – than would have been the case had you seen them on time. The more we wait for something, the greater its perceived importance. In *Waiting For Godot* by Samuel Beckett, for instance, the importance of Godot derives largely from the fact of waiting for him.

This can be explained by a psychological phenomenon, *cognitive dissonance*, first described by an American psychologist named Leon Festinger. In an experiment he paid students either $1 or $20 to lie about a tedious, routine chore which they had just completed. He bribed them to tell students still waiting to perform the task that it was very interesting. Later he asked them how interesting they had found the job. Those paid $20 still regarded it as very dull. But, intriguingly, the ones who received only $1 to lie reported it as being quite interesting. Festinger suggested that the students who received $20 were able to tell themselves they had lied because they were well paid to do so (the experiment was carried out in the fifties). Those receiving just $1, however, couldn't accept that they were prepared to lie for so little. This created a conflict between their self-image and actual behaviour. To resolve this conflict, or dissonance, they came to believe that the task really must have been interesting.

If we are kept waiting we can only explain our behaviour by seeing the reason for our wait as being increasingly important. 'Who likes to eat in an empty restaurant?' asks Robert Levine. 'We tell ourselves we choose the restaurant with the long line because it serves better food. But the wait itself is an important part of the attraction.'

The second reason for keeping people waiting is that, as we have already seen, by controlling their time you diminish their status while enhancing your own. Forcing a person to wait automatically makes you more important than they are. The most obvious characteristic of powerful people is their ability to dictate the way others spend their time. The most obvious characteristic of lesser mortals is that they are obliged to wait. 'Keeping someone waiting probably does more to reduce someone's stature than telling the person verbally how you feel,' comments N.M. Henley in *Body Politics*.

A vivid illustration of this tactic in action was provided by Boston *Globe* reporter Mary McGrory when she described how a congressional subcommittee chose to demonstrate the insignificance to them of the then Secretary of State, Henry Kissinger:

'"I have to wait?" It was more of a wail than a question. Should the Secretary of State . . . destiny's own man, be asked to cool his heels while the African Affairs Subcommittee went off to the Senate floor for a vote? It seemed unconscionable, but it was happening.'

The rule is simple: Control Over Time = Power = Status = Dominance.

You can apply this rule to dominate somebody in two ways. The first is to keep them waiting in some public area. This has the advantage that a constant passage of busy people – secretaries, colleagues, assistants and the like – serves to make them feel both conspicuous and idle. This further reduces their perceived status. Then, after allowing your visitor to cool his heels for a while beyond the office, invite him into your presence but immediately take a phone call, sign some letters or finish reading a document so as to delay the encounter a few moments longer. Apologize mildly: 'I shan't keep you a moment, it's been absolute hell today.' Make certain you have seated your visitor first, however, otherwise your power of domination is diminished in two ways: first, he can move around the room, so filling his time by studying your view, your pictures or your books. This allows him to look occupied and feel less of an intruder; second, he is standing while you are sitting, and he therefore has the advantage of greater height, so putting *you* at the disadvantage. Once seated, however, most people – especially in a strange office – are too anxious to do anything other than stay put. To make doubly certain offer him a coffee but make sure the only place to put the cup is on his lap. This both anchors him firmly in the seat and restricts his own body language, especially the use of gestures.

Many people become mildly anxious when trapped in a seat – psychologists refer to this as the Barber Chair Syndrome – and by triggering their Red Light reflex you automatically undermine feelings of confidence and self-worth. At the same time increased arousal impairs recall, making even familiar facts and figures elusive and liable to be inaccurately remembered. Thus you make it more likely your visitor will blunder, so decreasing his perceived status and increasing a sense of inadequacy and vulnerability.

It's worthwhile ensuring that you take at least one phone call immediately after the visitor has sat down. This further emphasizes how limited your time is and so increases its perceived value.

How long should you keep a person waiting? Fifteen minutes is about the longest most people are willing to wait, in the absence of a very valid reason, without becoming anxious, irritated or distressed. This makes the twenty-minute tactic a useful status cruncher. If your visitor is still patiently waiting five minutes into injury time you will have achieved a significant psychological advantage. While there is some slight risk of the person walking out, cognitive dissonance arising from the feeling, 'I've waited this long so my visit must really be important, therefore I should wait even longer', makes it far more probable he'll remain. In addition he or she must consider the time, trouble, expense and difficulty of rescheduling the meeting and, perhaps, losing a valuable contract or sale.

If your visitor does seem about to depart, train your secretary immediately to offer tea or coffee. What *she* must never do is phone you in a panic and beg you to see your visitor immediately. What *you* must never do is give in and see him, since either response weakens your hand and transfers the advantage back into his hands.

All this may sound extremely unpleasant, devious and manipulative. And, of course, it is. But remember we are talking about zero-sum games where winning is all that matters.

RULE TWENTY-FOUR FOR SILENT SPEECH SUCCESS

To dominate another person first take control of his or her time. The longer you compel them to wait – up to a point – the greater the dominance you demonstrate. Use the Twenty-minute Test. If he or she is still patiently waiting for the meeting you will have dominated them to the point where their perceived status is significantly undermined.

Countering time manipulation

To ensure co-operation on equal terms, or if you wish to dominate the meeting, it is essential to counter the waiting-game ploy. Here's how you do so:

Always take work – or something which gives the appearance of work – to a meeting where you are likely to be kept waiting. Papers are good on their own, but documents and a calculator together make an even more powerful combination. Better still is a portable phone on which you make or receive calls from the waiting area. You can then give the impression of being so absorbed in your work that you fail to respond when the secretary invites you in to the meeting. 'Please tell him I shan't be a moment,' you reply courteously. 'I've got to finish these calculations,' or '. . . take this call'.

Even without a portable handset the telephone can still be a powerful ally. Ask the receptionist or secretary if you can use their phone – you'll rarely be refused – and then make a lengthy call – preferably one which extends into the time when you are invited into the meeting. Arranging to have an 'urgent' call put through to the office, again shortly after the meeting has started, is another excellent strategy. In each case you counter attempts to dominate you by encroaching on the other person's time.

Be ready to counter comments about how busy the person is – his ploy both to justify keeping you waiting and to provide a further demonstration of how valuable his own time is. You can do this

202

non-verbally, by simply smiling and producing your own work, which should be continued for a short while *after* the other person wishes to begin the discussion.

How long should you wait? The only answer is to adhere strictly to the fifteen-minute maximum. Never allow the person to keep you waiting a minute longer. By doing so you reduce your status and place yourself in a submissive posture. As a general rule it's usually far better to cancel the meeting – even one which has been tough to set up – than continue on these unfavourable terms.

Exceptions should, of course, be made when the other person is a friend or colleague with whom you have enjoyed a warm, co-operative relationship in the past; if there is a genuine reason for the delay; or when you simply cannot arrange another meeting. In the latter case be ready to use some of the dominant silent speech strategies described above to assert yourself once the meeting starts. By doing so lost status can often be recovered.

Under most circumstances, however, you should continue to wait and work up to the fifteen minutes then calmly pack away your things and announce that you have another meeting. A well-trained secretary will offer you tea, coffee or some other inducements to remain. All such blandishments must be politely but firmly refused. Say, 'I'll get my secretary to phone for another appointment, perhaps when I get back from Europe.' Suggesting you will not be able to attend a further meeting for some time will panic all but the best-trained secretaries into calling their employers and all but the most steel-nerved employers into seeing you immediately. Either way you have gained an important psychological advantage.

RULE TWENTY-FIVE FOR SILENT SPEECH SUCCESS

Counter attempts to waste your time. Keep busy and turn the tables by making the other person wait for you. Stick to the fifteen-minute rule for being kept waiting. At the end of this period, unless there is an obviously valid and genuine reason for the delay, abort the meeting.

The co-operative meeting

This is a far more agreeable affair than the ploy and counter-ploy found in dominant encounters. One should generally seek to turn meetings or negotiations into co-operative exchanges as soon as possible. Sometimes this can be most easily achieved by allowing the other person to score a few trivial points unchallenged. By 'giving to get' in this way, you allow an individual whose basic lack of confidence and self-esteem creates a need to bluster and bully to work things out of his system – it is mostly males who feel the need to behave in this way. Then, after the preliminary skirmishes, you will often find he is prepared to co-operate. Allowing him minor victories should cause you no regret, since the main object is to win the war.

Signal your desire to co-operate by postural echoing, as described in chapter eleven. Subtly reflect back some of the other person's gestures, as well as stance and posture. Maintain eye-contact, especially when listening, and keep your expression relaxed but friendly. When it is possible to arrange the seating always be sure to sit at right angles to the person with whom you wish to co-operate.

While making proposals, lean forward and offer steady eye-contact. As the other person starts speaking continue leaning forward if you agree with what he or she is saying, but lean away while objections are being raised. This will distance you from the criticisms.

The submissive meeting

You may wish to submit in order to defuse some of the anger being expressed by a superior after you have made a bad blunder. Lowered gaze and a contrite expression can often help ensure an angry individual calms down more quickly. It is usually best to let a person's rage burn itself out naturally, rather than protest or interrupt while he or she is in full flow.

You may also wish to submit when faced with a dominant individual, but this time as a tactic for gaining the upper hand at a later date. Here the submission should be made, whenever possible, from a position of strength. To do this start by responding with dominance signals of your own. Then suddenly, and when the other person is not expecting it, concede a point either verbally or non-verbally. By giving way on a relatively unimportant point after a sustained period of dominance you make subsequent co-operation more likely.

To signal submission, break eye-contact by glancing downward rather than to left or right. Restrict your silent speech signals and avoid any expansive gestures. Be sure you have a very good reason before allowing yourself to get involved in a submissive meeting. They not only damage your actual status within an organization, changing for the worse the way others view you, but also reduce your perceived status; how you see yourself. Confidence, assurance and self-esteem are all undermined. What's more being submissive can quickly become a habit that's extremely hard to break.

CHAPTER FOURTEEN

Reading Others Right

He that has eyes to see and ears to hear may convince
himself that no mortal can keep a secret. If his lips are silent,
he chatters with his fingertips; betrayal oozes out of him at
every pore.

Sigmund Freud

Walking down a quiet city street you encounter a group of tough-looking youths. How will you react? The most common response is to assume a neutral expression and avoid eye-contact. You are silently saying, 'Please leave me alone. I want no part of this.' Under most circumstances your signals will be seen and accurately interpreted. But if they are prone to violence these youths are more likely to read your expression as one of hostility or disgust than as a desire not to get involved. The result is you may unwittingly provoke the very attack your silent speech was intended to avoid.

This conclusion stems from a study by Drs Sean Austin, from Hancock County Medical Clinic in Findlay, Ohio, and William McCown, of the Loyola University in Chicago. They asked adolescents aged thirteen to sixteen to identify the expressions on illustrations depicting happy, disgusted, surprised, sad, fearful and neutral faces.

While all the youths came from similar social and economic backgrounds, some had convictions for violent assaults. Austin and McCown found that while non-violent youngsters had no difficulty in accurately matching feelings to faces, violent teenagers were extremely poor at the task. They frequently confused neutral or even friendly faces with expressions of aggression or contempt. The researchers blame this lack of skill on the youngsters' inability to use gaze correctly. They never looked long or hard enough at the faces to form an accurate impression. Why did they find it so hard to use gaze in

205

social situations? Probably because their deprived home backgrounds meant they had never learned to use their eyes to read or communicate positive feelings. Furthermore angry or disgusted expressions were more familiar to them than loving ones. As a result of their discovery, Austin and McCown were able to create a programme designed to improve body talk skills. Delinquents watched silent films and had to try and identify the emotions portrayed. Austin and McCown report that, after training, the youths became significantly less violent.

It is not only aggressive teenagers who are bad at reading others right. Based on my own researches, I consider only one person in ten has any great fluency in this vitally important language. For most people even a brief encounter can be filled with mistaken judgements and misinterpreted messages.

Who uses silent speech most successfully?

The ability to send and read non-verbal signals successfully is influenced by many different variables, including age, gender, status and occupation. Let's review each in turn to see the part it plays.

Your age
When you were a toddler, silent speech was your main method of communication. Expression, gesture, posture and proximities all played their part in enabling you to play with other infants and get what you wanted from grown-ups. You also paid close attention to adult silent speech, accurately detecting looks of love, irritation or frustration. Not every infant is equally proficient at body language, however. During my studies of nursery non-verbal communication I found that children who learn to speak at an early age are more interested in chatting vocally to adults than silently to their friends. As a result their body language fluency declines sharply, a premature loss of skill which can impair their sensitivity to these signals when adults. After the age of about three, the spoken word increasingly becomes the dominant method of communication and silent speech gradually becomes less apparent to us.

According to Dr Carol Malatesta of Long Island University, we retain greatest proficiency when decoding 'the emotional expressions of peers or adjacent age groups'. This, she speculates, may be because we are most experienced at, or interested in, the facial expressions of people our own age. But we tend to be least successful when observing people much older or younger than ourself. The middle aged often have great difficulty reading the body language of adolescents, while teenagers find it difficult to interpret their seniors' silent speech accurately – a finding which may help explain the communications gap between generations. One possible explanation for this break-down lies in status differences between young and old, a point we'll consider in a moment.

Older faces are harder to read correctly than young ones because wrinkles and poor muscle tone make their expressions less obvious and so more difficult to observe.

Your sex

Women are more sensitive to silent speech than men, possibly because they are also far more socially skilled at all ages. When pairs of eleven-year-old girls and boys were filmed solving problems, it was found that the boys talked mainly about finding solutions while the girls were interested in discussing their feelings about the task. Such differences could well be due to play experience in infancy. Girls tend to be given dolls to whom they talk, while boys get train-sets and building blocks which they manipulate.

Although it is not known why, independent and assertive females do better at reading the silent speech of both women and men. More traditionally feminine women, by contrast, read male body language more effectively.

Your status

The greater the difference in status the less successfully mutual body language is read. The junior clerk finds it hard to interpret the silent speech of the managing director, while he in turn misreads the non-verbal signals from his clerk. This is simply because, as we have seen, high-status people pay less attention to those regarded as their inferiors: they are just not of any great interest to them. Low-status people gaze very little at their superiors, out of concern that this will be interpreted as impudence or aggression. The failure of young and old to read each other right may be explained by this status difference. Many adults regard their juniors as having lower status, while young people frequently assume that age automatically confers superior status.

When, in 1973, David Rosenhan and his colleagues feigned schizophrenia to have themselves admitted to mental hospitals in order to study treatment from the patients' viewpoint, they discovered a horrifying lack of communication – both verbal and non-verbal – between staff and patients. Eye-contact, for instance, was given by only 23 per cent of doctors and 10 per cent of nurses. The patients' low status was emphasized by a lack of privacy. Staff could come into their rooms at any time without permission, and bathrooms lacked doors. 'Staff members sometimes acted as though the patients were invisible, non-persons whom they did not have to take into account,' comments University of North Carolina psychiatrist Barclay Martin.

'One nurse unbuttoned her uniform to adjust her brassiere in full sight of an entire ward of men. She was not being seductive; patients were simply not the same as real people.'

Perhaps as a result of this non-verbal indifference, none of the pseudo-patients was ever detected by medical staff, although the genuine patients spotted them almost immediately. Some asked if they were journalists preparing a story on mental hospitals!

Your occupation
Certain jobs offer special training to heighten employees' sensitivity to silent speech. Police officers, for instance, are taught how to recognize hostility and deceit and psychotherapists to identify anxiety or depression, while actors or actresses learn how to portray all types of emotions convincingly.

How sensitive are you to silent speech?

Score each statement on a scale of 0–4, where 0 = Neither agree nor disagree, 1 = Agree slightly, 2 = Agree to some extent, 3 = Agree strongly and 4 = Agree very strongly.

1. I make a real effort to be liked when introduced to somebody new.
2. It makes me sad to see somebody alone at a party.
3. I like talking things over with a friend.
4. I get angry when I see somebody being badly treated.
5. I believe in showing my feelings openly.
6. I become very involved when watching a film.
7. I enjoy meeting new people.
8. I cannot feel happy in the company of miserable people.
9. I like making friends.
10. If somebody is upset I usually know right away.
11. I would sooner work with others than on my own.
12. The words of a love song often move me deeply.
13. I would sooner go to a party than a film.
14. I do not mind going on holiday alone.
15. I get upset at seeing people cry.

Score
0–25: You seem to be a rather self-sufficient person who dislikes emotional scenes and prefers to keep your feelings under tight control.

This will make it harder for you to read other people's silent speech signals accurately. During encounters you are probably more concerned about the sort of impression *you* are making than the effect another person is having on you.

26–45: You are moderately high on affiliative tendency – that is the desire and ability to get along with others – and show a fair degree of empathy. However it seems likely that you make little effort, at present, to exploit your latent skills at reading silent speech. You rely on interpreting obvious expressions of mood while giving greater attention to verbal than non-verbal messages.

46–60: You either are, or could easily become, highly skilled at interpreting body language. Your score shows a great interest in and empathy towards others, essential qualifications for reading silent speech successfully.

No matter what your score, however, you certainly possess the latent ability to become proficient in using and understanding silent speech provided you take the time and trouble to do so.

Certain signals are easier to read than others

Most people can identify basic emotions accurately, even when seeing them very briefly. Harvard psychologist Robert Rosenthal found people could correctly interpret facial expression in one twenty-fourth of a second.

We are also skilled at detecting the obvious signs of anxiety. In a study by Barbara Jeffrey, a student of mine at the University of Sussex, subjects were shown silent videos of inexperienced public speakers making a presentation. When the anxiety levels of speakers, as rated by themselves and by the audience, were compared, a very high degree of agreement was found. When a speaker was nervous both he and those watching him were painfully aware of the fact. Anxious speakers were also considered inferior to relaxed ones, both by themselves and by their audience.

But when people – especially those experienced in deceit – set out deliberately to fool us, the chances are high that we will be taken in. Such expertise is found not only among professional gamblers and confidence tricksters, but across a wide range of perfectly respectable occupations including medicine, the legal profession, politics, public relations and salesmanship. In fact among any workers for whom honesty may not always be the best policy. Yet it is during such encounters, of course, that we are most interested in finding out whether we are being told the truth.

Is a politician's promise reliable? Is a salesman being truthful about his products? When your doctor assures you there's 'nothing to worry about' is she concealing her true diagnosis? Should a business executive's assurances be taken at face value?

You might cynically retort that the obvious response is 'No' in every instance. But can one be more certain about truth or falsehood? The answer is that silent speech often provides the insight we seek. So why are most people so easily fooled? The most common explanation is that we rely too much on people's expressions. Our culture is overly 'face focused'. We even talk of taking people at 'face value'. Unfortunately . . .

Faces are hard to read

Many people see the face as a barometer of a person's innermost feelings. We say someone has an 'open face' or an 'honest look', accuse them of 'lying through their teeth' or talking with their 'tongue in their cheek'.

In the ancient Greek theatre actors wore a mask called a *persona*, from which the modern word personality is derived. Thus personality and the human face have long been linked. Studies have shown that when viewing young, attractive faces people tend to make extremely positive judgements about those portrayed. They are regarded as more likely to be rich than poor, with a high status, happy marriages, warm personalities, good social- and excellent sex-lives. Ugly people, however, are considered to be unsuccessful, have lower status, poor relationships, cold personalities and little social or sexual attraction. It is a distorted view they may even come to share themselves: American sociologist Robert Agnew, of Emory University, believes some delinquents act in an ugly way because they regard themselves as having disagreeable faces. He reports that boys rated 'fair' or 'poor' on appearance were more likely to behave antisocially than those rated as 'excellent' for looks.

A team of psychologists and political scientists from Dartmouth College suggested that an important part of Ronald Reagan's 1984 presidential campaign success lay in his superior skill in using facial expressions. When video tapes of his 'happy-reassuring' look (eyebrows raised, head tilted upward, teeth displayed) were shown to non-partisan audiences they created very positive and enduring feelings towards him. The other candidates were much less successful in communicating strength, happiness and reassurance via their faces.

The faking face

The difficulties we face when reading faces accurately were intrigu-

210

ingly demonstrated by psychologist Peter Thompson of the University of York. Glance at the picture below. You should have no difficulty recognizing politician Margaret Thatcher. It appears to be a straightforward portrait, until you turn over the page: then the effect is horrific.

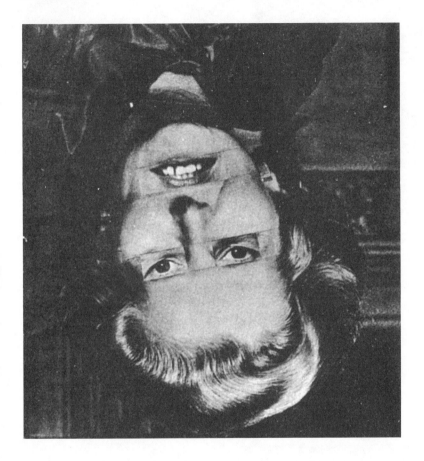

The seemingly normal portrait has, in fact, been doctored by cutting the eyes and mouth from the original and sticking them back again upside down. When seen inverted the horrible expression passes unnoticed. Peter Thompson calls this the 'Margaret Thatcher Illusion', but the same effect can be obtained with any smiling face. What's going on? Why should an agreeable expression when inverted become so disagreeable the right way around?

 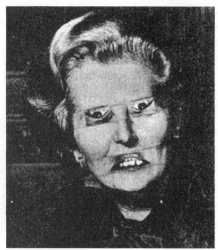

Psychologist Irvin Rock of Rutgers University believes the illusion demonstrates a key fact about how we make sense of complicated shapes. The crucial thing is what we assume to be the top. The geometric figure below helps illustrate this point.

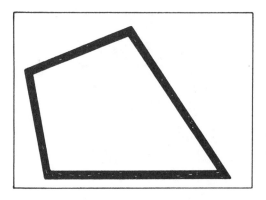

At first sight it appears to have an irregular shape. But if I tell you the 'top' is located in the upper right-hand corner, the figure instantly assumes the regular outline of a child's kite.

In the face too we make assumptions about what we *believe* we are looking at. 'It is not the whole face, per se, that we recognize, but only the form of each part – that the mouth is smiling for example,' comment psychologists Drs Theodore Parks and Richard Coss of the University of California. You can verify this by covering everything except the mouth in the photograph. But the whole face is important

212

because it tells us where the *top* is located, which is the upper and which the lower lip for example. Denied these clues by the faked-up image we misinterpret it.

As Parks and Ross point out, artists have long had problems dealing with upside-down features. Michelangelo, for example, could only depict the unfortunate St Peter, who was crucified upside down, by painting his face in such a way that the expression couldn't be clearly seen.

The importance of this illusion is that it emphasizes what a significant role expectations have on perception. We see not so much what is there as what we believe *ought* to be there. Here's an illustration which makes this difficulty apparent. Study the design below and note down what you see.

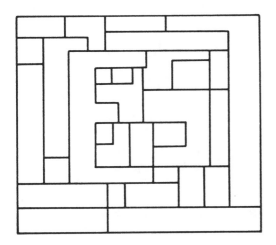

When I present this image at workshops, the answers given range from 'a maze' or 'a group of lines' to 'a bunch of rectangles'. So allow me to alter your expectations, and at the same time your perception, by suggesting that you look for letters of the alphabet.

Now what do you see?

The chances are that it's a letter E. Once you've noticed it you'll see it immediately each time you return to the drawing. Your perception has been shifted by changed expectation.

RULE TWENTY-SIX FOR SILENT SPEECH SUCCESS

Approach each encounter with an open mind. Avoid too many preconceptions about what you are going to see.

Reading others right

Let's now look at the secrets to be discovered from silent speech in all its many and varied guises. We'll start by continuing the previous chapter's theme of power-plays and considering ways of assessing status.

Reading status right

To manage an encounter you must create the impression of having status which is equal, or superior, to the other person's. This, of course, demands accurate knowledge of what his or her true importance within the relevant organization is. Appearances, as we have seen, can be deceptive. After all if your true status is lower than that of your companion you should be working to create an impression of equality. He or she could, of course, be doing exactly the same thing!

When visiting somebody's place of work you can gain a more accurate insight into their status by scoring an individual on the following ten factors. Use a scale of 1–5, where 1 = 'little or none' and 5 'the maximum possible'.

1. Privacy in the workplace
The more privacy a person enjoys at work the higher their status.

2. Location
High corner offices with picture windows and spectacular views get the highest score. Small, windowless offices or partitioned areas within a general office the lowest.

3. Wasted space
Recall that large areas without anything in them of practical value indicate high status.

4. Proximity to power

The closer their office to the seat of power the higher the status. A door leading directly to the chairman's suite indicates the highest status short of total mastery.

5. Difficulty fixing the appointment

As we saw in the previous chapter, the harder it is to arrange a meeting the greater the perceived differences in your relative status. The more reclusive an individual the higher their ranking in that organization. Related to this is the other time factor mentioned in the previous chapter: how long you are kept waiting once an appointment is made. The longer the delay the greater the difference in your relative status.

6. Personal possessions

The more personal possessions the greater their control over that space. However be cautious of a person who keeps framed qualifications on the walls. This usually reveals a low-status person trying to make an impression. The same applies to photographs depicting the occupant with celebrities. You will be dealing with a person of low self-esteem but considerable self-importance.

7. Window size and view

The larger the window and the better the view the higher the status.

8. Desk size and decor

The size of the desk, and the other furnishings, their lavishness and cost may provide additional clues. But be careful here, for there has been a recent trend away from big desks and elaborate decor to a more spartan, high-tech image. The offices of today's top ranking CEOs often contain slimline power symbols. Desks are frequently replaced by tables, which may be circular, occasionally oval, sometimes oblong but hardly ever square. On them you might find a couple of telephones, a computer terminal and some small but costly work of art. 'The crucial image,' says psychologist Adrian Furnham, 'is one of space, lack of clutter, indeed almost emptiness.'

9. Layout

The significance of office lay-out has already been described in the previous chapter. As I explained there, the key point to observe is the positioning of the desk and chairs. Here, again, are the six main office lay-outs identified by Duncan Joiner together with the level of status revealed.

1. The desk forms a diagonal barrier across the corner of one room, facing the door. *Status rating*: Low to moderate.
2. The desk faces the door and creates a barrier across the width of the room. *Status rating*: Low to moderate.
3. The desk still creates a barrier across the room, but there is greater space down one side. *Status rating*: Low to moderate.
4. The room is open on the door end, with the desk forming a barrier within the room. *Status rating*: Low to moderate.
5. The desk, pushed against one wall, no longer offers any sort of barrier. *Status rating:* Moderate to high.
6. The occupant looks out of the window rather than towards the door. *Status rating*: Very high.

Take account of occupations
The job a person does also influences the positioning of his or her desk. Academics are the most likely group to have desks facing away from the door, and government officials the least likely. Out of fifty-five offices where the owner was unable to observe the door, Duncan Joiner found that thirty-two occurred in universities, seventeen in commercial organizations and only six in government departments. This can be explained by the fact that academics, who spend a lot of time in their rooms talking to students, organize the furnishings in such a way as to reduce the distance between people and diminish the leadership role implied by a higher status. They want to avoid making the students feel inhibited during tutorials and discussions. However the seniority of the faculty member also has an effect on office lay-out: in one study it was found that while twenty-four out of thirty-three senior faculty members kept a desk between themselves and their students, only thirteen out of fourteen junior faculty did so. 'Unbarricaded' professors were rated by students as being less likely to show 'undue favouritism' and more prepared to allow students to voice different opinions. 'Conversely,' notes Joiner, 'commercial and government occupants had arranged their rooms so that during discussions their dominant role was sustained by maintaining social distance across their desk tops.'

Only very high-status individuals feel sufficiently self-assured not to create artificial barriers between themselves and their visitors. Two assumptions can be drawn from this. The first is that they only expect to meet individuals who, being of equal status, would consider such a barrier insulting; the second is that, on those few occasions when lower-status individuals do enter their presence, other carefully stage-managed aspects of the encounter will prove effective in keeping them at an appropriate distance.

Award the highest points for occupants who prefer to face the window rather than the door and the lowest for those whose desks directly face the entrance.

There is one additional way in which you may gain an insight into a person's status, and that is a clue which often presents itself long before you ever meet: it is the way they sign their names.

10. Signature size and status

An intriguing way of conveying status by commanding space can be found in people's signature style. Research by Dr R. Zeeigenhaft has shown that the more important a writer feels him- or herself to be the larger – and often the less legible – his or her signature becomes.

Celebrity signatures are on average nearly 50 per cent larger than those of non-celebrities, a difference clearly shown in the two examples below: the first was made by Rudolph Nureyev when he was at the New York Ballet academy, the second belongs to a tea lady from the same school.

When the mighty fall from power, however, their signature often shrinks in proportion to loss of status. The triumph of victory and the humiliation of defeat are clearly seen in two of Napoleon's signatures illustrated below:

The first is taken from a document signed when the general was at the height of his power; the second was made soon after his surrender at Waterloo. The illegibility of many high-status signatures seems to reflect a feeling on the part of the writer that he or she is so important that those reading the signature should *know* who they are without having to be told. Low-status individuals, or those lacking confidence and possessing poor self-esteem, by comparison, usually sign their names with great care.

Rating status
Total the score and refer to the table below.

Score	Status
45–50	Very high
35–44	High
30–34	Moderate
15–29	Low
10–15	Very low

Watch out for exceptions

Rating status in the way I have described offers a useful guide to the kind of person you will be dealing with, and the sort of encounter likely to occur. However be on your guard for exceptions to these guidelines. They are *most* likely to apply in normal commercial organizations, large companies which have a distinct hierarchy, a fondness for status symbols and the financial resources to reward attainment in the ways described above. The smaller the organization, the less perks there are for anybody to enjoy, although even here *relative* differences between the highest and the lowest can be found. I know of one three-person firm operating from two small rooms above a grocery store where the boss still manages to enjoy slightly more space, privacy and prestige than his two secretaries.

You will also find some important differences in government departments, where furnishings and lay-out are determined by bureaucratic rules rather than personal preferences. Here it may be necessary to look for more subtle indications of status. Is there a hat-rack? What pictures decorate the walls – originals or mass-produced prints? Are there any personal possessions on the desk? Is the floor covered with carpet or lino? If carpeted, does it cover the whole area or stop short a few inches from the skirting-board? That short, uncarpeted space can signify a considerable reduction in status.

The rating system is most likely to fail in academia, where status depends on reputation and publication. A *Newsweek* reporter sent to interview Stephen Hawking, Lucasian Professor of Mathematics at Cambridge University and, in the view of many, the most brilliant theoretical physicist since Einstein, was surprised by the surroundings in which the great man worked: 'Hawking seems not to rate many perks,' he noted. 'His office is a narrow, cluttered cubicle in . . . a building as charmless as its name.' He missed the point that if the occupant's name and title don't instantly confer status, at least to other academics, he or she probably has very little. Indeed there is often a reverse effect in universities, with dons trying to demonstrate their lack of material interest by occupying the drabbest and most cluttered surroundings available.

Assessing your own status

Now compare your own status *so far as the other party's organization is concerned.* This is essential since what matters is not the standing you have in your own particular sphere but how you rate in the other's world. A professor who is highly respected by colleagues and shown great deference by students might have little status in her bank manager's office if she happens to be a poor credit risk, or in her publisher's office if the wretched woman's last book sank without trace!

Bear in mind, however, that your actual status is often far less important than your *perceived* status; in other words the status which others consider you to possess. This is frequently as much a reflection on effective Impression Management as anything else.

In the absence of other information your status will be measured by the way you look (see chapter fifteen) and how successfully you sell yourself non-verbally.

Status and encounter management

If your status actually is, or appears to be, equal to your companion's you have the choice of dominance, co-operation or submission during the encounter. Where each of these might be most appropriate was discussed in the previous chapter.

If your status, actual or perceived, is higher than the other person's, dominance or co-operation will be the most effective strategies. There is, however, one possible exception to this rule. That is when dealing with low-status people who nevertheless have it in their power to inconvenience you. This includes receptionists, security guards and petty officials of all kinds. Here some small token of submission, after your superior status has been firmly established, can make life easier by pandering to their need to feel important.

Where your status is significantly lower than that of the person with whom you are dealing, co-operation is probably the best to hope for.

Reading personality right

Silent speech signals can be used to determine whether the person you are with is outgoing and extrovert or intense and introverted. This is not always apparent from their behaviour, since even introverts let themselves go from time to time while extroverts will occasionally withdraw into their shells. Watch for the following signs:

Greater use of silent speech
Extroverts usually use more extravagant gestures and seek to occupy greater space than introverts. They prefer closer proximity during encounters.

Use of gaze
Extroverts use more direct eye-contact, looking at people longer and with greater frequency than introverts.

Direction of gaze break
An important signal is the direction in which eye-contact is broken. Gaze can be ended by a person glancing away either to left or right. Research suggests that the direction preferred is not haphazard but a reflection of the way their brains work and, consequently, an indication of personality. Extroverts tend to break gaze by looking away to the left, while introverts break right.

Reading memory right

Eye movements can also help you discover what sort of memories people are accessing when answering questions. There are several types of memory: one type is for the recalling of sights and sounds which have actually been experienced – for instance remembering a room at home or the sound of your child's voice, but there are also manufactured memories, that is images and noise which you construct, mentally, by combining ideas from fact and fantasy. You can test this for yourself by watching a friend's eye movements carefully while asking him to think hard about the following:

Please imagine the sight of . . .

A man cycling down the road
You are likely to see his eyes move upward and to the left while picturing this scene. This is because he is recalling some actual image from the visual storehouse. When visual memories are being accessed, brain activity causes the eyes to move in this direction on most occasions.

A pink elephant riding a bicycle along a tight-rope
The eye movements generated by this request are more likely to be upward and to the right. This is because the bizarre image is being created by fantasy instead of retrieved from memory.

Please imagine the sound of . . .

A brass band playing
Eye movements now are most likely to be sideways and to the left as an actual sound memory is retrieved.

A brass band playing underwater
The probable eye movement this time is sideways and to the right, as the sound has to be *constructed* rather than remembered.

These differences in eye movements can provide important clues when deciding whether or not you are being told the truth. If you ask somebody to describe what they were doing last weekend, for instance, you would expect a upward movement to the left as memories are retrieved. A movement upward but to the right suggests that imagination rather than recall is being brought to bear on the task. This would not necessarily reveal a deliberate lie, of course; it could simply be that the person has forgotten some of what he had done and is filling in the gaps with unconscious fantasy.

Reading anxiety right

He looks cool and collected, the master of this situation. His features are relaxed, his gaze steady, hands folded placidly in his lap. But is he really as calm as he appears?

In many situations knowing how tense or laid-back a person really is could prove of considerable benefit. As we have seen, blatant anxiety is easy to detect. But when a person has learned to control his feelings, the features may betray not a trace of discomfort or self-doubt. What, then, should you look out for?

The clues are to be found in non-verbal *leakages*. Tense people betray themselves by a variety of slight, but unmistakable, silent speech signals. These 'leaks' can easily be seen once you know what to watch for. Here are the most important signs . . .

Fidgeting feet
When standing, anxious people often make small, shuffling movements. They scuff their toes on the ground, rub one foot against the other, tap the ground and fidget in other ways as well. If sitting cross-legged, the upper foot may jiggle up and down.

Fiddling fingers

An anxious person is more likely to play with his pen, pencil, cigarette or lighter; fiddle with his hair, pick specks of invisible fluff from a lapel or tug at an ear. Hand-rubbing, as though washing with invisible soap, grooming checks – smoothing and patting at invisible wrinkles in skirt, blouse or jacket – nail-biting and finger-sucking are all *displacement* activities, ways of displacing inner tensions through subconsciously inspired activity. Nervous airline passengers may be seen constantly checking their tickets, boarding cards or passports, patting pockets to make sure their wallets are still there or going through the content of handbags again and again. Desmond Morris reports that while only 8 per cent of railway passengers were observed performing such displacement activities, 80 per cent of those at an airline check-in desk did so.

Smoking is an important displacement activity. Watch for the 'ashless tap', when a cigarette is tapped frequently on the ashtray despite there being no ash to remove.

Anxious smiles

As we saw in chapter eight, smiles have a complex language all their own. In addition to signalling warmth and friendship they can also be used to deceive (see below) or cover anxiety. Identify the anxious smile by its tentative, fleeting nature. It is a low intensity, simple smile (see page 88), which does not involve the rest of the face. Teeth remain covered.

RULE TWENTY-EIGHT FOR SILENT SPEECH SUCCESS

Detect anxiety by looking at feet and hands rather than faces. Watch for 'leakage' as inner tensions are relieved by small, subconsciously controlled movements.

Reading buying-signs right

We are all in the business of selling. Men try to peddle their physical charms to women, job hunters their skills to interviewers, crooks their honesty to police officers and therapists their ability to clients. Which makes reading buying-signs right a matter of importance to everybody.

Buying-signs are the silent speech signals which tell you that somebody has swallowed your sales pitch and is willing to close the deal; by making a date, offering you a job, signing up for therapy or paying the price you asked. Unfortunately buying-signs can easily be missed, which means you may carry on pitching past the psychological moment to close the deal – and lose it as a result.

I remember attending one workshop on closing runs by an ebullient Chicago-based trainer. 'What do you do', he demanded of his audience of largely professional salespeople, 'when the client is on the point of closing.' There was a long silence. 'Right!' he exclaimed. 'That's right. That's just what you do. You shut up!' The skill, of course, lies in knowing exactly *when* to shut up. Many salespeople consider that deciding when to 'close' is their greatest challenge, and fortunes have been made training them in this supposedly Byzantine art. Here are the silent speech signals which will help you judge this critical moment:

Relaxation
As they reach a buy decision, people become suddenly more relaxed. Up to that moment there may have been considerable tension caused by mental conflict. Once they've made up their minds all tension vanishes.

Be on the look-out for a sudden *absence* of the anxiety signals described above. An agitated foot grows still, a fidgeting hand becomes motionless.

Chin touch
According to leading sales-trainer Georges Patounas, a potential buyer touching his chin represents a very powerful buy-sign, and the salesperson should immediately try a trial close.

Closer proximity
The person on the point of closing a deal moves closer to you when standing or leans forward if seated.

Greater eye-contact
While you are talking the other person is likely to avoid giving too much eye-contact. It's their way of not seeming too involved in what you have to say. Once a buying decision has been made gaze becomes longer and more frequent.

The opposites of these signals represent a resistance to your proposals. Greater bodily tension, more displacement activities, increasing the distance by moving or leaning away and a refusal to look you in the eye all indicate a lack of interest in the proposals. Your most sensible response is to change tactics or abandon the selling attempt – at least for the moment. As the oilman wisely remarked, 'If there's no hope of striking oil – stop boring.'

Reading friendship right

'I just want to be your friend', the other person pleads. Does he, or are there darker motives behind these overtures of friendship? Only time will tell for certain, but meanwhile silent speech can offer helpful insights. Watch for . . .

False smiles
When a photographer orders his subject to 'say cheese' it produces the sort of false smile you sometimes find during feigned assurances of friendship. When looking at a high intensity upper smile (see page 91) watch for the presence of two small folds of flesh rising beneath each eye. These are produced by cheek muscles which wrinkle into little pouches whenever we are genuinely amused or happy. They can clearly be seen in the photograph below.

The presence of small folds of flesh beneath each eye confirms that a smile is genuine.

Since these muscles are not under our voluntary control it's impossible to fake the folds; there has to be genuine feeling behind the smile. So if your presumed friend's welcoming smile lacks cheek swellings you can be reasonably certain that his or her greeting lacks sincerity.

Hostility disguised by a friendly smile can often be detected by, among other signs, an aggressive lower smile. In this the bottom teeth are uncovered while the top row remain largely concealed. The eyes are usually wide open, the gaze intense and the eyebrows remain level.

Unconscious mirroring
I have already described how you can deliberately copy another person's stance and stand in order to develop empathy. As we saw, friends often spontaneously and unconsciously mirror one another's silent speech signals. Watch for mimicking of your movements. While these are fairly easy to fake, when they occur together with other non-verbal expressions of friendship they can be trusted to reveal sincere feelings.

Greater touch
While unwritten cultural and social rules determine how much touch is permissable between friends, one usually finds a greater desire for physical contact of some sort between people – even same sex companions – who feel genuine warmth towards one another. Such contact may involve no more than a slightly prolonged handshake, perhaps combined with a touch to the upper arm, or occasional touches on the hand, arm or shoulder.

Head tilt
A slight sideways tilt to the head when talking reveals a desire for greater closeness. This unconscious signal is a strong indication of liking and empathy.

RULE THIRTY FOR SILENT SPEECH SUCCESS

To check a friendship is sincere look for cheek folds revealing a genuinely warm smile, increased touching, unconscious copying of your stance and gestures and a tilted head during conversations.

Reading deception right

Many people believe a liar is easy to spot – but they are wrong. This holds true even for professionals such as police officers. Drs Bella DePaulo of the University of Virginia and Roger Pfeifer from the Federal Law Enforcement Training Center in Glynco, Georgia, asked students and policemen to listen to tape recordings of people telling some lies and making some true statements. While the policemen were confident of their ability to distinguish truth from lies they proved to be no more accurate than the students.

People develop pet theories about how to tell when someone is lying. Often this means judging by appearance. When psychologists Drs George Rotter of Montcalir State College in New Jersey and Naomi Rotter of the New Jersey Institute of Technology asked people to sort photographs of men and women into honest, dishonest and ambiguous categories, they found considerable agreement over what constituted an 'honest' or 'dishonest' face. Gaze was only important in men, with those looking directly into the camera being seen as more honest. Women who looked straight at the lens were rated as *dishonest*. But the single most important factor was whether or not the individual was smiling. Both males and females who smiled were rated as honest, while a sour expression produced a verdict of dishonesty.

What happens when the liar can be seen in action instead? Surely then any deception is easily spotted. Unfortunately this is not the case. A practised deceiver will nearly always fool those unversed in silent speech. But if you do know just what to look for, lies are often fairly easy to detect. Here's what to watch out for:

Fewer gestures
Because of subconscious fears that hand movements will somehow reveal their deception, liars tend to restrict their use of gesture. Hands may be kept out of sight behind the back or thrust into pockets. Even here, however, the tension caused by lying may betray itself through the displacement activity of jiggling coins or fiddling with keys.

The ear-rub.

Increased face-touching
Self-touching increases significantly, with the chin, neck and ear being favoured target areas. The *ear-rub* is a subconscious attempt by the speaker to block out his deception. It reflects a conflict between his self-image as an honest, dependable person and the lies being told.

The *neck-scratch* is a sign that the words spoken run contrary to the speaker's real feelings. 'I entirely agree with you . . .' the person says. But his silent speech signals contradict this assurance. They disclose doubt, uncertainty or downright deception. The finger usually scratches the neck exactly five times. Seldom more and rarely less.

The neck-scratch.

The collar-pull.

The *collar-pull* may be caused by increased physical tension stimulating nerves in the neck and producing a tingling sensation. By tugging at the collar, the irritation gets massaged – and the deception is unwittingly exposed.

The *nose-touch* is an especially revealing gesture since it is a modified mouth cover. The subconscious desire is to guard the mouth, perhaps out of fear that the deception will be spotted. But at the last moment the movement changes to a light nose brush. This is a different action to that made when the nose itches, when a firm and obvious rubbing movement is made.

The *eye-touch* reflects a desire to cover the eyes and avoid looking at the person being deceived.

Men touch or rub the eye energetically and then usually glance away and stare at the floor. Women make a more tentative movement, gently rubbing the flesh directly beneath the eye before glancing upward. In general the more vigorous the eye-touch the bigger the lie.

The nose-touch.

The eye-touch.

Eye movements

Having 'shifty eyes' is a traditional sign of deception and one which professional liars work hard to overcome. They can gaze at you confidently while telling the biggest falsehoods in the world. Less polished deceivers, however, really can betray themselves by their eye movements, so these are worth watching for. The main eye signals are:

Evasive eyes: Looking away, usually for long periods, while talking. A refusal to meet your gaze. This is more often seen in deceitful children and adolescents than in adults.

Shifting eyes: Glance rapidly away from your face and back again.

Stuttering eyes: Eye-contact is given, but the eyelids flutter.

Stammering eyes: Similar to the above, but the lids remain closed for what can often seem like several seconds.

Hostility signals

Occur when the person either feels angry with himself for deceiving you or, not uncommonly, angry with you for 'compelling' him into falsehood. 'If only my wife was more understanding, I wouldn't need to lie all the time,' a client once told me angrily.

Hostility signs to look for are:

Foot jabs: A modified displacement signal, only instead of fidgeting, as in anxiety, the foot jabs angrily against the floor or some other object.

Face picks: Involve attacking parts such as ears, hair, or cheeks, which are pulled, pinched or tugged.

Lip bites: The person sucks, chews or even bites his own lips, usually the lower one.

RULE THIRTY-ONE FOR SILENT SPEECH SUCCESS

Liars betray themselves in several ways. Watch for fewer than normal gestures and increased self-touching. This usually involves the hands rubbing, pulling or stroking ears, nose or cheeks. The nose-rub and eye-touch are especially revealing. Deceptions involving hostility can be detected by aggressive movements of the feet, hands or mouth.

How obvious these silent speech signals are may depend on whether or not the person telling you lies finds you attractive. By secretly observing people instructed to lie, Dr Bella DePaulo and her colleagues at the University of Virginia discovered that deceptions practised on good-looking people and members of the opposite sex are far easier to spot than lies told to either same sex individuals or those considered unattractive. 'Lies were more transparent in just those conditions in which subjects may have been especially motivated to make their lies less transparent,' they report.

Why? Probably because the greater one's desire to be believed the more stress and anxiety is generated. What's more the liars are concentrating so hard on being convincing that their control over silent speech signals is reduced. So the next time somebody tells you an obvious untruth maybe you should feel flattered at being found so attractive.

Perhaps the most appropriate response when you detect a falsehood is to use this silent speech emblem from deaf-and-dumb sign language:

It means — bullshit!

CHAPTER FIFTEEN

Dress Success

A well-tied tie is the first serious step in life.

Oscar Wilde, *The Importance of Being Earnest*

You can learn unexpected things from the least likely people. I once held many long and fascinating conversations with a high-class West End prostitute. I should make clear she was a client of mine rather than the other way around! I asked her how she could tell, out of all the thousands of males who thronged her Mayfair hunting grounds, which would be able to afford her substantial prices. 'I look at their shoes,' she explained. 'A man with limited resources wanting to put on an impressive front will spend money on an expensive suit, silk tie and even a hand-made shirt. But unless he's loaded he'll skimp on his shoes!'

While this doesn't mean you can only make a good impression by investing in hand-crafted shoes at £1,000 a pair, her comment emphasizes a vital factor in dressing for success. Never forget the small details in your concern over the big picture. Unpolished shoes or a careless shave can lower your status every bit as much as a shabby jacket and creased trousers.

Earlier in the book I mentioned the executive who would never employ people turning up at interviews with dirty fingernails. Others have expressed similar distaste for untidy hair, carelessly-applied make-up, dandruff-specked collars, frayed cuffs and laddered tights. 'Unless people are prepared to take time and trouble over the way they look,' one CEO told me, 'I'll never believe they are going to spend time and effort on the work they do for us.'

As we have seen, first impressions are vitally important and the way you package what you've got on offer is usually central to success. Only two types of person can get away with ignoring social expectations when it comes to what they wear: the super-wealthy who have nothing to prove and the super-poor who have nothing to lose. For the rest of us dress success is a matter to be taken very seriously indeed.

Dressing the part

'Unlike the contents of a wallet or one's personal values, clothing is highly visible and is brimming with clues about the wearer's background,' comments Dr Michael Solomon, social psychologist and associate professor of marketing at the Graduate School of Business Administration at New York University. 'We are expected to draw conclusions about a person's identity from such symbols and to act accordingly.'

In one of the earliest experiments to demonstrate the link between clothes and status, Monroe Lefkowitz and his colleagues investigated the willingness of pedestrians to copy a jay-walker breaking the law by crossing the street against a red light. When the offender was dressed in a suit many followed his lead. But when a shabbily dressed individual broke the law nobody was tempted to do the same.

In a more recent experiment, an actor was employed to beg for money at New York's Grand Central Station. On different days he dressed smartly, casually and scruffily. In each case his story was the same. He had lost his wallet and wanted a few dollars to get home. As a neatly and conservatively dressed business type he collected $513 in just one day. Many sympathetic commuters pressed him to accept twice the money asked for so that he could 'get himself a drink' to recover from his unfortunate experience. In casual but smart clothes he managed to raise $150, but when shabbily clothed his take dropped to just $10 for a full day's begging and nobody offered him a drink!

In a similar study, a small coin was deliberately left in the tray of a pay-phone. A man or woman, dressed in two different ways, approached phone users and inquired, 'I think I might have left some money in this phone booth a few moments ago. Did you find it?' Half the time the man had a suit and tie and the woman a smart dress and coat. The other half the man wore working clothes and the woman a shabby skirt and faded blouse. You will not be surprised to learn that when the couple looked as though they could ill afford to lose the coin it was least likely to be returned to them.

So does this mean you should always wear formal clothes? Is this what writers mean when they speak of a 'power outfit'? The high status uniform that will open any door?

The answer is *no*.

What really matters is dressing in a way that matches the impression you wish to convey. In one situation this might call for a conservative

232

pin-stripe or severely cut costume, in another designer jeans, in a third grubby overalls.

Let's take an extreme case. Suppose you are up in court on a serious charge. How should you dress? With suit and tie or well-cut dress and smartly pressed blouse, or jeans and casual shirt?

Your decision must depend on how you want judge and jury to perceive you. Many male defendants, especially in fraud or drunken driving cases, feel that a suit will make them appear respectable and trustworthy. A young jury, however, might feel far more empathy with somebody casually dressed and more like themselves. But choosing what to wear is no trivial matter. In some cases it really could mean the difference between a guilty and a not guilty verdict. In their classic study of the American jury, Harry Kalven and Hans Zeisel noted that a variety of characteristics could provoke a sympathetic response from the jury. The elderly, the good-looking and, overwhelmingly, ex-servicemen who appeared in court wearing their medals were able favourably to influence the results of their trials.

During Watergate top Nixon aides Haldeman, Ehrlichman and Mitchell appeared before the televised Senate hearings wearing pin-stripe suits. According to American clothing consultant John Molloy this conveyed exactly the right image of credibility to the millions of viewers. 'The pin-stripe suit has been traditionally the most credible apparel for a man to wear when selling something important,' he explains. But by the time they went on trial, the impression they needed to make had changed. Their Senate appearances had destroyed much of their credibility and the audience they now had to persuade of their innocence were not senators and TV viewers but a judge and jury. 'During the Watergate hearings the credibility of the pin-stripe suit shrank', says Molloy. His suggestion would have been sporty but non-authoritarian neck ties with light-coloured suits. 'If you are trying to visually communicate to a jury that you weren't the man in charge, wearing non-authoritarian clothes could be a plus'.

Even without this advice, the defendants did change their appearance. Ehrlichman sported a light-blue suit and spectacles with a fine gold frame, which looked a good deal less threatening than his former dark-rimmed half glasses. Haldeman abandoned his cherished crew cut, with its militaristic, authoritarian overtones, and allowed his hair to grow longer, so conveying a more laid-back and liberal image.

Dressing the part means . . .
1. Wearing clothes which are right for the impression you are seeking to make.
2. Avoiding anything which might contradict that impression.
3. Considering every aspect of your appearance, from hair length for males to the amount of make-up worn for women.

You are what you wear

Clothing has the power to influence not only how others perceive you but also the way you regard yourself. Therapists sometimes suggest that depressed clients go out and buy themselves new clothes in order to lift their moods. When we feel good about the way we look we feel better about ourselves as well.

Psychologist Dr Michael Solomon demonstrated this by constructing a fake corporate office at the University of North Carolina and conducting mock job interviews with students. No instructions as to dress were given, but by arranging appointments carefully Dr Solomon was able to ensure that some came directly from lectures while others had time to change into formal clothes.

At the end of each interview the students were asked to say how they felt the interviewer had evaluated them. As he had predicted those wearing the appropriate interview 'uniform' of suit and tie believed the interviewer had a higher opinion of their abilities than those informally dressed. What is more, when asked to suggest an appropriate starting salary for the job, formally-dressed students asked for £2,500 more than those who were casually attired.

In many companies employees are expected to conform to an unwritten but strictly enforced dress code. For men this usually means jackets and ties and for women short hairstyles, moderate use of make-up and plainly tailored clothing. The sultry, seductive look is definitely out. As one executive told psychologist Thomas Cash during his study on corporate grooming styles, 'A sexy looking woman is definitely going to get a longer interview, but she won't get the job.'

Dressing to win

There are many excellent books on dressing for success. Two I can especially recommend are *The Winner's Style* by Kenneth Karpinski and *Colour for Men* by Carole Jackson. You'll find details of the publishers in the reference section. Here I am simply going to list the seven most vital do's and don'ts of dressing to win:

1. DO ensure that what you wear creates the impression you must make to gain the benefits you desire. When job-hunting, for instance, always dress for the job you *want* rather than the one you've already got. If you have any doubts about that organization's dress code, pay them a visit prior to the interview and see what people already working there wear. Hang around outside the premises, if necessary, and observe people going in or leaving. Bright colours may be essential for one vacancy and the kiss of death at another.
2. DON'T wear black. Perhaps as a result of all those cowboy films

where the villains wore black hats, it arouses very negative emotions. You are likely to be seen as untrustworthy, sinister and potentially violent. In a study of the effect of colour in sport, Thomas Gilovich and Mark Frank of Cornell University found that footballers wearing black were more likely to be considered aggressive and blamed for any violence on the field.

3. DO be restrained in your manner of dress. Avoid wearing bright colours, loud checks or other flamboyant clothing unless, of course, that is the organization's accepted dress. Women should be especially careful of using too much perfume. In a study by Dr Robert Baron of Purdue University, two women were given mock interviews by male and female interviewers. The candidates altered their behaviour in various ways, either using or avoiding empathic silent speech signals such as smiles, eye-contact and leaning forward, sometimes wearing a highly noticeable perfume and sometimes not. Baron found that when the women wore perfume and used positive body language they were rated more negatively by male, although not by female, interviewers. It seems likely that the men were distracted by the women's behaviour and appearance and felt less effective as interviewers. 'Efforts by applicants to enhance their "image" can go too far,' Baron suggests. 'From a practical point of view . . . the best strategy for job applicants to follow appears to be one of careful moderation.'

4. DON'T have *anything* in the top jacket pocket. Pens, pencils, a spectacle case, glasses, a calculator and so on are signs of a loser, not a winner. The only permissible item for the man's breast pocket is a neatly folded, and spotless, handkerchief.

5. DO think carefully about wearing a beard and longer than average hair when dealing with commercial organizations. They tend to create an image which, while acceptable to the arts, theatre and academic world, can arouse negative responses in most branches of industry and commerce. They could even lessen your chances of reading the news on television. A British TV producer once told me there was a strong prejudice against allowing bearded presenters because it was believed they appeared less credible to viewers. While this might sound improbable, there is clear evidence from American research to support the claim that a presenter's look really *does* influence the way their message is received. This was demonstrated by psychologists at Texas Tech University who simulated sixty-second news bulletins using male and female professional broadcasters. The news story remained the same but the presenters' clothes ranged from formal to casual. When viewers were asked to rate the broadcasters on competence and honesty it was found that dress style exerted a strong effect. The formally dressed presenters received the highest credibility ratings.

Beards and long hair, perhaps because of their association in many people's minds with a Bohemian lifestyle, diminish an individual's status in some circles but may greatly enhance it in others. A survey conducted among university students showed that beards were considered to make the male look more masculine, mature, self-confident, dominant, liberal, courageous, nonconformist and industrious. It is doubtful that such views extend beyond the campus.

6. DO choose your glasses with care if you are a spectacle wearer. The right frame can enhance your looks by emphasizing good features and disguising those which are less attractive. The choice depends on the shape of your nose and face. If you have a long nose, select spectacles with a low bridge. For shorter noses a high bridge gives the best appearance.

   Round face: Frames with straight tops and sides which angle inward to a straight bottom. This strengthens the cheekbone.

   Square face: Frames which are slightly rounded or curved to lengthen your face.

   Oblong face: Frames which are large, wide with straight bottoms and thick, rounded sides which will add width while making your features appear shorter and more angular.

   Diamond shaped: The wide cheeks and narrow chin can be disguised by glasses which are oval in shape with wide tops and straight sides.

   Triangular shaped: The broad forehead and narrowed chin of this face need to be balanced by light frames with curved bottoms.

7. DON'T overlook the details. Small points make a big difference when it comes to Impression Management. Here are the four things people most often miss when checking their own appearance, but immediately spot in others:

   a. Dirty, chewed or poorly trimmed fingernails. Both men and women, unless they work in jobs where hands get rough treatment, should take care of their nails.

   b. Unhealthy complexion. Your skin is an accurate reflection of your overall health. When you are over-tired, too stressed or eating incorrectly your complexion is certain to be poor. Correct diet and healthy exercise can do much to improve its appearance. Males should be just as careful over their facial care as women, and these days more and more men are recognizing this fact.

   c. Badly polished shoes. If you can't be bothered to take time cleaning and buffing your own shoes, spend a little money on a professional shoeshine. It's a worthwhile investment. Take special care with the back of the heels, an area many otherwise well-groomed people – especially males – seem to miss.

CHAPTER SIXTEEN

The Rules of Silent Speech Success

First meetings

RULE ONE
Manage every second of a first meeting. Do not delude yourself that a bad impression can be easily corrected. Putting things right is a lot harder than getting them right first time.

Eye power

RULE TWO
Always initiate the eyebrow flash whenever possible. *Always* respond to another's eyebrow flash unless your deliberate intention is to signal hostility.

RULE THREE
Always break eye-contact downward, unless it is your deliberate intention to convey a lack of interest in the other person or to throw them temporarily off balance by a disconcerting upward eye-break.

RULE FOUR
Never normally hold gaze for more than three seconds during the Initiation stage. Look, then break eye-contact briefly. Any violation of this rule can generate a negative impression, even though the person receiving the message is unable to explain the reason for their feelings. The only exception is during a power-play when it is your deliberate intention to disconcert your opponent.

Smile power

RULE FIVE
Use the smile most appropriate to the situation. Smiling inappropriately can create as negative an impression as not smiling at all.

Using space – while standing

RULE SIX
Be careful never to invade another person's Intimate Zone unintentionally. If you do so deliberately, as a power-play strategy, be aware that you will provoke a powerful increase in arousal. (See rule twenty-three.)

RULE SEVEN
Make sure you are working at the correct distance to achieve the results you require. Take into account individual and cultural differences, as well as the nature of the relationship. Learn to work at a variety of distances without feeling alienated or uneasy. The more flexible you can be in manipulating another person's various Zones the greater control you will be able to exert over the encounter.

RULE EIGHT
Under certain circumstances deliberately violating someone's personal space can enhance mutual liking. But only do so if you are rewarding the person with verbal praise and/or warm, encouraging silent speech signals. Under these conditions closing the distance between you will enhance their liking, interest and willingness to co-operate with you.

RULE NINE
Never stand directly opposite an unknown male or adjacent to an unfamiliar female. With a man start at a more side-on position and gradually work your way around to a more frontal one.

With a woman, adopt the opposite approach by starting the encounter in a frontal position and then moving slowly to a more adjacent one.

RULE TEN
Never stand when somebody else is sitting, unless it is your intention to dominate or intimidate them. Height is a powerful dominance signal (see chapter thirteen).

Using space – when sitting

RULE ELEVEN
Avoid, if possible, deep arm-chairs which compel you to sit well back in them, since this will limit your ability to send out a number of important posture signals.

RULE TWELVE
When chairs can be moved, the rules for personal distance described above apply, although you can get away with sitting closer to another person than you could if standing. This is because the chair increases our sense of security, especially when its arms provide a physical barrier between us and other people.

RULE THIRTEEN
Avoid sitting immediately *beside* a female stranger or *in front of* a male stranger. Whenever possible follow the movements described above by starting the encounter sitting adjacent to a man and facing a woman.

While shaking hands

RULE FOURTEEN
Keep your hand dry and apply a moderate pressure. Hold the handshake for around six seconds – under most circumstances.

RULE FIFTEEN
To communicate dominance use the Great Man Grip, stronger than normal pressure and slightly longer than usual grasp. To convey friendship and a desire for co-operation use the Get Together Grip, moderate pressure and normal grasp time. If you want to add a little assertiveness to your signal then apply slightly greater pressure.

Enhance friendship by retaining the hand for slightly longer. Smile and keep your expression relaxed, lean slightly forward. Maintain eye-contact throughout the handshake.

To convey submission, employ the Give-in Grip. Grasp and duration should be normal. Eye-contact is reduced. Break the glance by looking downward.

RULE SIXTEEN
Unless there are medical reasons for wearing them, avoid tinted, dark or reflecting glasses. If you want to be seen as warm and empathic wear contact lenses rather than spectacles to correct vision defects.

Encouraging co-operation

RULE SEVENTEEN
Use a head-tilt, together with eye-contact and a warm smile, on first meeting to increase the warmth and impact of your presence. Use the same gesture whenever you are asking for help or co-operation.

RULE EIGHTEEN
When speaking to a group ensure your gaze includes them all. Avoid reading from a script. Either memorize what you wish to say or use brief notes.

Power-plays

RULE NINETEEN
The secret of a successful power-play depends on your ability to control the other person's time and space.

RULE TWENTY
Walk slowly, walk deliberately and walk tall. Take the time to review your surroundings. Adopt the manner of a proprietor, not the furtive air of somebody who doesn't really belong there. Imagine you own the place and move accordingly. Never allow yourself to be hurried.

RULE TWENTY-ONE
Use prolonged gaze to disconcert others. But refuse to return a prolonged eye-contact. Break gaze either left or right but never downward.

RULE TWENTY-TWO
Whenever possible choose where and how you sit. Select a chair without sides which is easy to get out of and puts you at the same height as the other person. Avoid the trap of the deep but confining punishment chair.

RULE TWENTY-THREE
Your ability to dominate others can often be enhanced by a deliberate invasion of their personal space.

RULE TWENTY-FOUR
To dominate another person first take control of his or her time. The longer you compel them to wait – up to a point – the greater the dominance you demonstrate. Use the Twenty-minute Test. If he or she is still patiently waiting for the meeting you will have dominated them

to the point where their perceived status is significantly undermined.

RULE TWENTY-FIVE
Counter attempts to waste your time. Keep busy and turn the tables by making the other person wait for you. Stick to the fifteen-minute rule for being kept waiting. At the end of this period, unless there is an obviously valid and genuine reason for the delay, abort the meeting.

Reading others

RULE TWENTY-SIX
Approach each encounter with an open mind. Avoid too many preconceptions about what you are going to see.

RULE TWENTY-SEVEN
Do not pay too much attention to faces. While they can provide some valuable clues, their silent speech signals are the most often concealed, the easiest to fake.

RULE TWENTY-EIGHT
Detect anxiety by looking at feet and hands rather than faces. Watch for 'leakage' as inner tensions are relieved by small, subconsciously controlled movements.

RULE TWENTY-NINE
No matter what you are trying to sell, silent speech buy-signs can tell you if the other person wants to do a deal. The key signs to watch out for are a sudden release of tension, increased eye-contact, greater proximity and touching the chin.

RULE THIRTY
To check a friendship is sincere look for cheek folds revealing a genuinely warm smile, increased touching, unconscious copying of your stance and gestures and a tilted head during conversations.

RULE THIRTY-ONE
Liars betray themselves in several ways. Watch for fewer than normal gestures and increased self-touching. This usually involves the hands rubbing, pulling or stroking ears, nose or cheeks. The nose-rub and eye-touch are especially revealing. Deceptions involving hostility can be detected by aggressive movements of the feet, hands or mouth.

This concludes our discussion of the secret language of success and failure. As you have seen, there is a great deal more to even the briefest encounter than meets the ear. By taking the time and trouble to prepare yourself non-verbally as well as verbally for an encounter you greatly enhance your chances of gaining from that situation all you hoped to achieve. By working to manage the impression you create it becomes possible to retain control of situations, so sustaining your self-confidence and self-esteem.

When it comes to selling either your personal charms or professional abilities, body language talks loudest of all.

Bibliography

Allport, G.W., & Vernon, P.E., *Studies in Expressive Movement* (New York, Macmillan, 1933).

Anderson, N., 'Re-Theorising the Selection Interview', paper at the BPS Annual Occupational Psychology Conference (January 4–5 1988).

Argyle, M., *Social Interaction* (London, Tavistock, 1969).

Argyle, M., *The Psychology of Interpersonal Behaviour* (Harmondsworth, Penguin, 1967).

Argyle, M. & Cook, M., *Gaze and Mutual Gaze* (Cambridge, Cambridge University Press, 1979).

Baron, R.A., *Journal of Applied Social Psychology* Vol. 16 (1987), pp. 16–28.

Birdwhistell, R.L., *Kinesics and Context* (Harmondsworth, Penguin, 1970).

Bramson, R.M., *Coping with Difficult People* (New York, Anchor Press, 1981).

Carnegie, D., *How to Win Friends and Influence People* (Tadworth, Cedar, 1953).

Cook, M. & Wilson, G. (Eds), *Love and Attraction* (Oxford, Pergamon Press, 1979).

DePaulo, B. et al, 'Good-looking lies', *Psychology Today* (January 1986), p. 12.

Ekman, P., 'Universals and cultural differences in facial expressions of emotion', in J.K. Cole, Ed., *Nebraska Symposium on Motivation*, Vol. 19 (Lincoln, University of Nebraska Press, 1972).

Fast, J., *Body Language* (London, Souvenir Press, 1971).

Fisher, J., Bell, P., & Baum, A., *Environmental Psychology* (New York, Holt, Reinhart and Winston).

Goffman, E., *The Presentation of Self In Everyday Life* (Harmondsworth, Penguin, 1969).

Goffman, E., *Gender Advertisements* (New York, Harper and Row, 1979).

Hall, E.T., *The Hidden Dimension* (New York, Doubleday and Co., 1966).

Hall, J., 'Gender effects in decoding nonverbal cues', *Psychological Bulletin*, 85 (1978) pp. 845–57.

Hall, J., 'Gender, gender roles and nonverbal behaviour' in

P. Rosenthal (ed.), *Skill in nonverbal communication* (Cambridge, Oelsgeschlager, Gunn & Hain, 1979).

Hamachek, D.E., *Encounters With Self* (New York, Holt, Reinhart and Winston, 1978).

Hanna, T., *Somatics* (Reading Massachusetts, Addison-Wesley Publishing Company, 1988).

Henley, N.M. *Body Politics* (New Jersey, Prentice Hall, 1977).

Jackson, C. & Lulow, K., *Colour For Men* (London, Piatkus, 1984).

Kalven, H. & Zeisel, H., *The American Jury* (University of Chicago Press, 1966).

Karpinski, K.J. & Trupp, P.Z., *The Winner's Style* (Washington, Acropolis Books, 1987).

Knapp, M.L., *Essentials of Nonverbal Communication* (New York, Holt, Reinhart and Winston, 1980).

Kunz, M., 'Clothes Make the Defendant', *Globe* (Boston, 12 October, 1974).

Lamb, W. & Watson, E., *Body Code* (London, Routledge, 1979).

Levine, R., 'The Waiting Game', *Psychology Today* (April issue 1987) pp. 24–33.

Malatesta, C.Z., *Psychology and Ageing* vol. 2 (1987) pp. 193–203.

Martin, B., *Abnormal Psychology* (New York, Holt Reinhart and Winston, 1981).

Mayo, C. & Henley, N.M. *Gender and Nonverbal Behaviour* (New York, Springer, 1981).

Mehrabian, A. *Nonverbal Communication* Chicago, Aldine. Atherton, 1972).

Morris, D., *Manwatching* (London, Jonathan Cape, 1977).

Noller, P., *Non-Verbal Communication and Marital Intervention* International Series in Experimental Social Psychology, Vol. 9 (Oxford, Pergamon Press, 1984).

Parks, T.E. & Coss, R.G., 'Prime Illusion', *Psychology Today* (October 1986) pp. 6–8.

Patounas, G., *Silent Language* (Allied Training International Ltd, 1986).

Pease, A., *Body Language* (London, Sheldon Press, 1981).

Proshansky, H.M., Ittelson, W.H. & Rivlin, L.G. (Eds), *Environmental Psychology* (New York, Holt, Reinhart and Winston).

Rosenthal, R. et al, 'Assessing Sensitivity to Nonverbal Communication: The PONS Test', *Division 8 Newsletter,* Division of Personality and Social Psychology of the American Psychologica Association (January 1974), pp. 1–3.

Rosenthal, R. et al, 'Body Talk and Tone of Voice: The Language Without Words', *Psychology Today* (September 1974, vol. 8., no. 4), pp. 64–8.

Sapir, E. 'The Unconscious Patterning of Behaviour in Society' (1927), in D.G. Mandelbaum, ed., *Selected Writings of Edward Sapir* (Berkley, University of California Press, 1949).

Scheflen, A.E., *How Behaviour Means* (New York, Doubleday and Company, 1974).

Solomon, M.R., 'Dress for Effect', *Psychology Today* (April 1986) pp. 20–8.

Wieman, J.M. & Harrison, R.P. *Nonverbal Interaction* (Beverly Hills, Sage Press, 1983).

Zunin, L. & Zunin, N., *Contact – The First Four Minutes* (New York, Ballantine Books, 1972).

Acknowledgements

My grateful thanks to Dr Peter Thompson, Department of Psychology, University of York, for permission to use his Margaret Thatcher illusion which appears on page 211. This first appeared in the journal *Perception*, 1980, volume 9. The line illustrations are by Richard Armstrong and the photographs, with the exceptions of those on pages 29, 30, 101, 102, 180, 183, which are from my own research files, were taken by Derry Robinson. I should also like to thank my two research associates, Shandy Mathias and Len Armour.